Toe the Mark

Running programs in Chico in the 1970s were similar to those elsewhere. Famed University of Oregon coach Bill Bowerman had introduced the sport of jogging; American Frank Shorter was the winner of the marathon at the 1972 Olympics; and Steve Prefontaine, running for Oregon, drew thousands of fans to see him race. A distant 384 miles south of Eugene, Oregon, lay Chico, a small rural town in northern California. In these exciting times, a high school coach there put together the top Cross Country teams and developed the best collection of distance runners the town had seen, then or since. Included among the male and female athletes were the "Charlie's Angels" — seven high school girls which, in 1977, *Harrier* magazine ranked second in the nation. Five years earlier, an elite miler at the local college had the community abuzz with his quest to break the magic four-minute barrier. Meanwhile, two feisty marathoners (former college boxers) were leading the road-racing contingent in town. While doing so, they met the existing Olympic Trials qualifying standard for the 26.2-mile race. This book transports readers back to an age of innocence and excellence to run in the footsteps of the athletes of that era. One hundred and fourteen photographs add value to this work.

To coach Chuck Sheley, former Chico High teammates and other Panthers; Wildcat runners across the street at then Chico State College, in the 1970s; and rival Pleasant Valley Vikings across town.

Toe the Mark

David D. Bruhn

HERITAGE BOOKS
2022

HERITAGE BOOKS
AN IMPRINT OF HERITAGE BOOKS, INC.

Books, CDs, and more—Worldwide

For our listing of thousands of titles see our website
at
www.HeritageBooks.com

Published 2022 by
HERITAGE BOOKS, INC.
Publishing Division
5810 Ruatan Street
Berwyn Heights, Md. 20740

Copyright © 2022 David D. Bruhn

All rights reserved. No part of this book may be reproduced or transmitted in any form or by any means, electronic or mechanical, including photocopying, recording or by any information storage and retrieval system without written permission from the author, except for the inclusion of brief quotations in a review.

International Standard Book Number
Paperbound: 978-0-7884-2402-1

Heritage Books by Cdr. David D. Bruhn, USN (Retired)

Battle Stars for the "Cactus Navy":
America's Fishing Vessels and Yachts in World War II

Enemy Waters:
Royal Navy, Royal Canadian Navy, Royal Norwegian Navy,
U.S. Navy, and Other Allied Mine Forces Battling the
Germans and Italians in World War II
Cdr. David D. Bruhn, USN (Retired) and Lt. Cdr. Rob Hoole, RN (Retired)

Eyes of the Fleet:
The U.S. Navy's Seaplane Tenders and Patrol Aircraft in World War II

Gators Offshore and Upriver:
The U.S. Navy's Amphibious Ships and Underwater Demolition Teams,
and Royal Australian Navy Clearance Divers in Vietnam

Guns Up, Depth Charges Readied:
U.S. Navy, Commonwealth, and Other Allied Escort Ships
Shepherding Convoys, and Battling German and Italian Air
and Naval Forces in the Mediterranean in World War II

Guns Up:
Naval Action in the Yellow Sea off Korea, 1950–1953

Home Waters:
Royal Navy, Royal Canadian Navy, and U.S. Navy
Mine Forces Battling U-Boats in World War I
Cdr. David D. Bruhn, USN (Retired) and Lt. Cdr. Rob Hoole, RN (Retired)

Ingram's Fourth Fleet:
U.S. and Royal Navy Operations Against German Runners,
Raiders, and Submarines in the South Atlantic in World War II

MacArthur and Halsey's "Pacific Island Hoppers":
The Forgotten Fleet of World War II

Nightraiders:
U.S. Navy, Royal Navy, Royal Australian Navy, and
Royal Netherlands Navy Mine Forces Battling the
Japanese in the Pacific in World War II
Cdr. David D. Bruhn, USN (Retired) and Lt. Cdr. Rob Hoole, RN (Retired)

On the Gunline:
U.S. Navy and Royal Australian Navy Warships off Vietnam, 1965–1973
Cdr. David D. Bruhn, USN (Retired) and
STGCS Richard S. Mathews, USN (Retired)

Ready to Haul, Ready to Fight:
U.S. Navy, Royal Australian Navy, and
British Merchant Navy Cargo Ships
in the Pacific in World War II

Salvation from the Sky: U.S. Navy, Royal Australian Air Force, and
Royal New Zealand Air Force Heroic Air-Sea Rescue in the Pacific in World War II
Cdr. David D. Bruhn, USN (Retired) and Stephen Ekholm

Send Some King's Ships:
U.S. Navy, Royal Naval Patrol Service, and Royal Canadian Navy Ships
Combating German U-boats off North America's Eastern Seaboard, and
RNPS and South African Naval Forces Vessels in African Waters as well, 1942–1945
Cdr. David D. Bruhn, USN (Retired) and Lt. Cdr. Rob Hoole, RN (Retired)

Support for the Fleet:
U.S. Navy and Royal Australian Navy Service
Force Ships That Served in Vietnam, 1965–1973

We Are Sinking, Send Help!:
The U.S. Navy's Tugs and Salvage Ships in the African,
European, and Mediterranean Theaters in World War II

Toe the Mark

Turn into the Wind:
Volume I: US Navy and Royal Navy Light Fleet Aircraft Carriers
in World War II, and Contributions of the British Pacific Fleet

Turn into the Wind:
Volume II: US Navy, Royal Navy, Royal Australian Navy, and Royal Canadian Navy
Light Fleet Aircraft Carriers in the Korean War and through End of Service, 1950–1982

Wooden Ships and Iron Men:
The U.S. Navy's Ocean Minesweepers, 1953–1994

Wooden Ships and Iron Men:
The U.S. Navy's Coastal and Motor Minesweepers, 1941–1953

Wooden Ships and Iron Men:
The U.S. Navy's Coastal and Inshore Minesweepers,
and the Minecraft that Served in Vietnam, 1953–1976

Contents

Foreword by Professor emeritus Walt Schafer	xi
Foreword by Professor Britton Brewer	xiii
Foreword by Coach Bill Gregg	xv
Acknowledgements	xvii
Preface	xxiii
1. Attempt to Break the 4-Minute Mile	1
2. Identification, Recruitment, and Development of Runners	9
3. The North Section's Best Distance Runners	19
4. Pleasant Valley High School, and One Chico High Panther	25
5. 1972-73 Sophomore Year at Chico High	31
6. Road Racing in Northern California	43
7. 1973 Cross Country Season	53
8. 1973 Wildcat Cross Country	59
9. 1974 Track Season	63
10. 1974 Wildcat Track & Field	73
11. Second Chico North Section Varsity Cross Country Title	77
12. 1975 Track Season	83
13. 1975 Wildcat Track & Field	95
14. Chico Running Club, and Visit of Peter Snell to Chico	97
15. 1975 Cross Country Season	101
16. 1976 Track Season	111
17. 1976 Wildcat Track & Field	119
18. CHS Boys Strongest Ever; Charlie's Angels More So!	121
19. 1977 Track & Field Season	135
20. 1977 Wildcat Track & Field	149
21. Second in the Nation 1977 Charlie's Angels	151
22. Suzanne Richter 5th at State Meet	163
23. 1978 Wildcat Track & Field	171
24. 1978 Cross Country Season	175
25. Chico High Graduates' Seasons	181
26. 1979 Track Season	187
27. 1979 Cross Country Season	193
28. Jill Symons and Greg Williams' 1979 Cross Country Seasons	195
29. End of the 1970s, End of a Dynasty	199
30. What Came Later	203
Postscript	223

Appendices
  A. Top Times of CHS Boys Track Athletes in the 1970s   225
  B. Top Times of CHS Girls Track Athletes in the 1970s   227
  C. Best Times by Panthers on Chico's Home Course in the 70s 229
  D. Assistant Coaches, and Athletes who later Coached   231
About the Author   233

PHOTOS AND SKETCHES

Acknowledgements-1: Kent Pease, and Pat and Mike Buzbee	xvii
Acknowledgements-2: Professor emeritus Walt Schafer	xviii
Acknowledgements-3: Professor Britt Brewer as a young runner	xix
Acknowledgement-4: Coach Bill Gregg	xx
Preface-1: Baton Pass from Chuck Sheley to Charlie Moseley	xxiii
Preface-2: Chuck Sheley in parachute harness, and later as a coach	xxiv
Preface-3: Chico State Wildcat Bob Noe, and later Coach Noe	xxv
Preface-4: Olympic gold medalist Jack Yerman	xxvi
Preface-5: Dale Edson and Wildcat Coach Cherrie Sherrard	xxx
1-1: Wildcat Kim Ellison running a 4:01 mile	1
1-2: Wildcat Scotty Bauhs breaking the 4-minute mile	5
1-3: University of Texas El Paso track star Kerry Ellison	6
1-4: Wildcat Gene Meyers competing in a cross country race	7
2-1: 1971 Chico Junior High Cross Country (XC) team	10
2-2: Panther Cross Country runners at McKinleyville's Clam Beach	11
2-3: Twins Mike and Pat Buzbee	17
3-1: Toni Ruggle as a Chico State Wildcat	19
3-2: Paradise's Rob Erb leading Pleasant Valley's John Barneson	22
4-1: Pleasant Valley's Tim Holt and Charlie Griffin	25
4-2: Pleasant Valley's 1971 Boys' Cross Country team	26
4-3: Dave and Jim Scott	28
4-4: Western States 100-miler belt buckle	29
4-5: Luanne Park racing	30
5-1: 1972 Chico High Varsity and Junior Varsity XC teams	34
5-2: Panthers Pat and Mike Buzbee on the starting line	36
5-3: Mike Buzbee leading the eventual winner, Robert Robles	37
5-4: Pat Buzbee, who would finish in fourth place	37
5-5: 1966 Chico High Cross Country teams	38
5-6: Mark Burch and Dave Bruhn finishing one-two in a mile race	41
6-1: T-shirt awarded to Pat Buzbee for the 1971 Pepsi 20-mile run	43
6-2: Christmas Relays cup, and race-associated long-sleeve t-shirts	50
7-1: 1973 Chico High Cross Country teams	53
7-2: 1973 Chico High Varsity Cross Country team	58
8-1: Chico State 1973 Far Western Conference team champions	59

8-2: Mark Shuman running to a 23rd place finish at the Nationals	62
9-1: Robert MacKay breaking the tape in the 440-yard dash	65
9-2: Kent Pease and Dave Bruhn running repeat 440s barefoot	67
9-3: Dave Bruhn, Paul Ryan, and Bill Gregg in a mile race	69
9-4: Kent Pease winning the jayvee mile	71
9-5: Doug Avrit winning the freshmen 1 ½-mile race	71
10-1: Wildcat Pat Stordahl stalking an opponent on the track	73
10-2: Tom Brown clearing a steeplechase barrier	74
10-3: Calvin Lantrip competing in the Nevada Union Invitational	76
11-1: Chico High Panthers on the starting line before a race	77
11-2: Doug Avrit at the 1974 League Championships	80
12-1: Kent Pease winning the mile at the Section Championships	83
12-2: Pat Buzbee running the Trail's End Marathon in Seaside	85
12-3: Doug Avrit and Dave Bruhn in a varsity 2-mile race	88
12-4: Kurt Graves finishing a jayvee race on the track	93
14-1: Walt Schafer running the Seaside, Oregon, marathon	97
14-2: Walt Schafer finishing a high school Cross Country race	98
14-3: Walt Schafer running on the Great Wall of China	100
15-1: 1975 Chico High Boys Cross Country teams	101
15-2: Mike and Pat Buzbee at Avenue of the Giants marathon	102
15-3: Chico High Boys Cross Country team toeing the line	104
15-4: Doug Avrit leading Kent Pease during a race at Lassen	106
15-5: Seven Panthers finishing abreast to win the race	106
16-1: Panthers' training on Chico High School's dirt track	111
16-2: Ticket to the 1976 U.S. Olympic Track & Field Trials	114
18-1: Chico High's strongest ever Boys Cross Country team	121
18-2: Paradise High School's Larry Greer	122
18-3: Chico High School's Charlie's Angels	123
18-4: Varsity boys team at the San Ramon Invitational	125
18-5: Sketch by Bob Noe related to the McKinleyville Beach Run	126
18-6: Greg Williams and Doug Avrit	129
18-7: Awards Night in Chico High's Lincoln Hall	132
18-8: 1976 Chico High Boys Cross Country team's top runners	133
19-1: Runners at the starting line of the Bidwell Classic Marathon	136
19-2: Woman marathoner Merill Cray	137
19-3: Kurt Graves nipping teammate Doug Avrit at the finish	138
19-4: Seth Roberts of Paradise edging teammate Larry Greer	140
19-5: Doug Avrit racing to victory	142
19-6: Entrants in the 2-mile on the starting line at the State Meet	144
19-7: Two-mile race in progress	144
19-8: Pat and Mike Buzbee at Avenue of the Giants marathon	145
19-9: Vintage Humboldt Redwoods Marathon t-shirt	146

19-10: Jim Price, Jack West, and Toni Ruggle on the track	147
21-1: 1977 Chico High School's Girls Cross Country team	151
21-2: Runners competing in the Chico Invitational Meet	152
21-3: Chico's Gregg Williams, Chris Johnson, and Steve Growdon	155
21-4: Charlie's Angels with their coach, Chuck Sheley	158
21-5: Britt Brewer at the 1977 National Junior Olympics Meet	160
21-6: 1977 All-Golden Gate Conference team	160
21-7: Pepsi 20-Mile Race jacket earned by Mike Buzbee	162
22-1: Suzanne Richter finishing a race	163
22-2: *Chico Enterprise-Record* sports page drawing of Bidwell Park	164
22-3: Suzanne Richter	168
23-1: Toni Ruggle competing as a Wildcat on the track	171
23-2: Toni Ruggle leading the "Devil Mile" at the Cow Palace	173
24-1: Chico High Panthers relaxing on race day	175
24-2: Steve Growdon finishing a race	176
24-3: Greg Williams leading Central Valley's John Frank	178
24-4: Cindy Claiborne and Greg Williams running together	180
25-1: Jill Symons as a Wildcat, and younger Aqua Jet member	181
25-2: Lady Wildcats competing in a cross country race	183
25-3: Mike Leonard, Mike Fornaciari, Pat Finn, and Scott McVay	184
25-4: 1978 All-Golden Gate Conference Cross Country team	186
26-1: Jack West winning a race on the track for Butte College	187
27-1: Mural by Ed Logan adorning the CJHS gymnasium	194
28-1: West Valley Cross Country team, circa 1979	197
28-2: Steve Growdon, and his bike packed with gear	198
30-1: Doug Avrit on the track competing for West Valley College	203
30-2: Yuba City High School Coach Mike Buzbee	207
30-3: Pat Buzbee racing at a San Jose State charity event	209
30-4: Kurt Graves in a 10,000-meter race	210
30-5: Kurt Graves and friends relaxing on the water after a race	211
30-6: Craig Larsen at the top of Mt. Haleakala in Maui	212
30-7: Kent Pease rock climbing	215
30-8: Additional climbing-related, and fishing activities	215
30-9: Suzanne Richter after completing a 5,000-meter race	216
30-10: Cindy Claiborne and Suzanne Richter	218
30-11: Tom Cushman competing in a road race	220
30-12: Jim Walker competing in a relay race	222
Appendix A: Britt Brewer leading EAL Championship 2-mile race	226

MAP

Preface-1: Northern California: Yuba City to the Oregon border xxxvi

Foreword

When I arrived in Chico in 1975, I was excited to join a community with a strong culture of running—at all levels, from high school through college to post-collegiate adults, from jogging for health and pleasure to focused competitions. Beyond Chico, running had taken off throughout the country from the late 60s into the 70s, owing in part to wildly popular books like Bill Bowerman's *Jogging* (1967), Dr. Kenneth Cooper's *Aerobics* (1977) and Jim Fixx's *The Complete Book of Running* (1977). Locally, high school and college track was reaching new levels with many performances that remain in record books to this day. The same was true for road racing, from 5Ks to marathons. It was not only those at the top who flourished, so did middle-of-the-pack finishers. Large numbers of non-competitive joggers were seen on the trails of Bidwell Park and throughout the Chico-area flats and foothills.

During the summer of 1975, weekly evening track meets were held at the Chico State track, mixing high schoolers with collegians, and adults of all ages. Events varied week to week. One of those events was a 3-mile, leaving the track to run on nearby athletic fields and streets, returning to finish at the track. That's when I first met David Bruhn, a successful high school miler/2-miler. During my high school and college days, I had been an 880/mile specialist. By then, I was an enthusiastic distance runner, with an occasional foray back on the track. Mainly, I was training for marathons. That summer, I also met many others featured in this book. As you will read, the Chico Running Club emerged from those meets, continuing to this day.

Holding the stopwatch at some of those meets was Chuck Sheley, an inspiring, highly successful Chico High track and cross-country coach who had already mentored a host of successful athletes with many more to come. His career extended over more than four decades. His influences continue to this day, in the lives of individual runners (male and female) and on the high school programs at Chico High and beyond.

In this book, David Bruhn has documented training and racing performances of Chico-area runners through their high school years and, in many cases, extending through college and later. It is remarkable history. There are stories of outstanding racers, like Doug Avrit whose Chico High mile record stands today and who went on to a successful collegiate and post-collegiate career, including high finishes at the 1983 New York City Marathon and the 1984 U.S. Olympic Trials. Toni Ruggle from Oroville's Las Plumas High School was outstanding 50-some years ago and continues to run to this day, often with others featured in this book such as Jim Walker and Tom Cushman. We learn about outstanding high schoolers Suzanne Richter, Darcy Burleson, Luanne Park, and Jill Symons. We get to know the racing twins, Mike and Pat Buzbee, along with many others.

This book is truly a treasure of running and racing history, focused on one community but with tales that will appeal to readers far beyond, especially those who lived through and still appreciate that era. The book is engaging, informative and inspiring. Enjoy your read!

Walt Schafer

Foreword

Astronomers gaze outward from Earth into the heavens, scanning the galaxies for planets with environmental conditions conducive to the existence of life. Now, consider what might have happened if one had taken a similar approach in the 1970s, looking outward from Eugene, Oregon, the quintessential distance-running hotbed (both then and now) in search of another community with similar characteristics. It's quite likely that a small city 384 miles to the South would be identified as a prime candidate for supporting a distance running haven. That city is, of course, Chico, California.

The physical environment of Chico resembles that of Eugene in several key running-relevant ways. Like Eugene, Chico is situated in a predominantly flat, agriculture-intensive river valley with ample access to hills. Further, like Eugene, Chico has relatively mild winters and is rich in natural beauty, with an abundance of scenic roads and soft-surface trails. The physical features that the two cities have in common are, not surprisingly, facilitative to year 'round running and training for both speed and strength in pleasant surroundings.

Of arguably greater importance than the physical similarities between Chico and Eugene were commonalties in their social environments. Like Eugene, Chico was (and still is) a university town, free of big city distractions, with a regular influx of talent, energy, and enthusiasm to boost the rolls of runners. During the running boom of the 1970s, Eugene and Chico both evolved strong social networks of clubs (both with "tree" logos, no less), teams, gifted coaches, dedicated race directors, devoted volunteers, and generous sponsors to support the activities of runners. Above all in the social realm, however, it was the combined efforts of individual people who helped make Eugene and Chico into the running meccas they became.

Eugene had Phil Knight, and the Bill Bowerman's legendary waffle iron; Chico had, late in the decade, Sally Edwards and Fleet Feet Store #2. Eugene had Dyrol Burleson; Chico had Darcy Burleson. Eugene had the McChesney brothers; Chico had many dynamic sibling combos of its own, including the Buzbees, the Greggs, the Growdons, the Navas, the Parks, the Richters, the Scotts, the Zickers, and...

Literally hundreds of active individuals across the youth, junior high school, high school, college, open, and masters levels—from Greg Williams and William (Bill) Gregg to Toni Ruggle and Everett Riggle (and beyond)—contributed to the colorful tapestry of Chico distance running in the 1970s.

In *Toe the Mark*, David Bruhn chronicles a golden decade of distance running in Chico with the careful attention to detail befitting the work of a naval historian. Interweaving personal observations with information gleaned through interviews, media accounts, and primary source materials, David breathes new life into a bygone era. Chico had a heck of a run—and was a heck of a place *to* run—in the 1970s. Eugene's running star may have shone more brightly, but its California cousin a quarter-day's drive down I-5 had a luminous running glow of its own in the 1970s. Thanks to David and *Toe the Mark*, we need neither a telescope nor a time machine to view a collection of stellar moments that resonate to this day in the hearts, minds, and legs of those who experienced them.

Britt Brewer

Foreword

My journey to being an athlete at Chico High School started from a different location than almost every other Chico High runner in *Toe the Mark*. I did not attend Chico Junior High School.

The journey began at Sierra View Elementary School, with stops at Bidwell Junior High School, and Pleasant Valley High School.

We did the Presidential Fitness Test in elementary school. I wasn't very good at the 50-yard dash, but discovered an ability to push hard over the longer haul in the 600-yard run.

I was on the track team at Bidwell Junior High in 9th grade. My event was the 1320-yard run, the longest offered in junior high. Such an odd distance!

Fast forward to 10th grade at Pleasant Valley High School. At the beginning of the track season in 1972, it was determined by the coaches that I needed a haircut in order to be a member of the track team (some sort of grooming code that I did not understand). I did not cut my hair, so I was removed from the team.

As a 16-year-old, being cut from a "no cut sport" was a very unpleasant and confusing experience, so much so that I transferred to Chico High School for my junior year in the fall of 1972. That was when I met my new coach, Chuck Sheley. Luckily for all of us, Chuck knew that the length of a runner's hair was not a reflection of the runner's character or ability.

Chuck is one of the most prepared and detail-oriented coaches I have ever met. He asked his athletes to trust him, to be disciplined, and to be dedicated to the team above and beyond individual goals. Chuck would not let us veer off path and held everyone accountable. In the moment, being held accountable by Chuck could feel harsh, but in hindsight, his manner was a blend of tough love, compassion, and truly caring about all of us.

I have been fortunate to be a successful high school coach. My success doesn't stem from a unique coaching philosophy or a distinctive training plan that I created. My coaching is a product of the incredible influence and impact my coaches had on me and all of the athletes they taught and trained. My coaching roots are born from the seeds planted and nurtured by my coaches.

In *Toe the Mark*, David Bruhn describes in vivid detail the development, growth, and success of the running programs at Chico Junior High and Chico High under the guidance of Chuck Sheley. In the book's preface, David acknowledges the Chico Aqua Jets swim team's contributions to cross-over athletes who became part of "Charlie's Angels" along with the accomplishments of other Chico swimmers who were successful at national and international levels. The Aqua Jets were coached by Chico State's Ernie Maglischo. I was fortunate to be a member of the team and swam side by side with many of the swimmers David mentions. I owe much of my success to the fact that I was mentored at a young age by these two great coaches, Sheley and Maglischo, in the small town of Chico, CA. The book also tells great stories about Chico State runners, Gene Meyers and Kim Ellison. Both men coached me at Butte College and I am grateful to them for sharing their wisdom and experiences.

Like a family tree, a coaching tree shows the relationship between coaches. The term coaching tree can also refer to any idea or set of ideas originated by an individual or group. In both senses, I am a descendent of coaches Sheley, Maglischo, Meyers, and Ellison. Other younger branches on the tree include long time coaches Doug Avrit (Calaveras), Seth Roberts (Paradise), and Bobby Hastings (Las Plumas). Davis High alum, Drew Petersen, now coaches at UC Davis. My children, Kaitlin and Brendan, have developed thriving online coaching businesses. I firmly believe that a healthy portion of Chuck Sheley's coaching DNA lives on in their coaching today.

In recent correspondence with Chico High grad, Kurt Graves, we acknowledged how lucky we all are to be able to call Chuck Sheley "our coach." Those two words are magical!

David Bruhn has woven a beautiful fabric, full of detail and richness in *Toe the Mark*. I trust you will enjoy traveling back to those enchanted running times in the 70s.

Bill Gregg (Chico High Class of '74)

Acknowledgements

Photo Acknowledgements-1

At left: The meeting of two Panther Mile Record Holders—Horace Brakebill, CHS record holder in the 1920s, with Kent Pease the new record holder in the mid-1970s. Many decades earlier, in 1927 while competing for Chico State, Brakebill had marks of 4:35 and 2:04 for the mile and half-mile, respectively. At right: exchange from Mike to Pat Buzbee (leg six to the final anchor leg) at the 1993 Tahoe Relays. Photographs courtesy of Chuck Sheley and Pat Buzbee

Many people involved in running in Chico in the 1970s assisted with *Toe the Mark*. Knowledge and even written information about events which occurred decades ago are perishable. Nevertheless, sufficient records and remembrances of key individuals were available to provide readers an accounting of what transpired to produce the greatest groups of distance runners ever spawned by this small, northern California city.

The collective efforts of those involved, some highlighted in these acknowledgements, serve as a spirited handoff of running heritage to following generations—as some were passed by Horace Brakebill to Chico High miler Kent Pease in the 1970s. The former Chico State great was the teacher/principal at the elementary school in Stirling City for many years, later named Horace Brakebill Elementary School. Horace was a guest at Chico High Cross Country Awards events, and he came to at least one Chico High track meet at Butte College, as shown with Kent.

Before acknowledging the many individuals, who contributed to or influenced the book, I would first like to thank Debbie Riley, Heritage Book's editor and book designer for her sensational cover art. Pictured on the front cover are Jill Symons and Kim Ellison and, on the back, Pat Buzbee and Doug Avrit. (Readers will learn much more about these individuals in the preface and text of the book.) For those who like "old school," (who doesn't?) the medals depicted on the cover are California North Section Cross Country gold team medals from 1971-1974.

I am deeply appreciative of professors Walt Schafer and Britton Brewer, and Coach Bill Gregg's generosity in reviewing the text, as well as penning forewords for the book offering their very unique and valuable perspectives. Walt was an outstanding college and post-collegiate athlete. After arriving in Chico to take up a Professor of Sociology faculty position at Chico State, he was instrumental in the formation of the Chico Running Club.

Photo Achnowledgements-2

Professor emeritus Walt Schafer.
Courtesy of Walt Schafer

A well-known expert in stress management, Walt has authored many books and articles on this subject including the authoritative standard, *Stress Management for Wellness*. His research publications include a study showing that among more than 500 northern California adult distance runners, the frequency and seriousness of running injuries were associated with greater clustering of stressful life events in the recent past. His other studies of hundreds of college students showed that the more frequent the exercise, the lower the stress level. Now in his 80s,

Walt stays active as a cyclist. He serves as president of the Honey Run Covered Bridge Association near Chico and as a member of the Board of Trustees of the Enloe Medical Center in Chico.

Photo Acknowledgements-3

Springfield College

**Professor of Psychology
Head Cross Country Coach
(1993-2001)**

Chico Junior High School Cougar Britt Brewer racing to an individual win in the 1977 Eastern Athletic League Freshman Cross Country Championship race, while leading his team to victory. There were six creek crossings in the race.
Courtesy of Britt Brewer

Britt is uniquely suited to offer his perspective on the subject matter of *Toe the Mark*, having been a champion runner at Chico Junior High School, Chico High School, and in road racing before his family moved away to Spokane, Washington, in the middle of his sophomore year of high school. After departing from Chico, he won the 1980 National Junior 20 Kilometer Championship, was a member of the Washington State AAA state champion cross country team, placed third in the 1980 National Postal 3-Mile Run, and claimed the 1981 Washington State AAA title in the 3200-meter run. His involvement in running after high school was injury-filled and otherwise unremarkable.

Britt earned a doctorate in clinical psychology from Arizona State University and has been a professor at Springfield College in Massachusetts since 1991, serving as Head Cross Country Coach at the school from 1993-2001. An extraordinarily prolific researcher and writer, he has authored or co-authored over 200 book chapters and articles in peer-reviewed journals, many at the intersection of sport and health psychology. Britt co-authored the text *Psychology of Sport Injury* and edited a volume on sport psychology for the International Olympic Committee Medical Commission.

Photo Acknowledgements-4

Davis High School Head Cross Country and Track & Field Coach Bill Gregg.
Courtesy of Bill Gregg

Bill Gregg is an extraordinarily successful coach, and his laudable accomplishments in this area were achieved despite fulltime demands on his time outside the school environment; first as the owner of a ski equipment shop, and later as an account manager and account analyst at an educational non-profit and at UC Davis. Almost all highly successful coaches are employed as teachers at the school in which they engage with athletes after the school day is over. Bill, serving in what some term an "off-campus coach" capacity, meaning not from within on-campus teacher ranks, aptly demonstrates that greatness is greatness, whatever the source.

As introduced in his foreword, and expanded on in *Toe the Mark*, Bill ran cross country and track & field, was a member of the ski team, and competed in age group swimming while a student at Chico High school. He competed in cross country and track for Butte College, and ran cross country at UC Davis from which he graduated, and following college, competed in road races. His first coaching experience came in 1978 as head swim coach for a summer program in Quincy, California.

From 1983-1989, Bill served as Assistant Women's Cross Country and Track & Field coach at U.C. Davis. With this experience in hand, he then turned to developing prep athletes at Davis High School; first as alpine ski team coach (1989-1997), before transitioning in 1997 to his first love, coaching cross country and track through the present time.

Coach Bill Gregg's many accomplishments are too lengthy to list here. They include his "Blue Devils" garnering twenty-two Sac-Joaquin Section Cross Country Championship Team titles, and finishing in the top ten at the California State Championships fifteen times. Bill's girls cross country teams were runner ups at the Nike National Cross Country championships in 2015 and 2016. Three former Blue Devils, his children Brendan and Kaitlin, and Chelsea Reilly Sedaro, competed in the U.S. Olympic Track & Field Trials. Recently, Coach Gregg was inducted into the Sacramento Running Association Hall of Fame in 2020. Individuals thus honored have made significant contributions to the sport of long distance running either through excellence in the sport or significant contributions to the sport.

Much thanks to Mike Wolcott and Justin Couchot, editor and sports reporter for the *Chico Enterprise-Record*, respectively, for their interest in and support of this book, which included allowing the use of photographs and material from the 1970s.

This book would not have been possible without access to the meticulously compiled and maintained records of coach Chuck Sheley. Chico State coaches Oliver Hanf and Gary Towne, and former Wildcat Toni Ruggle provided much information related to Wildcat track & field and cross country. Similarly, Scott Fairley and Tom Cushman contributed North Section prep athletics historic data and records.

Finally, a tip of the hat to the many individuals, some former teammates, who provided important information, perspective, and from scrapbooks, photographs and newspaper articles. These include: Doug Avrit, Dale Edson, Kurt Graves, Bill Gregg, Rich Gregg, Charlie Griffin, Steve Growdon, Craig Larsen, Bob Noe, Pat O'Connell, Luanne Park, Kent Pease, Suzanne Richter, Dave Scott, Jim Scott, Jill Symons, Jim Walker, and Greg Williams.

Kim Ellison, serving as content editor for *Toe the Mark*, added much personal knowledge, perspective, and expertise to the work, in addition to improving structure and syntax.

My longtime editor Lynn Marie Tosello did the final burnishing, probably grateful to be reviewing something besides naval history.

Preface

Missed the greatest ever female athlete from Chico [Tonya (Alston) Burns]—CIF High Jump Champion, UCLA Track, walk on to UCLA women's basketball, NCAA High Jump Champion.

—Response by Chuck Sheley to the author's query about whether I had correctly identified all the Chico High School coaches and distance runners associated with the sports of track & field and cross country in the 1970s, who had been inducted into the *Chico Enterprise-Record* Athletic Hall of Fame. I omitted Tonya Alston who, although not a distance runner, deserves special mention for her accomplishments.

Photo Preface-1

Baton Pass from Chuck Sheley to Charlie Moseley (University of Alabama 4th NCAA 1962 high hurdles and long jump) at all-comers meet in Medford, Oregon, 1964. Gobi Track Club consisted of Siskiyou U.S. Forest Service Smokejumpers.

It would be disingenuous to write a book about distance running in Chico in the 1970s and not highlight the significant achievements and influence on this era by Coach Chuck Sheley. Chuck is a legendary figure in the world of running in northern California and rightly so. He was, when he started what would be a fifty-year coaching career, and remains today, a focused, no-nonsense, all-business individual. If you phone him at home and get his recording, you will hear, "This is Chuck Sheley. Leave your message please."

We, his athletes in the 1970s, generally knew that Chuck had been a hurdler. He was listed on the Chico High School Track & Field Record Board with a time of 19.3 for the 180-yard low hurdles (an event no longer run), and we knew that he had run a 49.2 second quarter mile while an athlete at Chico State. We did not know that the quarter mile capped off his senior year at Chico State in 1960, nor that he had competed in the NAIA national championships his freshman year, and the equivalent of today's Division II the remaining three years. We also knew that he had a bum knee from being a former smoke jumper (someone who parachutes out of a plane to fight forest fires in remote areas), and thus could no longer run.

Photo Preface-2

At left: Chuck Sheley in parachute harness, with helmet at the ready, being airlifted somewhere to "jump fire." Right: Years later, Coach Sheley observing a track meet. Courtesy of Chuck Sheley and Dale Edson

When the decade of the 1970s began, Chuck was a physical education (PE) teacher at Chico Junior High School and also head of the PE Department. One of the other PE teachers, Keith Lockwood, had also been a smoke jumper, and there was an ex-Marine on the PE staff as well—all devoted to ensuring that we got our full allotment of exercise each day. In the fall of 1971, Chuck took over as head Chico High School Cross Country Coach from Jack Yerman, and in spring 1972, as head Track & Field Coach as well, while retaining his teaching position at Chico Junior High School. When this occurred, Bob Noe, Chuck's assistant coach at Chico Junior High, assumed those duties, aided by Al Holzhey, a math teacher at the school, as assistant coach.

Photo Preface-3

At left: Chico State Wildcat Bob Noe, pictured in 1967 as a member of the Block "C" Society, composed of Varsity letter winners. He played baseball. Right: Coach Bob Noe, squinting in bright sunlight, and sporting the long sideburns and mustache style common among many young males in the 1970s.
The Record 1967 – Chico State Yearbook Collection, and courtesy of Bob Noe

Coach Yerman had earlier succeeded the legendary Mel Jones in these positions. Melvin Richard Jones had served as a Radarman aboard the amphibious attack transport USS *Mellette* (APA-156) in World War II, and earned the Purple Heart Medal for being wounded in combat. Following the war, Jones first attended Marin Junior College, then transferred to Chico State, where he participated in baseball, track, and boxing, becoming a Far Western Conference boxing champion in 1950. Mel was the founder of the Chico Invitational Track Meet in 1958 and in 1998 the Chico High Track was dedicated as the "Mel Jones Track and Field Complex." Mel passed away on September 3, 2019, at age 94, greatly beloved in the Chico community.

An even more legendary figure at Chico High in the 1970s was Olympic Gold Medalist Jack Yerman. Then a history teacher, he had, years earlier in 1960, teamed with Earl Young, Glenn Davis, and Otis Davis at the Rome Olympics to win the 4 x 400-meter relay in 3:02.2. While I was a student at Chico High School (1973-1975), I did not have the pleasure of having Mr. Yerman as a teacher, but I remember him occassionally showing up at track practices in his Olympic sweats and running workouts with our quarter-milers.

Photo Preface-4

Jack Yerman, circa 1962.
Star Presidian, Volume 10, Number 39, p. 7

As anecdote to this overview, I recently discussed with Mike Buzbee (someone readers will become acquainted with later), what it was like having had Yerman as a cross country coach in the late 1960s. Mike remarked, "Well, he was not a true distance coach. He thought we were slow." After I stopped laughing, I responded, "Well, if you were a 46.3 400-meter runner," (Yerman's time in winning this event at the 1960 U.S. Olympic Trials at Stanford University), "you might also think that high school cross country runners were slow."

Before progressing on with this overview of *Toe the Mark*, it is important to highlight that Chico was a relatively small community back in the 70s. In 1970, the population of the city proper was 19,580. Over the decade, the number of people living within the city limits grew to 26,716 by 1980. At that time, Chico was mostly known for Chico State College (later University) which, founded in 1887, is the second oldest campus in the California State University system; and Bidwell Park, one of the largest municipal parks in the nation. Currently, it is also known for the Sierra Nevada Brewery, which was established in 1979; and as the hometown of Aaron Rodgers, quarterback of the Green Bay Packers professional football team.

THE NORTHERN SECTION

For high school athletic competition, the State of California is divided into the ten sub-divisions, termed Sections, which are identified in the following map.

CALIFORNIA'S CIF SECTIONS

2) North Coast Section
1) Northern Section
3) Sac Joaquin Section
4) San Francisco Section
7) Central Section
5) Oakland Section
6) Central Coast Section
9) Southern Section
8) Los Angeles Section
10) San Diego Section

Chico High School, and crosstown rival, Pleasant Valley High School, are in the Northern Section (commonly called the North Section), which begins to the north-northwest of Sacramento, and extends to the Oregon border minus the northern coastal region.

LASSEN HIGH SCHOOL DOMINANCE IN THE 1960s

As shown in the following table, Lassen High School dominated the sport of Cross Country in the North Section (NSCIF) in the 1960s. Lassen High is in the town of Susanville, located 101 miles to the northeast of Chico, at an elevation of 4,186 feet. This elevation, in conjunction with the hilly terrain, is conducive to developing very good Cross-Country runners. In the 1970s, Chico High had a relatively short and flat 2.55-mile home course. Following a two-and-a-half-hour van or bus ride along winding canyon roads, you arrived in Susanville for competition, and were often treated to cold and very windy weather, along with as many steep hills as the geography allowed Lassen High School's coach to incorporate into their home course.

We liked to get the Grizzlies (Lassen runners), who were our major competitors, down to Chico and on our flat, fast course; whereas they liked to get Panthers (us) up there in their thinner air and hilly terrain.

CHICO HIGH SCHOOL AND CHICO JUNIOR HIGH CROSS COUNTRY SECTION CHAMPIONSHIPS

NSCIF BOYS CROSS COUNTRY CHAMPIONS

Year	Varsity	Junior Varsity	Small School	Freshman
1965	Lassen	Lassen		
1966	Lassen	Chico		
1967	Lassen	Lassen		
1968	Lassen	Lassen		Chico Jr.
1969	Lassen	Lassen		Lassen
1970	Lassen	Lassen		Lassen
1971	Lassen	Lassen		Chico Jr.
1972	Lassen	Chico		Chico Jr.
1973	Chico	Chico		Chico Jr.
1974	Chico	Chico	Weed	Chico Jr.
1975	Chico	Chico	Weed	Chico Jr.
1976	Chico	Chico	Weed	Chico Jr.
1977	Pleasant Valley	Paradise	Weed	Chico Jr.
1978	Chico	Lassen	Weed	Chico Jr.
1979	Paradise	Anderson	Big Valley	Nova

NSCIF GIRLS CROSS COUNTRY CHAMPIONS

Year	Varsity	Junior Var
1974	Enterprise	
1975	Lassen	
1976	Chico	
1977	Chico	Chico
1978	Shasta	Lassen
1979	Shasta	Chico Jr.

Chico teams made a couple of inroads in the 60s when the Chico High junior varsity won the section meet in 1966, and Chico Junior High freshmen won it two years later in 1968. However, things did not begin to change until autumn 1971 when the Chico Junior High School team, of which I was a part, won the Freshman Section Championship. This was followed by a Junior Varsity Championship the following year after we had moved on to high school, and then two consecutive Varsity Championships in autumn 1973 and 1974.

This string of wins by basically the same group of runners—there was some shuffling around, with both departures and new additions—might appear reasonably impressive, and we were proud of our accomplishments. However, we barely squeaked out some of the team wins over Lassen, and the best group of Chico runners ever, had not yet left their mark on the northern California and national high school running scene. These were the "Charlie's Angels" (a nickname derived from a popular television series at the time, and Chuck Sheley's first name, Charles). This collection of extradinarily talented, dedicated, and disciplined young ladies included:

- Suzanne (Richter) Reade: finished 5th in the mile at the State Meet in Bakersfield in 1978 with a time of 4:52.42; future stand-out UC Cal-Berkeley runner and All-American
- Jill (Symons) Hernandez: holder of swimming age-group world records and Olympic Trials competitor in 1976, and later Chico State All-American in Cross Country
- Luanne Park: competitor in the 1984 U.S. Track & Field Trials and later a triathlete and legendary ultrarunner
- Darcy Burleson: daughter of Chico State Track & Field Head Coach Larry Burleson, and niece of Dyrol Burleson, a several-time Olympian and former U.S mile record holder; ran Cross Country at Chico State
- Joan Gregg: Swam for UC Davis and also ran Cross Country
- Julie Selchau: Post-high school accomplishments unknown
- Stacey Shols: Post-high school accomplishments unknown

More about these individuals later in the book. It's worthwhile here to highlight the local swimming program from which Jill Symons, and other cross-over athletes, such as Joan Gregg, emerged. As previously mentioned, Chico was then relatively small and offered no elite athletic facilities. The Chico Aqua Jets trained at a modest-sized swimming pool at Bidwell Junior High School (the cross-town of Chico Junior High School), but from this "patch of water" came a host of champions.

These included: Jill Symons, who at age sixteen, competed in the U.S. Olympic Swim Trials in the 100-meter butterfly (16th) and 400-meter individual medley (13th); and David Santos, whose chance to make the Olympic Team was denied by the U.S. boycotting the 1980 Summer Olympics because of the Soviet Union's invasion of Afghanistan. His brother Roque Santos did make an Olympic Team, and competed in the 1992 Games in Barcelona, Spain. Finally, in 2004, Haley Cope won a Silver Medal at the Olympics in Athens, Greece.

CHICO HIGH TRACK & FIELD

Track & Field programs at high schools, colleges, and universities with "powerhouse" cross country programs are greatly advantaged by having distance runners who can collectively "rack up" many points in the middle-distance and distance events at track meets, thereby contributing significantly to their teams' overall scores. However, each of these events takes a lot out of the athletes, so most distance runners run a single race at a meet or perhaps two.

Sprinters, who by virtue of their leg speed are usually also jumpers, typically compete in four events. Accordingly, an exceptional athlete can individually score a lot of points. Their efforts are often rewarded by much public acclaim and recognition.

To the credit of the *Chico Enterprise-Record* Hall of Fame, of the below listed six athletes associated with Chico High School Cross Country and Track & Field in the 1970s, three are distance runners. Chuck Sheley believes that Jamie Starmer and Tonya Alston are the greatest all-around track athletes ever produced by Chico High School. The distance runners listed were the top three members of "Charlie's Angels" who, in addition to being ranked second in the nation in cross country, were exceptional track athletes.

Chico Enterprise-Record Hall of Fame

Coaches	Distance Runners	Sprinters/Jumpers
Chuck Sheley	Suzanne (Richter) Reade	Jamie Starmer
Bob Noe	Luanne Park	Tonya (Alston) Burns
Dale Edson	Jill (Symons) Hernandez	Mike Sherrard
Cherrie Sherrard		

Photo Preface-5

Above: Chico State Women's Track Coach Cherrie Sherrard (wearing a track suit), pictured with Trainer Tara Lepp in 1980. *The Record 1980* – Chico State Yearbook Collection

At left, Chico High School Girls Track and Field Coach Dale Edson holding a stopwatch with one of her team members standing alongside her.
Courtesy of Dale Edson

Cherrie (Parish) Sherrard, a superlative athlete and Olympian who competed in the 80-meter hurdles at the 1964 Summer Games in Tokyo, coached at both Chico High School and Chico State College. Her son Mike Sherrard—who later played professional football as a wide receiver for the Dallas Cowboys, San Francisco 49ers, New York Giants, and Denver Broncos—was a football/basketball/baseball player in high school, but ran sprints his senior year.

I believe that former Chico High distance runner Doug Avrit should also be inducted into the Hall of Fame. He is the greatest male prep distance runner to ever come out of Chico, setting school mile and 2-mile records of 4:16.5 and 9:11.9, respectively, in 1977 (which, as of this writing, remain unbroken). He was twice an All-American while at Cal Poly San Luis Obispo, and finished 13th in the marathon in the 1984 U.S. Olympic Track & Field Trials. Also competing in these trials were former Chico High athletes Luanne Park, Tonya Alston, and pole vaulter Jerry Mulligan. Suzanne Richter qualified for the trials, but was unable to participate owing to an injury.

THE IMPORTANCE OF DISTANCE RUNNERS

The following table identifies the high schools that won North Section Varsity Boys and/or Girls Track & Field Team Championships in the 1970s. Even a cursory look at it reveals the close relationship between Chico High's previously identified dominance in cross country (XC) and associated track and field (T&F) prowess. Section Championships in T&F coincided with or followed those in XC. Nearly all of the members of championship cross country teams returned, in the spring of those same school years, to compete in track & field, and score lots of points.

NSCIF (NORTH SECTION) VARSITY BOYS AND GIRLS TRACK & FIELD TEAM CHAMPIONS

1970	1971	1972	1973	1974
Lassen V Boys	Pleasant Valley V Boys	Pleasant Valley V Boys	Chico V Boys	Shasta V Boys
			Wheatland V Girls*	Wheatland V Girls**

1975	1976	1977	1978	1979
Chico V Boys	Chico V Boys	Chico V Boys	Enterprise V Boys	Chico V Boys
Lassen V Girls	Lassen V Girls	Chico V Girls	Chico V Girls	Chico V Girls

* First NSCIF Girls Semi-Final Championships
** First NSCIF Girls Section Championships
Shaded area indicates there were no Girls Championships these years

An outlier to this pattern was Pleasant Valley High School winning the 1971 and 1972 North Section Track & Field Championships without great success in the preceding sport of cross country. This signifies that these track teams had very talented individuals scoring a significant number of points in many events other than distance running.

ROAD RACING; MIKE AND PAT BUZBEE'S VENUE

Nor-Cal Running Review
JULY 1973 (No. 42)

NCRR POINT RATINGS

Below are this month's leaders in the NCRR Long Distance Point Race. To figure your point rating, merely divide your average placing in races by the number of races run. Count a tie as an average (tie for 2nd is worth 2.5, etc.). For example, if your average placing is 4th over a total of five races, then your rating is 4/5 or 0.8. For our totals we count only the top ten finishers in each race (top six in the senior division...must have reached his 40th birthday). The NCRR reserves athlete, Bill Gookin. The top open and senior runners follow: OPEN: (Total races, Average place, Rating) -- (1) Dan Anderson (16, 3.625, 0.227), (2) Bill Seaver (10, 3.100, 0.310), (3) Phil Camp (7, 2.403, 0.347), (4) Darryl Beardall (13, 4.923, 0.379), (5) Jon Anderson (6, 2.667, 0.444), (6) John Butterfield (10, 4.600, 0.460), (7) Dave Garcia & Jim Nuccio (2, 1.000, 0.500), (9) Mike Buzbee (6, 3.167, 0.528), (10) Rich Kimball (8, 4.250, 0.531), (11) Ritchie Geisel (3, 1.667, 0.556), (12) Bob Darling, Steve Dean & George Stewart (4, 2.250, 0.563), (15) Mitch Kingery (4, 2.500, 0.625), (16) Pat Buzbee (5, 3.200, 0.640), (17) Ken Scalmanini (9, 5.944, 0.660), (18) Doug Butt & Ross Smith (7, 5.000, 0.714), (20) Duncan Macdonald (3, 2.167, 0.722), (21)

In 1973, the well-known "Buzbee twins," Mike and Pat, were college students at Chico State University, having graduated from Chico High School in 1969. They had run cross country and track in high school and continued to participate in these sports for a while at Chico State, but they then turned to road racing. They were also Chico High assistant coaches, which mostly involved their running workouts with us when they had the time. Mike and Pat worked to put themselves through college and graduated with double majors in Math and Biology and Math and Geography, respectively. They also boxed for Chico State and were conference champions in two different weight classes; but as Pat recently told me, "We mostly fought each other."

When I was a high school athlete, I once asked one of them how they ended up running the marathon (26.2-mile race), to which his reply was, "Well, if you don't have much speed, they move you up from the mile to the 2-mile, then the 3-mile, then the 6-mile, and pretty soon you're running the marathon." The Buzbees were scrappy, competitive, hardworking—but with little leg speed. Because of this, we sometimes referred to them as "one-speeders."

This joking did not diminish our respect for their accomplishments at the longer distances. A measure of how good they were can be gleaned from the rankings on the preceding table, excerpted from the July 1973 edition of the *Northern California Running Review*. The *Review* was a monthly magazine which evolved into the *California Track & Running News*, and later a website. As indicated, monthly rankings were calculated by dividing a runner's average place in a race by the number of races run (which had to be sanctioned by the *Review*). Readers who followed running in that era will recognize the names of many great runners. I will mention only three.

Three big names in California high school distance running in the mid-1970s were Roy Kissin, Mitch Kingery, and Rich Kimball. Kissin, from San Ramon Valley High School in the San Francisco Bay Area, would finish eighth at the 1975 IAAF World Cross Country Championships. This race was held during his senior track season on March 16th in Rabat, Morocco. A year earlier, Kissin had travelled to Chico to compete in the 1974 Chico Invitational Track & Field Meet hosted by Chico High School at Chico State. He won the 2-mile in 9:22.3, and I was a distant third with a time of 9:46.1.

In the *Nor-Cal Running Review* ratings, sandwiched between Mike Buzbee (9th) and Pat Buzbee (16th), were Rich Kimball (10th) and Mitch Kingery (15th). A little over a year later, at the 1974 California State meet, Kimball won the two mile in 8:46.6, then about one hour later, narrowly won the mile in 4:06.6. In the 1960s and 70s, road racing was a significant part of the "off-season" for many prep athletes, so it wasn't surprising that Kimball and Kingery were competing in longer races. Kingery was particularly well-suited for such. In 1973, though only a sophomore at San Carlos High School, he ran a 2:23:47 marathon, a new prep record.

Enough said about Pat and Mike, who will periodically reappear throughout the book.

CHICO STATE (CSUC) WILDCAT CROSS COUNTRY

The best performance by a Chico State Men's XC team in the 1970s came in 1973, with a Far Western Conference Championship. (There was then no Women's program.) The schools comprising the conference were Chico State, Humboldt State, Hayward State, Sacramento State, San Francisco State, Sonoma State, and UC Davis.

CSUC Men's Far Western Conference Team Finishes

1970	1971	1972	1973	1974
3rd	3rd	3rd	1st	3th

1975	1976	1977	1978	1979
no team	4th	5th	6th	7th

Mark Shuman was Chico's top runner at the conference race, with a 4th place finish. He and three teammates, identified below, made "All-Conference" by virtue of their top fifteen finishes.

Wildcats Garnering All-Conference Honors in 1973

Mark Shuman	Greg Griffen	Jim Price	Tom Brown
4th Place	7th Place	8th Place	10th Place

As evidence of the talent of members of that 1973 team, nearly fifty years later, Brown's best performance as a steeplechaser (competitor in a grueling 7 ½ lap race over mostly immobile barriers and a water jump) in track & field is still among those of the Top 10 Wildcats, ever.

My memory of Mark Shuman, from running workouts with Chico State athletes ocassionally, was that early in the season in XC and T&F, he ran behind his teammates as he worked into shape. "Shu," as the other runners called him, got better and better as a season progressed and, near the end, would qualify for the National Championships and compete in them. He was an All-American in cross country.

For the 1973 cross country season, Shuman went on to finish 4th at the NCAA West Regional Championships, and 23rd at the NCAA Division II Championships.

Five other Wildcats earned All-Conference honors in the 1970s; they are identified below, along with their respective finishes at the championship meet:

1970	1971	1972	1974	1978
Mike Dailey	Kim Ellison	Mark Shuman	Tom Brown	Tom Olson
7th	2nd	5th	7th	10th

WILDCAT TRACK & FIELD

Attending Chico State Track & Field meets and watching from the stands as Wildcats performed was quite exciting for Chico High athletes. The most electrifying event came in 1972, when Kim Ellison, in his senior year at Chico State, toed the starting line in preparation for an attempt to break the magical 4-minute mile mark. No Wildcat had ever accomplished this feat, and fans filled the stands, eager to watch the race—which had been well publicized in local media. This race, and an introduction of Kim and his brother Kerry's remarkable running careers, are the subject of Chapter One.

In addition to that of Tom Brown, the performances of three other 1970s-era Wildcats in middle-distance and distance events still rank (as of this writing) in the all-time top ten at Chico State.

Among Chico State Men's T&F All-Time Top 10 Records

Name	Time	800 Meter Run Year	Current Place
Gene Meyers	1:49.40	1969	5th

		1,500 Meter Run	
Kim Ellison	3:43.30	1971	3rd
Gene Meyers	3:47.10	1971	9th

		3,000 Meter Steeplechase	
Tom Brown	8:55.20	1974	4th
Karl Schaechterle	8:57.30	1976	6th

HALL OF FAME TEAMS AND ATHLETES

The scope of this book, and space limitations, only allow some coverage of Wildcat Track & Field distance runners, and not the full gambit of runners, throwers, jumpers and others that make up a team. It is noteworthy that the Chico State Athletic Hall of Fame includes under Team Recognition:

- 1970-79 Men's and Women's Track & Field teams
- 1975 Men's T&F NCAA Championships 3rd-place team

Three superlative distance runners who competed in the 1970s, earned Hall of Fame honors. Their names and year of induction follow:

- Kim Ellison – 2000
- Gene Meyers – 1999
- Toni Ruggle – 2016

With this overview of running in Chico in the 1970s complete, it is now time for readers to proceed into *Toe the Mark*. The book is written in the first person; not because I was a particularly noteworthy athlete, but instead to serve, hopefully, as a more personal means of introducing athletes and events and, in some cases, to provide additional context.

Map Preface-1

Section of northern California; from just south of Yuba City north to the Oregon border, and east to the Nevada border

1

Attempt to Break the 4-Minute Mile

I witnessed Kim's 4:01 race that very windy evening. I don't know what the extrapolation tables would calculate out to for running on a dirt track with 30 mile per hour winds but in my estimation, it was sub four.

—Observation by Toni Ruggle, a 4:08 miler while a track athlete at Chico State University, concerning the valiant, but unsuccessful attempt by Kim Ellison to break the four-minute mile before a very excited home crowd on a cold, brisk evening in 1972.

Photo 1-1

Wildcat Kim Ellison winning the mile race during a home meet on April 29, 1972.
Chico Enterprise-Record photograph

One evening in the spring of 1972, hundreds of spectators were present in the stands at the track stadium at Chico State University to witness a much-anticipated attempt by Kim Ellison to break the 4-minute mile. This feat had first been accomplished by Englishman Roger Banister at Oxford on May 6, 1954. Many others had subsequently also broken this barrier, but no "Wildcat" (Chico State track athlete) to date. At that time, Jim Ryun held the World and American Records of 3:51.1, set on June 23, 1967.

Ellison had a storied past as an elite runner, interrupted by military service in Vietnam. After graduating high school in 1965, as the three-time L.A. City Section Cross Country champion and the Los Angeles City Section 2-mile champion with a time of 9:20.0 and a second-place finish at the State Meet, he attended California State University, Northridge, for a time on a track scholarship, before leaving school to take a position with Adidas, then a fledgling shoe company.

One day his laidback lifestyle came to an end when, while hanging out on a beach with some friends, his brother, Kerry, came running up, waving an envelope, and yelling, "You got drafted." Kim's Army duty in Vietnam, at the Marble Mountain Army Airfield, south of Da Nang city, was, at first, as a clerk typist and later as a beach lifeguard. At the completion of his two-year obligation, Ellison was discharged from the Army and returned home.

Following the advice of Jim Roulsten, a former teacher and good friend, he headed to Chico, a small college town and agricultural community ninety miles north of Sacramento and enrolled at Butte College. Despite, understandably, not training in Vietnam, he retained his immense talent and competitive nature, and a return to fitness quickly followed. Within a year, he was on the Chico State track team and racing for a national championship in the mile, while pursuing a degree in English. In his final year at Chico State, Ellison wanted to break 4 minutes on his home track in front of hometown fans.

The stadium at Chico State is situated across Warner Street from the athletic fields and track at Chico High School. Because of this, there were close interactions between collegian and high school runners. They often encountered one another while training in nearby Bidwell Park, an expansive area stretching miles and miles from downtown Chico to the upper reaches of Chico Creek Canyon. The Wildcats were always very friendly and encouraging, and Chico High runners enjoyed attending Chico State home meets and cheering on the older runners.

One disadvantage of the open stadium at Chico State was that it was subject to mountain breezes (wind). To the east lay the foothills of the Sierra Nevada Mountains and, in the evening when the sun had set and it was cooler at higher elevations than in the valley, cold dense air would flow downslope to fill the void left by rising warm air. This is the definition of wind—the movement of air masses from areas of higher density to areas of lower density—and the winds often picked up in the evenings in Chico. Moreover, unlike today, with the athletic fields at Chico State reduced to provide space for new buildings constructed since 1972, there were then practically no impediments to buffeting winds. As a result of this geography, it was generally more-windy during evening track meets than daytime ones. Conversely, it was exciting for the athletes to compete under stadium lights with more fans in attendance coming out for an evening after work.

DUAL MEET AT HOME AGAINST UC DAVIS AGGIES

Wildcats Bury Aggies 120-51
Ellison Runs 4:01.4 Despite Cold Wind

—*Chico Enterprise-Record* headline in Monday's newspaper.

On Saturday night, April 29th, Kim Ellison made his attempt to break the magic four-minute mile barrier. The following description of the exciting race is from the *Enterprise-Record*:

> Chico State College's premier miler Kim Ellison didn't get his sub four-minute mile clocking at College Field Saturday evening but it was not because he failed to run a brilliant race.
>
> Despite a bitterly cold wind which swept the local track Ellison streaked to a 4:01.4 clocking and gave promise he'll crack the barrier in the near future.
>
> Paced by teammate Bob King, Ellison was under 60 seconds after the first 440 and at two minutes for the 880. Midway the third lap Ellison was forced to take the lead. He finished the 1,320 at three minutes then sprinted hard the last quarter. He tightened some coming down the stretch but his 4:01.4 was a great race. He broke the CSC mark of 4:02.9 set in 1969 by Duwayne Ray.

Ellison's clocking also broke the stadium record of 4:06.7, set the preceding year by Wildcat Gene Meyers. Finishing behind Ellison, UC

Davis' Dwayne "Peanut" Harms broke his school's record with a time of 4:07.1.

Two other Wildcat distance runners also garnered wins in the meet with UC Davis. Dave Wood won the 880 with a time of 1:55.1; and Pat Stordahl raced to victory with a 14:21.5 in the 3-mile.

Ellison's time of 4:01.4 on the dirt track would be the fastest mile of his life. Unfortunately, going sub-four wasn't in the cards for him. One week later, he tore ligaments in his foot from landing in pea gravel (in a French drain on the inside of the curb) during a race on Sacramento State's new all-weather track. The injury took about a year to heal, and Kim could not compete again at a high level.

A year later, while serving as a "rabbit" (pacesetter) for the open indoor mile at the Cow Palace (located in Daly City near San Francisco), and at the Bakersfield Invitational, Ellison found that he no longer had his "top-end gears." His ability to "kick" at the end of races was gone. Despite great disappointment that his competitive running was over, Kim finished school, earned his degree, and readily embarked on a teaching and coaching career.

In 1975, he married his wife Nancy, and took a job at Paradise High School (PHS), located less than twenty miles up the ridge from Chico, where he remained until retirement in 2008. In addition to teaching English classes, he coached track & field in the spring at Paradise High, and cross country in the fall at Butte College.

Kim ran right alongside the athletes he coached. Teams at Butte College called him "DAD." He continued running with athletes at PHS and Butte until, one day on a 10-mile run with his Butte team, he felt his hip grinding. December 1999 marked the end of his running days when he had a hip replacement operation. The orthopedic surgeon told him to walk, bike, swim, but DO NOT RUN.

As a result of the later involvement, and his previous competitive running, Kim was inducted into the Paradise High School, Butte College, and Chico State Athletic Halls of Fame as a coach and an athlete. Although no longer running and about to turn 75, his love for the sport has never waned and he can be found at local meets, assisting as needed, and cheering on athletes.

Following a career in the Navy, I returned to Chico in 2001 to embark on a ten-year teaching stint, in which I also coached cross country and track athletes. It was always a delight to encounter Kim at meets. On the night of his race in 1972, I was a 9th grader at Chico Junior High School. Thirty years later, upon seeing him at a meet, I commented that I had always greatly admired his class in not citing the challenging conditions that night as the reason for nearly, but not breaking the four-minute mile. He replied something like, "that was the day I had trained and peaked for, I was committed to it, and I have no excuses."

Kim Ellison's school mile record of 4:01.4 stood for thirty-seven years until April 12, 2008, when Scotty Bauhs broke it with a time of 3:59.81. In doing so, he became the 308th American to break the magical 4-minute mile barrier.

Photo 1-2

Wildcat Scotty Bauhs breaking the 4-minute mile.
Courtesy of Tom Cushman

Kim's brother Kerry was a member of the International Track Association (ITA), a professional track & field organization that existed in the United States from 1972 to 1976, which included many outstanding athletes of the day including Jim Ryun. At one time, Kerry Ellison and Kim Ellison held the world record for the combined mile times of brothers (3:57 in a relay and 4:01.4, respectively).

As an aside, Chico State University professor and outstanding runner Walt Schafer, introduced later in the book, attended an ITA meet as a spectator in San Francisco in 1973. He recalls about this event that, "The pole vault standards were replicas of Schick shavers. The pacing lights were first-ever at ITA meets. Now they're back and seen as respectable." Such lights, encircling the track, sequentially flashed one by one, as the runners progressed in a race, to visually show viewers how close to the pace for the desired final time, they were—and thereby increase the excitement for fans. The race time set into the pacing lights might be an American record or another exceptional standard.

Photo 1-3

University of Texas El Paso track star Kerry Ellison gracing the cover of the program for the 1972 Western Athletic Conference Track & Field Championships. His college running preceded subsequent involvement with the International Track Association. Courtesy of Kerry Ellison

Attempt to Break the 4-Minute Mile 7

CHICO STATE MILER PRECEDING KIM ELLISON

Photo 1-4

Wildcat Gene Meyers on the track, winning a race for Chico State.
Courtesy of Cathy Anderson-Meyers

In 1971 at the Far Western Conference (FWC) Track Championships, Wildcat Gene Meyers won the mile in 4:06.7, and the 3-mile in 14:07.2 (a new Chico State school record). Both races were battles to the end, with Meyers outkicking Hayward's Willie Eashman in the mile and Ed Haver of UC Davis in the three-mile. Evidencing how good Meyers' leg speed was in beating Eashman, the latter athlete came back with a 1:51.9 in the 880, narrowly losing to Chico's Jim Estes, whose 1:51.8 was also a new FWC record.

Placing third in the mile was Kim Ellison with a then lifetime best of 4:10.7. Other Wildcats distance runners scoring points in the meet:

- Bob Darling: Second in the 6-mile (29:25.7)
- Mike Dailey: Sixth in the 3,000-meter steeplechase

Gene Meyers best time in the mile came in his final race as a Wildcat, a 4:06.2 effort at the National Championships in Sacramento.

Eugene "Geno" Meyers (born and raised in Oroville, twenty-five miles from Chico) was inducted into the Chico State Athletic Hall of Fame in 1999. His athletic biography summarizes his qualifications for this great honor:

> Geno became the cornerstone of one of the greatest distance teams that Chico State has ever had. During his 4-year tenure in cross country, Chico State won the Far Western Conference Championship in 1968 and 1969. In track and field, he held the conference meet record in the mile and was an All-American in 1969 and 1971.
>
> Geno was one of the few athletes that could excel at all distance races. He held the school record in the 880-yard run, the mile run and the three-mile run. His converted times (from yards to metric distances) and ranking on Chico State's All Time Top 10 List exemplify how talented he really was thirty years ago! He is presently [1999] ranked second in the 800-meters, third in the 5,000-meters and fourth in the 1,500-meter race. His 800-meter record stood for 25 years and was finally broken in 1994.
>
> Gene Meyers is one of the best, if not the best, distance runners to wear a uniform for Chico State.

2

Identification, Recruitment and Development of Runners

The 1-2 punch of Mark Burch and Dave Bruhn. We would have become the first team to win the NSCIF Championship sooner if we had a four-year high school allowing you guys to run on the Varsity rather than at CJHS.

—Chuck Sheley alluding to the fact that as 9th graders, Mark Burch and I finished first and second at the 1971 North Section Freshman Cross Country Championships. In the spring, I won the 1½-mile race at the North Section Freshman 1972 Track & Field Championships, and Mark finished second in the 1,320-yard race (3 laps of the track).

In boys PE classes at Chico Junior High, we all ran two-thirds of a mile, two laps around the athletic field, and then went into the gym and climbed the rope before roll call. After roll call, we did calisthenics, then raced one more lap around the field to total a mile of running, before progressing to whatever we were doing that day. Our teachers were all gung-ho, particularly one who was an ex-Marine. Once, he had us do calisthenics for the entire period on a particularly hot day, after which he cooled us off by spraying us with a garden hose.

Needless to say, we were generally fit, and the running helped Chuck Sheley identify who he should recruit for his cross country and track teams. We also ocassionally raced a mile, three laps around the athletic field for time. When Mark Burch and I were in the 8th Grade, we both ran a time of 5:05. Chuck took us to the nearby Chico High School dirt track a couple of days later to see what we could do on it. Mark validated his previous time running 5:05, and I finished two-tenths of a second behind him. Mark may have already competed in cross country as a 7th grader, but I was then recruited for the sport.

Our standard daily workouts were initially running a 2.3-mile loop from the school through a portion of lower Bidwell Park, around a kids' playground called Caper Acres, and then back to the school. I thought these runs were long. Once they became easy, we progressed to 4-mile runs, referred to as "up to the dip and back." This meant running on a horse trail in lower Bidwell Park up to a dip in the trail, then turning around and coming back.

I don't recall racing much as an 8th grader, but we did participate in an invitational in Susanville, hosted by Lassen High School, at which I won my first medal. It was really small, but I was quite proud of it.

In the fall of the following year, 1971, seven 9th graders were recruited through Chuck's PE program and trained by him, Bob Noe and Al Holzhey. The group went on to win the NCSIF (North Section) Freshman Cross Country Championship. These individuals, standing in the back row of the photograph below, were from L to R: John Peterson, John Growdon, Pat O'Connell, Mark Burch, Dave Bruhn, Jim Walker, and Randy Hines.

Photo 2-1

AL HOLZHEY—BOB NOE
CHUCK SHELEY
COACHES

CHICO JUNIOR HIGH SCHOOL
CROSS COUNTRY
1971-72

N.S.C.I.F. CHAMPIONS
E.A.L. CHAMPIONS

Positioned directly in front of Pat O'Connell with bent knee is 8th grader Kent Pease. No one could then know that in high school, he would develop a devastating kick, be the North Section Track & Field champion in the mile twice, and set a school record of 4:19.1 in 1976.

This short-lived mark stood only until 1977, when Doug Avrit ran 4:16.5. Avrit was then a 7th grader, but apparently Sheley's system had not yet sifted him from the chaff in PE classes.

Bracketing the back row are assistant coaches Bob Noe on the left and Al Holzhey on the right, with Coach Chuck Sheley taking a knee in front of Noe. Bob Noe, although a former college baseball player, would become an outstanding track & field coach, and be inducted into the *Chico Enterprise-Record* Athletic Hall of Fame. Sheley once remarked to me about Noe; he is probably the only individual in California who coached both a boy and a girl State high-jump champion (Teak Wilburn in 2002 and Tonya Alston in 1979).

The freshmen trained with Chuck's high school runners, and Noe took care of the 7th and 8th graders. We ran on dirt trails in lower Bidwell Park and our workouts were fairly simple, try to hang with Mark Burch. There were only a few high school athletes out for cross country, and Mark could easily beat them, as well as all of us (his teammates). To say that he was dominant is an understatement. He won every race he was in that season, except two; I trailed one place behind him in each of them. The two exceptions were the Lassen Invitational in which he and I finished second and third, and the McKinleyville Invitational, third and fourth. The race at McKinleyville, California, was called the Clam Beach Run.

Photo 2-2

Panther cross country runners (a composite of seniors, juniors, and one sophomore) following the McKinleyville Beach run in autumn 1973. From L-R: Mark Burch, Craig Larsen, Dave Bruhn, Steve Nicholson, Bill Gregg, Kent Pease, Larry Day, Jim Walker, Mike McCulley, Pat O'Connell, Arnie Cervantes, and Nate Bunker.

McKinleyville was an interesting race where everyone runs barefoot on the beach and through shallow streams emptying into the Pacific. Before we competed, the coaches gave us a road trip adventure we never forgot. Sheley and Noe drove us in vans 250 miles north to Grants Pass, which lay across the Oregon border. Arriving there, we went to the Champion Store, which sold athletic gear seconds (mistakes made in team orders). I once bought a nice sweatshirt there for almost nothing, made for the University of Notre Dame. It had "Notre Dam" in large letters across the front. After we had purchased what we wanted, or could afford, Chuck took us to Abby's Pizza for dinner. Following sufficient pepperoni pizza and pitchers of Coke, we then traveled to the smokejumper camp at nearby Cave Junction, thirty miles to the south-southwest, our lodging for the night.

Having been a smokejumper there, Chuck was able to get whoever was in charge to agree to provide us bunkhouse lodging with the normal inhabitants. Smokejumpers are really fit and, out of necessity, tough, but not necessarily competitive runners. On this occasion, the best among them challenged Mark and me to a mile race in a straight line down the airstrip. We upheld the pride of our school.

In the morning, we drove down the coast and, upon arrival at McKinleyville—69 miles south of the Oregon border, but 90 miles by winding road—got out of the vans and raced. The race course was down the beach, around a pole and back. Following the race, Chuck took us to the Samoa Cookhouse in Eureka. At this famous cookhouse and logging museum, we sat inside on wooden benches, on either side of several picnic tables, and the servers brought us platters of food. You could eat as much as you wanted, and being usually hungry teenagers, and runners, we enjoyed this greatly.

Returning to the subject of Chico Junior High School's best XC runner, Mark Burch was very much an individual. He had long hair, played the drums, listened to Iron Butterfly and Black Sabbath (hard rock bands), and was involved to some degree in the martial arts. He also was assertive. Once, while in high school and running across an intersection during a workout, a car almost ran over us when we had the right-away. Mark, apparently eager to show his displeasure, ran up the hood of the car, over the roof, down the back—and then gave the male driver the finger.

FIRST NORTH SECTION XC CHAMPIONSHIP

At season's end in fall 1971, at the Section Meet in Anderson, Chico Junior High School won its first cross-country championship. Mark finished first on the 2.4-mile course with a time of 14:05, I was second at 14:07, and teammate Pat O'Connell third at 14:28. Our team score was 19 points. For readers not familiar with the sport of cross country, the finishing places of a team's first five runners across the final line are added together to arrive at an overall team score.

If a team's sixth runner beats the fifth runner of another team, one point is added to the other runner's place. If both the sixth and seventh runners beat the fifth runner, it results in two additional points. A perfect team score of 15 points signifies that the first five runners on one team crossed the finish line in the 1st through 5th places. Our score of 19 points was an indication of things to come in successive years.

1972 FRESHMAN TRACK & FIELD

It's important to highlight, before taking up freshman track & field, that the best marks we achieved as distance runners for Chico Junior High in 1972 and as high school athletes in subsequent years were only marks that succeeding yearly groups of runners developed by Chuck's program quickly swept away.

On the wall above the doorway leading from the locker room at Chico Junior High into the PE office was a Track & Field Record Board. My name made it up there in 1972 for two events: the Freshman 1½-mile (7:27.2) and 2-mile (10:07.2). Doug Avrit ran 7:26.3 two years later, surpassing one record. My 2-mile time had been a better effort, obtained after Chuck put me in a Varsity race at Anderson High School. I won the race but, being a junior high student, I did not score any team points. By virtue of that time, I was seeded (placed) into the Varsity 2-mile final at the Chico Invitational Track & Field Meet that year.

Greg Williams eclipsed my 10:07 with, to me, a stunning 9:50. He would go on to run a 4:21.6 mile at Chico High and, most impressively, later finish second at the California State Junior College Northern California XC Championship race while running for West Valley College. Kent Pease had a similar experience. A few years ago, I commented to him how impressive his 4:19.1 mile record was, to which he quipped, "It didn't last very long before Doug Avrit broke it [with a 4:16.5]." I would like to think that we were at least partially responsible for spurring later Panthers to greater heights; Avrit's accomplishments proved they were just better athletes.

During our Freshman Track season, Chuck had Mark and me (who were known collectively as "Burch and Bruhn") run different races, probably because I lacked leg speed. Mark ran the shorter 3-lap 1,320-yard race and I the longer 6-lap 1½-mile race. My assignment may have come about after being beaten in that event, early in the season, by an athlete from cross-town rival Bidwell Junior High.

His name was Matt Maderos, son of George Maderos, arguably the greatest athlete to ever don a Chico State uniform, who also played professional football for San Francisco 49ers. Matt later developed into a star basketball player at Pleasant Valley High and Butte College. While in high school, he occassionally took part in track meets and caused us some problems.

At the Northern Section Championships, Mark finished second in the 1,320 with a time of 3:29.7; I won the 1½-mile with 7:38.5. The other Chico Junior High School Frosh champion was Jamie Starmer, who prevailed in the 120-yard low hurdles with a time of 14.2.

INDIVIDUALITY AND LONG HAIR

> *The transfer of the Gregg family kids (Bill, Joan and Rich) to CHS because they [Bill and Rich] couldn't run at PV because of the length of their hair, cost the other side of town big time.*
>
> —Observation by Chuck Sheley regarding how the hair length-policy at Pleasant Valley High School benefited Chico High School. It didn't affect Joan obviously, who followed her brothers to CHS, and became a "Charlie's Angel." Bill and Rich both ran cross country and track, with Bill developing into a 4:32.1 miler.

Without delving into this subject too deeply, there was conflict between some high school and college male athletes and their coaches during this period. We were still in the Vietnam War, and there were strongly held beliefs on both sides regarding whether the United States should be in the war and whether there should be protests and other forms of expression against this involvement, particularly on college campuses.

Adult males, many World War II veterans, who didn't particularly care for members of the "younger generation" sporting lengthy locks, termed them "long hairs." Chuck Sheley did not care about the length of an athlete's hair, which put him at odds with some of the other male coaches at Chico High School. Two tried, unsuccessfully, to get him fired after the 1972 Season, because he didn't support their "if you want to be on this team, you must cut your hair" policy. There was also another inadvertent aspect to this; because Chuck allowed students with long hair to compete in track & field, some otherwise baseball players participated instead in the alternative spring-sport.

FORMATION OF THE NEW WAYS ATHLETIC CLUB

There was also some dissent and rebellion in the track & field program at Chico State, which resulted in the early 1970s in a group of athletes breaking away from the team, and forming their own athletic club. Its name, "New Ways," reflected their collective philosophy. Pat Buzbee recently recalled about the club:

> The New Ways AC started in the early 70's with the likes of several including myself, my brother Mike, Mike Porter, Daryl Brock, Denny Stemple, George Wright, Tom O'Conner, Juan Dura, Duwayne Ray, Paul Tjogas, Silas Sanchez, and many others. We were all dropouts from the [Coach Larry] Burleson program.

**At right: New Ways AC t-shirt design
Courtesy of Mike Buzbee**

Among this mix were two of the Chico State's greatest track athletes ever, Mike Porter and Duwayne Ray. As of this writing, their best marks remain among the Top 10 for their respective events:

	400 Meter Dash		
1st	Mike Porter	47.44	1971

	1,500 Meter Run		
6th	Duwayne Ray	3:44.80	1969

Their immense talent and significant accomplishments were formally recognized by the university when Duwayne Ray was inducted into the Chico State Athletic Hall of Fame in 1997 for Track (1968, 1969) and Mike Porter in 2009 for Track & Field (1969-1971). (Duwayne Ray was nominated for induction into the Hall of Fame by Bill Morris, who had run track with Chuck Sheley at Chico State. Morris went on and got his PhD and taught at Stanislaus State.) Information about Ray from the Hall of Fame website follows:

DUWAYNE RAY, Ceres
Track: 1968, 1969

Duwayne was an excellent distance runner in high school, junior college, and at Chico State University. He entered Chico State his junior year and set the school record in the mile of 4:02.9. Also, of that year, Duwayne was FWC Champion and went on to become the NCAA Division III National Champion in the mile in Ashland, Ohio. He graduated with a Bachelor's Degree in Physical Education then going on to receive additional credentials in biology and health. Following his graduation, he coached cross country and track at Beyer and Downey High Schools in Modesto. In addition to his coaching, he has taught biology and health for the last 24 years. The same work ethic and determination that made him a winner as a runner has made him a dedicated instructor and well respected coach. His nomination was made by Hall of Famer Bill Morris who has known and worked with Duwayne for almost three decades.

Pat Buzbee noted about his fellow New Ways AC members:

Duwayne Ray was a RUNNER, period! He could do it all, track, cross-country, and road races. Just ask Bill Clark a former Olympian now in his 80's. Duwayne doesn't get the respect he deserves because he and his coach didn't see eye-to-eye. Also, on this same list is Mike Porter. Probably one of the most raw, talented athletes ever to circle the Chico ovals. It was Mel Jones who plucked him from a PE class and auto shop [at Chico High School] to run track.

We did not know Duwayne Ray but were well familiar with Mike Porter after we moved on to high school, because he helped coach our quarter-milers during track season.

My only experience with the New Ways Athletic Club came during track season in 1972, when its members put on an All-Comers Meet at Chico High School. It was a calm, sunny day with no wind, and athletes and spectators enjoyed Rock & Roll blaring from rigged speakers and a sound system. I ran the mile in which the Buzbees also competed, finished with a time of 4:45, and beat one of them. In ensuing years, when the Buzbees (who were assistant distance coaches when we were in high school) periodically felt compelled to comment on my athletic failings, which included not having a kick, I would respond, "Wait a minute. Didn't I beat one of you when I was a CJHS freshman and you were college students?" Mike would then say, it was Pat; and Pat, it was Mike. Eventually this became, "It doesn't matter. You can't get both of us on the same day." In defending my lack of finishing speed in races, I once retorted, "I may only be able to outkick two people in the entire world, but if so, their names are both Buzbee."

In reviewing draft material, one of the Buzbees (I won't identify which one) protested inclusion of the above story in the book because he had only ever raced me on that single occasion, and it was not significant. "Moreover, if I wanted, we could toe the line right now." He softened the closing of this email missive with, "Just kidding." This story remains in the book because it makes a point. The Buzbees were not gifted with great leg speed, nor was I, but they had great heart, dedication and grit, and attained much success in longer races including the marathon. I have the utmost respect for them. Also, now 70 years old, at a time in life when some their age spend an inordinate amount of time talking about their ailments or embracing their senior status, the Buzbees remain feisty and are still training and racing.

Photo 2-3

L-R: Twins Mike and Pat Buzbee "back in the day."

IMPORTANCE OF COACHING

Some readers familiar with competitive running might be thinking at this point in the book, "Well, you guys were all right in your own little patch, but there were many, many much better prep athletes and teams in California than you." If so, they would be correct. This book is not a proclamation of the talents of former Chico Junior High Cougars and Chico High Panthers in absolute terms. Rather it is an accounting of what is possible when an energetic coach is able to identify, motivate, develop, and meld together a cohesive, competitive team from those individual athletes available to him or her.

The California State High School Cross Country Championships are currently, and have been for many years (since its inception in 1987), held at Woodward Park in Fresno, California. Located about mid-point between the far northern and southern boundaries of the state, it offers a wide, expansive course that can accommodate a lot of runners. There was no such championship meet back in the 1970s. Upon witnessing this event for the first time in 2004, what immediately caught my attention were the awnings erected by teams to provide their athletes shelter from the elements. Some proclaimed in stenciled or stitched-on lettering successive state division championships, seemingly year after year, with very few breaks in successful seasons.

Looking closer, one thing became apparent. Most of these schools were from large urban areas, where a championship program could draw runners wanting to be a part of it from dozens of other nearby high schools. Thus, greatness begets greatness. This phenomenon does not exist in the relatively sparsely populated and geographically large North Section of California. Coaches may benefit from students transferring from a rival school in their city or town to their own, but essentially, they must work with what they have.

Of course, if both good and very lucky, a coach might occasionally "catch lightning in a bottle," as occurred with "Charlie's Angels" at Chico High School in 1976-1977—a group of extraordinarily-gifted girls at the same school at the same time, participating in the same sport, and coached by the right person.

In addition to coaching practices discussed in subsequent chapters, Chuck Sheley was an early proponent of runners taking vitamin C and E supplements. We were also very fortunate to have access to the pool at Chico Junior High for post-run recovery. In addition, he had a library of books about famous runners which we could borrow and read. These great champions, almost forgotten today, included Emil Zatopek, Paavo Nurmi, Ron Clarke, Jim Ryun, Herb Elliott, Peter Snell, and Murray Halberg; as well as legendary New Zealand and Australian coaches Arthur Lydiard and Percy Cerutty—who counted Snell, Halberg, and Elliott among those they coached, respectively.

3

The North Section's Best Distance Runners

Photo 3-1

Toni Ruggle as a Chico State Wildcat.

The city of Oroville lies about twenty-five miles southeast of Chico, through which the Feather River flows. Seventy-five miles upstream through the Feather River Canyon is the mountain town of Quincy. What this means is there are a lot of hilly areas in which to train and facilitate the development of strong distance runners. In the early 1970s, two of the Northern Section's best distance runners emerged from Oroville, one each from rival schools Las Plumas High and Oroville High. These athletes were Toni Ruggle (principally a miler) and Calvin Lantrip (a 2-miler).

In 1972, Toni was the North Section mile champion with a time of 4:25.1 and Calvin the 2-mile champion with a 9:51.2. Calvin's best time that season was 9:30.2, a school record that stands to this day. By virtue of their wins, they represented the North Section at the

California State Track & Field Championships. That year, it took place on Oroville's new, 8-lane dirt track.

The stadium was not sited at either high school; instead, it was centrally located for use by both. Today, there is a National Guard Armory adjacent to the stadium. Back then, there was a drive-in movie theater. When done competing, athletes could (during evening meets) climb up to the top of the bleachers and, from there, view on the big screen whatever movie was being shown. There was no associated sound, of course, owing to an absence of car stand speakers.

NORM MACKENZIE
The track coach at Las Plumas High School, Norm MacKenzie, had a key role in getting the California State Track Championships to Mitchell Field in 1972. (Mitchell Field was later renamed Harrison Stadium in the late 1970s or early 1980s.) Norm was a 1948 graduate of Oroville High School and retired in 1995 after 39 years as a teacher, athletic director, and coach. He ran track and played football at Chico State. He was All-Conference one year in football and Conference Champion in the high and low hurdles his junior year. Most of his teaching time (1961-95) was at Las Plumas High, where he coached Track for 33 years. He was NSCIF Track Commissioner 1991-2017. In 1968, a group of track & field coaches in the North Section (Norm MacKenzie, Bob Russell, Bob Wall, and Chuck Sheley) established the NSCIF Track Advisory Committee which is still in operation today.

PREPARATION OF DIRT TRACKS FOR MEETS
For the 1972 State Championships, the dirt track at Mitchell Field was fast (a relative term if comparing it with today's all-weather tracks) owing to all the work that went into meet preparation. However, even "fast tracks" became much less so as a meet progressed owing to being torn up by long metal spikes affixed to the athletes' racing shoes (termed "track spikes") to provide better traction. This was particularly true for lane 1, in which multiple athletes circled the track while running the 880 and mile races. By meet's end, when the 2-mile and mile relay took place, the surface was pretty chewed up.

Chico High School did not have an all-weather track until well after Mark and I, and teammates ran there. Chuck Sheley recently described the effort it took, then, to prepare Chico High's track for a meet:

> The current day coaches have no idea of the amount of time it took to care for a dirt track and get it ready for a home meet. The CHS track was slanted so that water would run down and usually

pool in lanes 1-2. To counter that, I went around the track and dug "sump" holes 3-4 feet deep and filled them with gravel. That helped the water drain off the track and not pool.

Getting the track ready for a home meet was an all-day project. First, arrive at the track at 0-dark-thirty (usually about 5 a.m.), hook the 6-foot wide drag behind the motorized "tug" and drag the track to make it perfectly smooth. Next came the watering phase. There were four "quick couplers" located around the track, and I had 100 feet of hose to move and drag. That took the better part of hour number two, and it was time to head back to CJHS to get ready for first period.

After roll call, I would take eight students, pile them into the back of my pickup (illegal now days) and head over to CHS. My fellow instructors covered my class. We did not have a track lining machine, so I made eight "stamp" boxes. The boxes were about 3 by 6 inches, screened at the bottom and attached to a 3-foot aluminum handle. We filled each box with chalk, walked around the track, stopped every 3 feet, and "stamped" the box on the ground leaving a chalk mark. I had a rope that I placed on the curb with a student at the other end so that each of the "stampers" were in a straight line. If we moved fast, I could get it done in a single class period.

Most of the prior afternoon and evening the day before the meet was spent getting the field event areas ready, and getting all the result boards, measuring tapes, stop watches and other items ready for meet day.

LANTRIP, RUGGLE AND ERB

Calvin Lantrip had run 9:45.2 for the 2-mile in the Section Meet the previous year (1971), but narrowly lost to Lough from Lassen. Both athletes finished with the same time. After winning the mile at the Section Meet as a junior in 1972, Toni Ruggle defended his title the following year (1973) with a time of 4:27.4. At the State Meet, he finished fifth in his heat with a 4:23.6. Lantrip did not run track at Oroville High in 1973, and junior Bill Dyer from Lassen High won the race in 9:54.6. (Dyer was really strong on hills and, thus, was even better in cross country than on the track.)

Times for distance races at the 1972 and 1973 North Section Championship Meets at Lassen High School were relatively slow, because the track was at elevation (4,186 feet) and, as I recall, one of these meets was cold and windy and the other hot and windy. Toni won the mile at the Chico Invitational earlier that season with a time of 4:18.8. This Las Plumas High School record stood for forty-five years until finally broken by Brian Hastings in 2016. Calvin's best 2-mile time of 9:30.2, which he ran in 1972, remains an Oroville High School record for that distance.

In 1973, another local athlete, junior Rob Erb from nearby Paradise High, emerged as the North Section 880 champion with a time of 1:59.0. Erb had run second to Harder from Del Oro the previous year, with a 2:01.6 to the victor's 1:59.3 in the Section championships. Erb, pictured below in a XC race in autumn 1972 had fearsome speed. His best time came in his senior year, when he won the 880 at the Sub-Section Championship Meet (today, called Division Meet) with a 1:55.9, but that mark only provides an inkling of his talent. More about him later.

The top times for Las Plumas, Oroville, and Paradise High School champion distance runners in the 1970s—including those of Ruggle, Lantrip, and Erb—may be found on the second page of Appendix A.

Photo 3-2

Paradise's Rob Erb leading Pleasant Valley's John Barneson during a cross country race on the Vikings home course in Chico in 1972. The runners are splashing across, at that time of the year, shallow Big Chico Creek. Former Chico State great Gene Meyers (a 4:06 miler) was then the coach of the Pleasant Valley High School team. Pleasant Valley High School 1973 yearbook

THE TRACK HOUSE AND SUNDAY MORNING RUNS

Following the 1973 Track Season, Lantrip and Ruggle graduated from Oroville and Las Plumas High, respectively. That fall found the newly-minted Chico State freshmen running for the Wildcats and roommates at the "track house." Back in those days, some owners of historic two-story homes, and also more modest dwellings in college student areas around the campus, would endeavor to get as much rent money as possible. This was done by putting up partitions inside of rooms, to make smaller rooms. (I once shared a carpeted garage with a roommate; and my sister was one of about 20 coeds sharing a 3-story Victorian complete with attic and dwellers up there, as well).

Although called the "track house," this domicile housed members of both the track and soccer teams. Sometimes visiting teams, having completed competition with the Wildcats would "party" at the house on Saturday night, then stay over before departing on Sunday. Distance runners in general, including those of Chico State, traditionally do long runs on Sunday. At some point in high school, probably our junior year, Mark and I began joining the Wildcats on these runs. Upon showing up at the house on Sunday morning, the first thing I would see after entering the front door were lots of empty beer cans strewn around. At some point the Wildcat runners inside would assemble outside, and we would start off on the run.

The older runners alternated their weekly runs between running to Paradise via an ascent of Honey Run Road, about 16 miles, and a longer, approximately 23-mile run, to Magalia. I only did the runs to Paradise; but I believe Mark ran the longer, harder ones as well. The first 10 miles running out of Chico and into the Butte Creek Canyon to the Covered Bridge, were fairly flat and easy. From there it was six miles up Honey Run Road (a former Gold Rush wagon trail) to Paradise. There, we would find the Chico State coach waiting in his red pick-up truck, and we would pile into the back of it. (No one was particularly concerned about seatbelts back then, and parents routinely had kids ride in truck beds.) Errant runners that did not make it there by the appointed time were on their own, the coach having departed.

INTERACTION WITH THESE OLDER RUNNERS

During their senior year in high school (1972-1973), Toni Ruggle and Calvin Lantrip travelled to Chico every day after school to train with the Chico State distance runners. Recently, Kim Ellison recounted to me how this came about. Norm MacKenzie contacted him, told him that there were two outstanding distance runners from Oroville (Ruggle and Lantrip) with abilities well beyond those of their teammates, and asked if it was possible for them to train with the Wildcats. Kim replied in the affirmative, "Sure, they're welcome to join us."

As freshmen in 1972, Mark and I had seen Lantrip run at meets and knew that he was the section's best 2-miler. I was not then aware of Erb getting ready to burst onto the track scene in a big way, and I suspect my teammates were not either. We knew Calvin Lantrip and Toni Ruggle and had the most interaction with the latter individual.

Toni was an imposing athlete who, tall and with a long powerful stride, could quickly eat up the track. Both earnest and naturally quiet, he was always very friendly and encouraging to us. In 1973, when Mark and I were sophomores at Chico High, Chuck moved us up to Varsity, with the points we acquired doubling in the mile and 2-mile helping out the team. When we were competing against Las Plumas and entered in the mile with Toni as one of the other competitors, he was very gentlemanly. He would allow us to hang with him, until it was time for him to rack up a win (10 points) for his team. He would then leave us to finish in other places behind him. Toni always ran three events for Las Plumas: the mile, 880, and a leg on the mile-relay. He also set a school record with his best of 1:57 for the half mile.

CHICO HIGH VARSITY DISTANCE RUNNERS

Before leaving the subject of varsity distance runners in the early 1970s, when Mark and I and teammates were still Chico Junior High Cougars, it's appropriate to acknowledge the harriers at Chico High School. In the 1970 section finals at Del Oro High School, Dana Miller finished second in the mile with a time of 4:36.2; Dave Garner second in the 880 with a 1:58.1; and Bernie Fricke third in the 2-mile with a 9:59.9.

The following year, 1971, when the section finals were once again held at Del Oro High School, Craig Herendeen from Chico High School won the 880 with a time of 1:59.7; Dave Garner was fifth in that race, no time listed in the results. In the 2-mile, in which Lough from Lassen and Lantrip ran the same time of 9:45.2 to finish first and second, Bruce Eggleston was third in the race with a time of 10:08.6. As junior highers, we knew who Garner and Eggleston were and would ocassionally see them while running in Bidwell Park.

4

Pleasant Valley High School, and One Chico High Panther

Photo 4-1

At left: Tim Holt, and right Charlie Griffin (most valuable) in 1971. *1972 Valkyrie* yearbook

During the years in which the group of runners of which I was a part dominated North Section Cross Country with four consecutive championship wins, Pleasant Valley High School was not a strong rival.

North Section Boys Cross Country Team Champions

Year	School	Level
1971	Chico Junior High School	Freshman
1972	Chico Senior High School	Junior Varsity
1973	Chico Senior High School	Varsity
1974	Chico Senior High School	Varsity

They had some good runners, particularly John Barneson (pictured on the following page, and in the preceding chapter racing Rob Erb), but not the depth that we possessed and, thus, were unable to field strong teams. One reason for this was that as previously mentioned, Bill Gregg, younger brother Rich, and sister Joan, came to Chico High as a result of PVs policy that male athletes' hair could not touch their ears or their shirt collars. It appears, based on the following photograph from the *1972 Valkyrie* yearbook, that Bill was marginally in compliance at PV.

Photo 4-2

1971 PV High Boys XC team: Coach Denny Varley, Bill Gregg, Craig Larson. Kneeling: John Barneson, Tim Holt, Dave Brown. Not pictured Mike Cunningham. (The Craig Larson pictured is not the Craig Larsen that ran for Chico High School.) *1972 Valkyrie* yearbook

Jumping a little ahead in the chronology of this book, at the Eastern Athletic League Varsity Cross Country Championships in autumn 1973, John Barneson barely lost to Bill Dyer from Lassen, who had ascended to best distance runner in the North Section following the tenure of Calvin Lantrip. Bill Gregg led the Panthers to the team title with a third-place finish. Our other top five runners scoring for the team were: Mark Burch (4th), Craig Larsen (7th), myself (8th), and Pat O'Connell (10th). The top seven runners in the race made the All-League team. Rob Erb from Paradise finished 11th.

Among others not scoring for their teams were some future great athletes in different sports. Their places that day, and associated schools, are identified in the following table.

Other 1973 EAL Championship Meet Competitors

Chico High School		Pleasant Valley High School	
Place	Name	Place	Name
15th	Jim Walker	12th	Dave Scott
16th	Arnie Cervantes	13th	Tim Holt
17th	Larry Day	18th	Dave Brown
		26th	Matt Maderos

What's illustrative about this race regarding team depth, is that Chico High placed eight runners in the top seventeen; whereas the top five from Pleasant Valley High stretched from 2nd through 26th places. Tallying the combined finishes of each team's top five scoring runners, Chico High's score was 32 points, Pleasant Valley's 71 points.

However, if Bill had been wearing a Viking uniform that day, instead of the Red and Gold of Chico High, we would have only marginally beat Pleasant Valley with a score of 44 to their 48 points.

As previously discussed, Matt Maderos was a great high school and college basketball player; All-League in high school and a member of the Butte College team that won the California Junior College State title for a second time in the 1975-76 season. Legendary coach John Abell had notched the first win the previous year (1974-75). The players on one or both of these teams included: two-time state player of the year Paul Henderson of Paradise, Rocky Smith and Carl Whitfield, both of Oroville, Matt Maderos of Chico, and Steve Spooner of Willows. I don't believe that Maderos trained much as a runner, but PV used him to fill out XC teams and contribute points in track & field.

GREAT FUTURE SUCCESS

Dave Scott was a good runner who later became a world-class ultramarathoner. His brother Jim who also ran for PV, graduated in 1978 and also became an outstanding ultramarathoner. As an example of Dave's great success at this discipline, a summary of his results (from *Ultra Running Magazine*) for numerous annual Western States 100-mile races follow:

Dave Scott's Western States 100-Mile Race Results

Date	Time	Place	Date	Time	Place
6/27/87	20:34:11	13th	6/25/94	18:19:53	4th
6/25/88	18:22:29	7th	6/25/95	19:49:33	4th
6/30/90	17:14:23	2nd	6/28/97	19:08:32	6th
6/27/91	18:21:09	7th	6/27/98	19:05:14	7th
6/27/92	18:35:47	4th	6/26/99	22:24:27	32nd

Photo 4-3

At left: Dave Scott being greeted by race director Norman Klein, at the 1992 Western States finish line in Auburn, California. At right: Jim Scott out on the course the following year traversing a section of difficult terrain.
Courtesy of Dave and Jim Scott

Younger brother Jim ran the Western States race an incredible twenty times between 1992 and 2013.

Jim Scott's Western States 100-Mile Race Results

Date	Time	Place	Date	Time	Place
06/27/92	22:27:09	29th	06/29/02	20:07:19	18th
06/26/93	19:47:57	7th	06/28/03	23:28:14	80th
06/25/94	19:21:22	7th	06/25/05	22:09:15	53rd
06/25/95	20:33:07	8th	06/24/06	23:45:21	47th
06/29/96	23:24:11	54th	06/23/07	22:46:38	57th
06/28/97	21:16:03	32nd	06/27/09	23:40:16	68th
06/27/98	21:31:55	20th	06/26/10	23:15:40	91th
06/26/99	20:13:54	11th	06/25/11	22:49:27	84th
06/24/00	22:04:19	25th	06/23/12	25:03:57	161th
06/23/01	21:40:08	31st	06/29/13	26:39:44	146th

CHICO HIGH PANTHER

A great ultramarathoner is 1978 Chico High graduate Luanne Park, a former "Charlie's Angel" whom readers will meet later in the book. Her results in Western State 100-milers include her overall finish and, in parenthesis, among other women competitors.

Luanne Park Western States 100-Mile Race Results

Date	Time	Place	Date	Time	Place
06/27/98	23:07:16	35th (4th)	06/26/04	19:42:40	17th (2nd)
06/26/99	22:04:13	29th (3rd)	06/25/05	21:31:21	45th (5th)
06/23/01	21:48:56	37th (4th)	06/26/10	21:51:21	64th (13th)
06/29/02	20:48:22	27th (3rd)	06/25/11	26:08:55	156th (27th)
06/28/03	20:10:33	20th (3rd)	06/29/13	23:58:29	95th (18th)

For readers not familiar with the Western States 100-Mile Endurance Run, it is the world's oldest 100-mile-trail race. The run starts in Olympic Valley, California, near the site of the 1960 Winter Olympics, and ends 100.2 miles later in Auburn, California (33 miles northeast of Sacramento). In the decades since its inception in 1974, the grueling run has come to represent one of the ultimate endurance tests in the world. Competitors must climb more than 18,000 feet, before passing through Emigrant Gap in the Sierra Nevadas and descending nearly 23,000 feet to reach the finish at Placer High School in Auburn.

Those that complete the run in less than 24 hours receive one of the sport's oldest and most prized possession, a silver belt buckle, and those in 30 hours a bronze belt buckle. The Western States is one of the undisputed crown jewels of human endurance.

Photo 4-4

Western States 100-miler belt buckle awarded to finishers who complete the grueling race in less than 24 hours.

LUANNE'S CONSIDERABLE ACCOMPLISHMENTS

I have never been an All-American, Olympian or made it to Nationals. My claim to fame is that I started running at Chico Junior High School and haven't stopped since.

—Luanne Park's response to a query by the author regarding whether she was an All-American in addition to all her other accolades. Both her accomplishments and longevity are phenomenal.

As readers will learn, in addition to having requisite endurance in high school to do quite well in cross country races, Luanne was also very fast. In fact, she was the North Section champion in the quarter-mile. Competing for Butte College in 1980, the former Panther moved up to longer distances and ran a very swift 2:11.07 800 meters, and 4:37.94 for the 1,500 meters. These times are today, number one and number two, respectively, on the college's all-time Top 10 List. While at Butte College, she finished second in the 800 meters at the California State Community Colleges Track & Field Championships.

Photo 4-5

Luanne Park racing, and her worn-out Nike waffle trainers from "back in the day." Courtesy of Luanne Park

After finishing Butte College, Luanne accepted an athletic scholarship to Oregon State University for which she ran and played soccer. In 1984, she qualified for and ran in the inaugural U.S. Olympic Trials Marathon in Olympia, Washington. The time standard in 1984 was 2:51:16, which by the 1988 trials dropped slightly to 2:50:00. Luanne's best marathon time was 2:45:50; she qualified for, but did not participate in, the 1988 trials in Pittsburgh, Pennsylvania. By then, she had acquired a new passion—albeit one which included running 26.2 miles following a swim and bike ride.

In both 1987 and 1988, Luanne finished eighth among women at the Ironman World Championship in Hawaii, with times of 10:19:09 and 10:02:54, respectively. Her splits for the latter race (provided for interested triathlete readers) were 1:11:20, 5:23:54, and 3:27:40.

Apparently, the Iron Man was not challenging enough. In the late 1990s, Luanne began running annually the Western States 100-miler with other ultra-distance races sprinkled throughout the year.

5

1972-73 Sophomore Year at Chico High

The preceding two chapters introduced the North Section's top Varsity distance runners and also the program across town at Pleasant Valley High School. Some of the material moved out ahead of the story of our group of runners transitioning from junior high on to high school in autumn 1972. Hopefully, this straying off track is permissible as some of the athletes highlighted will not appear again in the book, so it was important to include their participation in the covered events.

It's my hope that *Toe the Mark* will offer some lessons learned for young runners, as well as a trip down memory lane for those who experienced Chico in the 1970s. If so, under the category of worst practices of athletes would be my decision as a high school sophomore to dramatically increase my volume of training. This action may have contributed to an injury to my left knee in 1976 while an athlete at American River College, which ended my competitive running.

My parents split up in 1972 and later divorced. Family dynamics resulted in my mother only being agreeable to picking me up after Freshman track practice once or twice a week in addition to meets. My father was a deck officer in the Merchant Marine who sailed out of San Francisco. As a result of going to practice only a couple of times a week, my training initially was very modest.

Many runners interested in their sport read *Runners World* magazine, the *Northern California Running Review*, or *Track & Field News*; and perhaps more than one of these periodicals. There were articles about high school athletes such as Rich Kimball and Mitch Kingery training 100 miles a week (14.3 miles per day) and achieving great success. So, I decided to run to and from school to solve the transportation issue. I would run additional miles in the morning, do regular afternoon workouts, and also run on the weekends.

On weekdays, I would get up early, put my clothes in a backpack, run the 3¼ miles to school; then I would put the backpack in a locker and run in Bidwell Park. Within a short time, this was to "the orchard and back," a six-mile run on top of the 3¼ miles. Following completion of the afternoon workout, I would run 3¼ miles home. If

I was really tired, I would walk part of the way, but I didn't like this because it was boring. Coach Sheley may have known I was doing some running in the morning, but I don't believe that he knew my average total mileage each week.

The upshot of this action was that I suffered two leg injuries in my sophomore year that changed my body mechanics. I hurt the quadricep on my left leg that fall but continued to train and race. I did not rest and let the injury heal properly. When I was finally mended, my left foot toed out during leg swing and foot plant; this put added stress on my left knee. Also, because I favored my left leg while injured, I later hurt the opposite muscle on the other leg, my right hamstring.

Some degradation to my running form wasn't the worst by-product of my high mileage. My memories of high school are of being tired, and I got more and more fatigued as a season wore on. As a result, my performance would degrade. This was called "being burned out." During each track season, I would run my best times about mid-season at the Chico Invitational; then, it would be downhill from there. After each cross country and track season, I ran more in order to do better (1,000 miles in the offseason) and this pattern would continue.

I did not grasp what was happening until a mile race at one of the first 1975 summer All-Comer meets at Chico State. I had been very disappointed in finishing second in the 2-mile at the Section Meet, and I didn't run a step for a month after graduating from high school. I had wanted to break 4:30 in the mile that season and couldn't do it. After a month of rest, and with no training, I ran a 4:28 mile.

JUNIOR VARSITY CROSS COUNTRY SEASON

> *Coach did a good job of keeping things interesting with variable workouts and in different locations. Some of the runs were also to train us for hills, especially for meets in Susanville and Paradise. In addition to the runs at Cohasset and Forest Ranch, I recall doing wind sprints up the pinewood derby hill in the upper park, including Bob McKay who was exceptionally fast—at least for the first couple of ascents. We ran rain or shine, and didn't take days off or retreat indoors like some teams.*
>
> —Kent Pease remarking on hill workouts and training in general.

At the beginning of our sophomore year at Chico High School, Bill Gregg showed up as a junior. I'm not sure when I first became aware of Bill's presence on campus, but you couldn't miss him and other blond-haired Aqua Jet swimmers. There must have been too much chlorine in the pool at Bidwell Junior High where they trained because the hair of the swimmers had a slight green tinge and was very shiny.

Bill recently remarked that what he remembers most about cross country was getting in vans and going somewhere—to Cohasset to run hills, to McKinleyville, etc. Jim Walker echoed this sentiment, asking, how many hours were spent in Sheley's green van? Chuck would drive us to the Bidwell Golf Course, located about six miles from Chico High School, on Mondays to run interval workouts barefoot on the fairways. We were cautioned to stay off the greens. Such workouts are no longer possible. Back then, the golf course was closed on Mondays for upkeep. Today, it's open for use seven days a week.

On a different day each a week, Chuck would transport us to either Cohasset, a mountain community seventeen miles north-northeast of Chico, or to Old Humboldt Road which paralleled Highway 32 on the east side of Chico. Arriving at Cohasset on the paved road, we would get out of the van and run the six-mile or so Vilas Road loop, basically a dirt logging road, and arrive back at the paved road at a different location, for pickup.

Running Humboldt Road, which paralleled California 32 (climbing up to the mountain community of Forest Ranch) for several miles before joining it, and which had very little automobile traffic, was tough, particularly when it was over 100 degrees in Chico. Some teammates referred to it as "Agony Hill." Chuck once quipped regarding the heat, "Don't worry. It will drive out all the evil spirits." On one of our early workouts there, Chuck gave us trash bags and instructed us to pick up aluminum cans during our run. I remember rebelling after engaging in this activity for a bit, saying, "I'm not going to repeatedly stop running to pick up cans, in order that your kids can go to college." In fairness to Chuck, he probably just believed that the roadside needed "policing" (cleansed) of discarded cans. He never asked us to do this again.

TRAINING AND RACING SHOES

In Chico in those days, most kids growing up wore canvas Converse brand shoes. The running shoes readily available to us were Adidas or Puma. The leather uppers gave you blisters until they were well worn in. To try to increase their suppleness, we rubbed mink oil into the leather. One of Chuck's innovations, and an important one, was finding a source of Japanese-made Koyo Bear racing flats and procuring them for us. These shoes had blue nylon uppers, very thin white rubber soles, and no padding for foot support, but you could run faster in them than would otherwise have been possible.

NORTH SECTION CHAMPIONSHIPS

Lassen High School of Susanville won its 10th straight North Section [varsity] cross country championship here Saturday while junior varsity laurels went to Chico High School.

Chico is the only team other than Lassen to win the North Section jayvee title. The 1966 li'l Panthers also won the jayvee title. Lassen has taken the championship nine times.

—*Chico Enterprise-Record* newspaper article describing the results of the 1972 Section Meet.

Photo 5-1

1972 Chico High Varsity and Junior Varsity XC teams. Back row L-R: Larry Day, Craig Larsen, Mark Burch, Clay Williams, Nate Bunker, Bill Gregg, and Chuck Sheley. Front row: John Petterson, Mike McCulley, Tim Berry, Jim Walker, Dave Bruhn, Pat O'Connell, and John Growdon.

In the preceding chapter, I used the word "dominance" to characterize our 1971 (Freshman), 1972 (Junior Varsity), 1973 (Varsity), and 1974 (Varsity) team victories over Lassen High in the North Section Championships. In absolute terms, we won; in actuality, on each of these occasions, we barely squeaked by our arch rivals.

In autumn 1972, Lassen's Bill Dyer won the varsity race with a time of 14:11, while Bill Gregg finished seventh to lead Chico's varsity team. The other Panthers to score were Larry Day (14th), Craig Larsen (29th), Clay Williams (33rd) and Brett Byers (60th). Their combined effort resulted in Chico's varsity team finishing fifth overall.

Las Plumas High's Toni Ruggle and Rob Erb from Paradise were third and sixth, respectively at the Section Meet. Calvin Lantrip was injured and did not compete in the varsity race.

In the 1972 Junior Varsity race, our top five runners finished in the top eight spots. Mark Burch won the race, I was second, Tim Berry fifth, Pat O'Connell seventh, and Jim Walker eighth. For this meet, Chuck had dropped Mark down to the jayvees, though he had been running varsity all season. He set a course record while capturing individual honors.

THE 1966 CHICO HIGH JV CROSS COUNTRY TEAM

> *Lassen Grizzlies Take NSCIF X-Country Title; CHS Captures JV Test.*
>
> —Headline of an *Enterprise-Record* article, which included details about Chico High's Junior Varsity team winning its first ever championship; something that wouldn't happen again until six years later.

We thought that we were the first Panthers to win the North Section Junior Varsity Championship, not knowing that a "two times Buzbee-led team" had first achieved this honor many years earlier. In the 1966 North Section Championships, at rain-soaked Bidwell Golf Course in Chico, Lassen High had swept to a perfect finish in the varsity race by taking the first five spots. Among local athletes, Dave Schoonover of Pleasant Valley was the highest finisher with a 7th place.

Chico's top varsity runner, Jim Gerber, crossed the line three places behind Schoonover in tenth. When Jim was still a student at Chico Junior High, Chuck took him and teammates to the Lassen Invitational Meet. On the way home, they drove into Lassen National Park, hiked about six miles back to a lake and camped over-night before returning to Chico the next day. Gerber went on to become a smokejumper for eight seasons while he was earning his PhD from UC Davis before becoming an Economics Professor at San Diego State University.

The Chico High Junior Varsity team led by Mike and Pat Buzbee, scored an upset victory over Lassen to win the Junior Varsity Section

Championship. The top ten finishers—all from Chico High, Pleasant Valley High, and Lassen High—are identified in the table.

Lassen High	**Chico High**	**Pleasant Valley High**
Robert Robles (1st)	Mike Buzbee (2nd)	Ted Fredenburg (8th)
Bittner (3rd)	Pat Buzbee (4th)	Duff (9th)
Read (6th)	John Staples (5th)	
	Steve Boosinger (7th)	
	Peter Mallory (10th)	

Photo 5-2

Panthers Pat and Mike Buzbee in the front row of the starting line with Mike wearing a t-shirt under singlet; John Staples in the front row next to Pat; Steve Boosinger behind, and to left of Staples; and to the left of Pat's head, slightly behind, Steve Ballinger.
Courtesy of Mike Buzbee

Photo 5-3

Chico's Mike Buzbee leading the eventual winner, Robert Robles.
Courtesy of Mike Buzbee

Photo 5-4

Pat Buzbee, who would finish in fourth place.
Courtesy of Pat Buzbee

Photo 5-5

Front Row: Larry Anderson, Pat Buzbee, Steve Ballinger, Mike Smith, and Mike Buzbee
Second Row: Ray Mayer, Steve Bossinger, Pete Mallory, Tom Fricke
Back Row: John Staples, Tom Petty, Jim Gerber, Jim Linville, and John White
(JV Team: Buzbee x 2, Ballinger, Boosinger, Mallory, Fricke, Staples, Petty, Mayer)
Chico High School 1966-67 yearbook

As described in the 1966-1967 Chico High yearbook, attrition of some team members had resulted in the Panthers being unable to field a complete varsity team:

> The Cross-Country team of 1966 showed great determination this season. They started out with a six-man varsity and an eight-man J.V. squad. As the season progressed, the varsity team dwindled to three men. This barred them from qualifying in any of the races as a team for they must have at least five men to start. The team was coached by Bill Peck, who spent long and hard hours working with the team. The only awards won were by individuals, but we are hoping for a better season in '67.

COACH BOB WALL AT LASSEN HIGH SCHOOL

Bob Wall had just begun his teaching career at Lassen High School as a social science and physical education instructor in 1966 when

Lassen's Varsity Cross Country team swept the first five places at the Section Meet. He taught and coached for 37 years and had a profound influence on students and athletes. In addition to coaching boys' sports, he started and coached Girls Cross Country, Track, Basketball and Golf. His dedication of time and energy to girls athletics opened up the world of sports for young ladies at Lassen High School, the state of California, and the nation.

As shown in the table listing North Section Championship teams, Lassen dominated the sport of cross country from inception in 1965, through 1972. Chico's subsequent run would come to an end in 1979.

Varsity	JV	Freshman	Varsity	JV	Freshman
	1965			1971	
Lassen	Lassen		Lassen	Lassen	Chico Jr.
	1966			1972	
Lassen	Chico		Lassen	Chico	Chico Jr.
	1967			1973	
Lassen	Lassen		Chico	Chico	Chico Jr.
	1968			1974	
Lassen	Lassen	Chico Jr.	Chico	Chico	Chico Jr.
	1969			1975	
Lassen	Lassen	Lassen	Chico	Chico	Chico Jr.
	1970			1976	
Lassen	Lassen	Lassen	Chico	Chico	Chico Jr.
				1977	
			PVHS	Paradise	Chico Jr.
				1978	
			Chico	Lassen	Chico Jr.
				1979	
			Paradise	Anderson	Nova

SOPHOMORE YEAR TRACK & FIELD

We were going after the JV Championship. I had run you and Mark on the Varsity for most of the season. Mark scored 78 team points, the number three scorer on the Varsity. You had scored 50 team points, the number six on the Varsity for the season as a sophomore. I moved you both down to the JV Division for the League Championships as I felt that taking the JV Division was the best option for the CHS program.

—Chuck Sheley recounting putting Mark and me on the Chico High Varsity T&F team for most of our sophomore track season.

As Mark and I began our sophomore Track Season at Chico High, we were the school's best distance runners. As such, we found ourselves moved up to varsity and ran a lot of mile and 2-mile doubles at league meets. Chuck Sheley recently described the 1973 Season generally and the practices he enacted then and which continued in future years:

> We (CHS) were starting to build a program. At the Varsity level we were 20th in the NSCIF in 1972. In 1973 we went from 20th to NSCIF Champions and only won one track & field event at the North Section Meet. Team contribution was always my goal—everyone is important! Over the next six years we won meets by one point, a quarter of a point and on.
>
> How did we do it? I subscribed to the home-town newspaper of every school in the league. We had a "scouting report" on every school before the meet. Bob Noe and I choreographed the meet and put it on the blackboard the day before the meet in a team meeting. Each athlete was given a goal to achieve for that meet. Every place was important. I remember that we beat Lassen in an important dual meet by ¼ point with a 4th place in the pole vault.
>
> By doing this every athlete had a goal. The person whose goal was a 4th place usually took 3rd. It worked. We were 59-1 in the league after this season.

My memories of these meetings are slightly different. The day before a track meet, team members would go into the wrestling room at Chico High and sit on the mats for a "chalk talk." If it was a three-way meet, Chuck had detailed on a blackboard what he expected athletes of the other schools to do performance-wise in each and every track & field event. Alongside them were what our athletes would have to do for us to prevail as a team. The projected team scores of all three teams were tallied before our arrival in the room. The places associated with each of our names were not goals; they were assignments.

Athletes such as Jamie Starmer normally had four assignments for each meet—he being a sprinter/jumper/hurdler/pole vaulter. Distance runners normally had two: the mile and 880, or mile and 2-mile. Assignments could change during meets. I remember occasions during my junior and senior years when Chuck would come to me near the end of a meet and say, "Dave, we can't win this meet unless we win the pole vault, 2-mile, and mile relay." I believe that Chuck's methodology for preparing for meets continues at CHS to this day.

On summer days in Chico, it is often hotter than 100 degrees. I recall showering between the mile and 2-mile races on at least one occasion, but not the details associated with this requirement. Chuck reminded me of this happening at the League Championships in 1973, after he moved Mark and me down to JV competition near season's end:

> I asked you and Mark to do the mile, two-mile double which would bring us many points and push league-leading Lassen back. This was not a normal double at the time as they ran the JV two-mile at the start of the meet and followed shortly with the mile which made a distance double almost impossible. Add to that, the temperature at Mitchell [stadium in Oroville] was 105 degrees.
>
> Heat and time were the obstacles. What did we do? I had both you and Mark shower in your running uniform just before the two-mile. Immediately upon finishing, you two went into the cold showers. It worked as Mark went 1st and you 3rd in the two-mile. In a very short time later, Mark won the mile in 4:43.5 and you took 3rd in 4:47.8. Pat O'Connell followed in 4th with a 4:52.9 and we won that meet by 24 points. None of the other placers in these two events did the "impossible" double. Keep the core temperature down and it will work.

Photo 5-6

Mark and me finishing one-two in the mile during a meet.
Chico Enterprise-Record photograph

Following the League Championships in track & field, comes the Sub-Section Championships, and then the North Section Meet. The Chico High Varsity did not miss Mark and me at the latter championships. Although scoring no points in the distance events, Chico's varsity athletes were so strong in other events that when the points were totaled, Chico had won the Section Meet. Pleasant Valley was eleventh.

In the Junior Varsity competition, Jamie Starmer won both the 70-yard high hurdles and pole vault, and I the 2-mile. Mark was fifth in the mile, two places behind Steve Henson from Big Valley. Henson would be my nemesis the following two years and into junior college competition. Pleasant Valley High had one individual champion: Matt Maderos in the 880. The Chico JVs finished fifth in the meet overall, and Pleasant Valley finished eighth.

In the Freshman competition, Kent Pease garnered a second place in the 1,320. Chico Junior High was fifth in the team competition and Bidwell Junior High sixth.

6

Road Racing in Northern California

Photo 6-1

T-shirt awarded to Pat Buzbee for the 1971 Pepsi 20-mile run. Today, many race organizers levy high enough entry fees for all participants to receive a t-shirt and participation medal. Fifty years ago, you had to finish very high up in the race, or your division, to receive a shirt, and they were considered "badges of honor."

In 1973, while we were participating in track meets, Pat and Mike Buzbee were fulltime college students at Chico State, working to support themselves, training, and running road races. When able, they also ran some workouts with us. Among Panther runners, I probably had the most interaction with them because, at some point in either my junior or senior year, they got me a job on Friday nights and weekends as a dishwasher in a restaurant where they worked.

Working for minimum wage, $1.65 an hour, we washed the dishes; we also bused tables for the waitresses and did other things, like pouring coffee for customers and whatever the cooks asked of us. The latter mostly involved them periodically declaring, "The health inspectors were just here, and they're going to shut us down if ... is not cleaned immediately." These proclamations usually resulted in one of us squeezing into a barely accessible area and scrubbing grease or some other substance off a wall or other surface.

To add insult to injury, the owner was not particularly generous regarding feeding employees. During an eight-hour shift, we were allowed one meal. From our perspective, if they were "working us like dogs," they should at least feed us adequately. There was a chill box in the back by our scullery, which allowed us to pursue this philosophy by availing ourselves of its contents. I don't recall what Pat and Mike enjoyed; they were very health conscious and on their own time, consumed a lot of rice cakes and raw vegetables. I liked the sliced roast beef and tapioca pudding.

Following our shifts, we would often do ten-mile runs together out Sacramento Avenue to the river and back.

Returning to the subject at hand, road racing, the Buzbees ran several such races in 1973, which are open to all who want to participate in them. In some, Mark Burch and I joined them. A sampling of these events is offered in this relatively short chapter.

NORTHERN CALIFORNIA RUNNING REVIEW

Portion of page 2 of the March 1973 issue of the *Northern California Running Review*.

The *Northern California Running Review*, formerly the *West Valley Newsletter*, was published on a monthly basis by the West Valley Track Club of San Jose, California. It was intended as a communication medium for all northern California track & field athletes, including age group, high school, collegiate, AAU, women, and senior runners. (For those readers interested, old copies are available online.)

MARATHON WIN AT PETALUMA, CALIFORNIA

<u>Mike Buzbee in PA-AAU Marathon Win</u>: (Dec. 10, Petaluma)

Even before 1973, Mike and Pat Buzbee were experiencing great success at road racing, particularly in the marathon. The above headline in the March 1973 issue of the *Northern California Running Review*, informed readers that Mike had won the Petaluma Marathon (a Pacific District AAU-sponsored race) on December 10, 1972. Petaluma is located along Highway 101, thirty-two miles north of San Francisco's Golden Gate Bridge. As alluded to in the brief article, if there had been a third New Ways AC member in the race, who did reasonably well, the Buzbees and company would have won the team competition.

> John Sheehan was the only person to split up the Buzbee brothers from New Ways AC in Chico at the District Marathon Championship. Mike won in 2:32:43, way off Jon Anderson's 1971 course record of 2:23+, followed by Sheehan (2:34:35) and brother Pat (2:36:21). New Ways, however, forgot to bring a third man and, consequently, the team battle boiled down to a three-way affair...

The top twenty-four finishers in the field included Nick Vogt (discussed shortly) and Bill Peck, who had been the Buzbees' coach when they were jayvees at Chico High School in 1966. Pat recalls this experience: "Coach Bill Peck was a decent coach and very good runner. He was one of the first coaches to run with his squads. Huge respect."

1 - Mike Buzbee (NewWays)	2:32:43	13 - Randy Buck (Modesto)(1stM2)	2:52:44
2 - John Sheehan (West Valley)	2:34:35	14 - Gary Chilton (SRC)	2:53:37
3 - Pat Buzbee (NewWays)	2:36:21	15 - Tom Mann (Marin AC)	2:53:43
4 - John Butterfield (US Navy)	2:36:41	16 - John Deer (Whittier Alum)	2:53:52
5 - Bill Pomadel (Pamakid)	2:40:40	17 - Barry Buck (Modesto)	2:55:00
6 - Nick Vogt (Gold Spike)	2:44:01	18 - Guy Artherbolt (Unat)	2:55:01
7 - Clark Rosen (Unat)	2:44:17	19 - Bill Peck (Unat.)	2:56:09
8 - Jim Bowles (West Valley TC)	2:45:48	20 - Ivan Boggis (Unat.)	2:56:13
9 - Dave Stevenson (SRC)	2:47:37	21 - Tony Garcia (Mather AFB)	2:58:09
10 - Joe Wood (Aggie TC)	2:49:15	22 - Fred Kenyon (VCMTC)	2:58:34
11 - Doug Oates (Un, Bakersfield)	2:51:06	23 - Gene Robinson (Hillsdale)	2:59:24
12 - Ernie Jeong (Pamakid)	2:52:12	24 - Wendell Seablom (King City)	2:59:47

EL DORADO 14-MILE BURRO TRAIL RUN

On April 21, 1973, having had an easy time of it in the annual El Dorado 14-mile Burro Trail Run, Pat and Mike decided to cross the finish line together. The Buzbees were excellent hill runners. This race took place in the little town of El Dorado outside of Placerville, about forty miles east-northeast of Sacramento.

```
 1 - Pat Buzbee (NewWays AC)       1:19:25    11 - Pete Hansen (Colfax RC)     1:30:23
 2 - Mike Buzbee (NewWays AC)      1:19:25    12 - Steve Williams (Gold Spike) 1:31:36
 3 - Skip Houk (West Valley TC)    1:21:37    13 - Fred Mansueto (Unat.)       1:34:22
 4 - Mike Cenary (Unat.)           1:21:43    14 - Ty Hadley (Unat.)           1:36:05
 5 - Ray Menzie (Marin AC)         1:24:23    15 - Paul Reese (NCSTC)          1:36:38
 6 - Jim Maslach (Unat.)           1:25:07    16 - Ray Cerankowski (Unat.)     1:37:35
 7 - Darryl Beardall (Marin AC)    1:26:17    17 - Lindy Valdez (Loomis HS)    1:37:36
 8 - Mike Eash                     1:28:18    18 - Unofficial Runner           1:37:40
 9 - Doug Butt (Marin AC)          1:29:04    19 - Wayne Stenberg              1:37:43
10 - Frank Krebs (GWTC)            1:29:18    20 - John French                 1:37:51
```

CHICO STATE WILDCATS ALSO RUNNING RACES

Some Chico State athletes were also occassionally running road races, as shown by the result for the Sacramento River Run in Redding (73 miles NNW of Chico) on June 3, 1973. As noted in the *Running Review*, "Chico State runners dominated the open division...with four in the first five finishers." Wildcat Pat Finn won the race, and the previous year's winner, Pat Stordahl, finished second. (Stordahl was one of Chico State's top distance runners, and competed in lots of road races.) In third place was Chico State's 4:01 miler, Kim Ellison; two spots back, Jim Price, another powerful runner; and in 14th, Dan Chapman.

In eighth was Mark Burch, the first junior runner, meaning the first competitor under nineteen years of age. Mark road raced more than I did, and I was not there that day. The first woman finisher, 18-year-old Deborah Finn, placed 25th with a time of 50:48.

```
 1 - Pat Finn (Chico St)           40:45    11 - Mike Larsen                  45:10
 2 - Pat Stordahl (Chico St)       41:21    12 - Mickey Brodie                45:37
 3 - Kim Ellison (Chico St)        41:46    13 - Rodney Smith                 46:14
 4 - Mark Elsa (Humboldt St)       42:13    14 - Dan Chapman (Chico St)       46:28
 5 - Jim Price (Chico St)          42:55    15 - Richard Gilchrist (SRJC)     46:51
 6 - Peter Hanson (Colfax RC)      43:06    16 - Don Feser                    47:41
 7 - Jim O'Neil (SF Olympic Club)  43:17    17 - Richard Scott (Alameda TC)   48:17
 8 - Mark Burch (1st junior)       44:19    18 - Bob Turner                   48:35
 9 - Richard Meyer (Six Rivers RC) 44:41    19 - Don Smith                    48:35+
10 - Dennis Butler                 45:09    20 - John Mansueto                48:54
```

APPARENTLY DRAFTED FOR A RACE

It appears that back in the 70s, some runners or groups of runners just created their own clubs. This may have been because it was fun. Pat and Mike occassionally made mention of their former Warner Street AC affiliation (when both members still lived in the Buzbee home on Warner Street) because club membership was necessary in order to compete in AAU-sanctioned road races.

On July 1st, Mark and I competed in the Hangtown Road Race in Placerville. I vaguely remember it being a hilly, tough course. We must have been drafted to join Pat and Roger Stordahl as part of a team, because we and they are listed in the results as being members of the Intermountain AA (Athletic Association). We were not members of this AA. Arthur Baudenistal finished a few spots ahead of Mark and me. We were later teammates at American River College. In 1977, after my departure to join the Navy, he ran a 9:08.4 time for the 2-mile. Art was really strong. He once declared that he could train 130 miles a week on asphalt roads and not get injured.

1 - Dave Garcia (Fresno State)	27:43	16 - Jim Bredy (Golden West TC)	29:19
2 - Steve Dean (Golden West TC)	27:57	17 - Mike Duncan (West Valley TC)	29:58
3 - Kevin Furey (Golden West TC)	28:22	18 - Bob Powell (Oceana HS)	30:06
4 - Donald Gregory (High Sierra TC)	28:25	19 - Dick Fenstra (Oregon TC)	30:11
5 - Pat Stordahl (Intermountain AA)	28:27	20 - Frank Krebs (Golden West TC)	30:14
6 - Terry Pintane (VOMTC)	28:29	21 - David Zumwalt (Un)	30:15
7 - Mike Conroy (Excelsior TC)	28:30	22 - Greg Sullivan (San Juan Str)	30:19
8 - Nick Vogt (Gold Spike Runners)	28:33	23 - Casey Culbertson (Un)	30:20
9 - Curt Duff (Golden West TC)	28:39	24 - Rudy Dressendorfer (KawMstrs)	30:21
10 - Butch Alexander (VOMTC)	28:41	25 - Jim Freeman (San Juan Str)	30:25
11 - Mike Tulley (Golden West TC)	28:46	26 - Roger Stordahl (Intermtn AA)	30:32
12 - Romero Mendoza (VOMTC)	28:49	27 - Bob Loux (Un)	30:34
13 - Timothy Jordan (CWTC)	28:55	28 - Jeff Jahn (Valley of Moon TC)	30:41
14 - Jim Howard (Golden West TC)	29:01	29 - Jim O'Neil (SF Olympic Club)	30:45
15 - Mark Dawson (Valley of Moon TC)	29:09	30 - Rod Read (Golden West TC)	30:50

TAHOE RELAYS, BUZBEE HANDS OFF TO TRACY

Tracy Smith, world indoor 3-mile record holder and a member of Athletes in Action, blitzed to a record 52.31 for his 9.4-mile leg, besting the oldest record for the Relays, that of the Olympic Training Camp's Eamon O'Reilly, who did 53:00 back in 1968.

—Excerpt from a *Northern California Running Review* article.

In the summer of 1973, Chuck Sheley enacted another innovation: high-elevation training and associated bonding between members of his cross country teams before the start of a new season in the fall. The means to accomplish this was via a week-long training camp put on by Nick Vogt in the Lake Tahoe area. Vogt was a former Chico State Wildcat, an accomplished road racer, and a teacher and coach at Nevada Union

High School in Grass Valley. The camp was quite rustic—you provided your own tents and sleeping bags, and brought and cooked your own food. Therefore, it was quite inexpensive to attend.

We trained twice a day at high altitude. We weren't right at Lake Tahoe but our training site was at about 6,000 feet where there was about 20 percent less oxygen to breathe than at sea level. In addition to training, we attended seminars put on by Nick about running-related themes. At the completion of the camp, we formed a team and participated in the Tahoe Relays. I remember it being smoky that year as described in an article in the *Northern California Running Review*.

> The day broke under LA-type smog-filled skies as a result of a huge forest fire burning east of Placerville. The first leg and most of the second were run in cool (because of the overcast) temperatures but difficult breathing conditions, as visibility was cut to about ½-mile in places. On the fifth and sixth legs the skies were again overcast (clear weather occurred on the third & fourth carries), but this time it was higher up, making the running quite comfortable because of the low temperatures, but quite unpleasant at times because of lightly falling ash. The last leg was about half-and-half ash and clear skies.

The 72-mile team race around Lake Tahoe (touted as the oldest distance relay race in the United States) had seven legs, and thus there were seven members on each team. These legs and associated distances of each are identified below:

1 – Lakeview Commons (9.6 miles)
2 – Cave Rock to Sand Harbor (13 miles)
3 – Sand Harbor to Kings Beach (9.5 miles)
4 – Kings Beach to Tahoe City (9.6 miles)
5 – Tahoe City to Meeks Bay (9.7 miles)
6 – Meeks Bay to Emerald Bay (8.6 miles)
7 – Emerald Bay to Lakeview Commons (10 miles)

1978 Tahoe Relays, Open Division 2nd place team ribbon

The lengths of the legs add up to 70 miles, so these figures were obviously rounded down for simplicity; the race around the lake being 72 miles in length. I ran the longest leg for our team (2nd); Mark the steepest and toughest (4th); and Pat O'Connell one on the Nevada side of the lake. Race results list names for only the members of the top five teams; I don't recall who our other members were.

The real excitement was associated with these top teams, some of which boasted world and national-class athletes. Mike Buzbee was part of a team which included Tracy Smith (as noted in the quoted material at the head of this section), then the world record holder for the indoor 3-mile. As further reported in the *Running Review*:

> Smith ran for the third-place Valley Printing TC squad, a team composed of [in addition to Tracy] Darren George, Mike Buzbee, and four South Africans who had been training in Tahoe for the summer.

Since Mike was a member of New Ways AC, and not the Valley Printing TC, he was probably recruited owing to his overall talent, and because he was particularly tough on hills. Both Buzbees were like mountain goats. At the end of his leg (the 4th), Mike handed off to Tracy Smith. Identified in the table are the names and split times for each Valley Printing TC member's leg of the race as well as the record splits at that time for each of the seven legs.

Leg	Name	Dist.	Split Time	Overall	Record Split
1st	Darren George	9.6 miles	70:25	70:25	62:02
2nd	Bernard Ross	13 miles	55:37	2:06:02	53:23
3rd	Mike Manke	9.5 miles	58:13	3:04:15	55:25
4th	Mike Buzbee	9.6 miles	60:34	4:04:49	55:20
5th	Tracy Smith	9.7 miles	52:31	4:57:20	52:31
6th	Leigh Reilly	8.6 miles	56:40	5:54:00	52:49
7th	Trevor Viljoen	10 miles	55:56	6:49:56	52:58

There were other famous runners in the race including Domingo Tibaduiza. In this race, he beat the previous record for the first leg, and already held the record for the second leg (62:02 and 53:23), as shown in the table. A Columbian attending the University of Nevada at Reno and team captain of the track team, he represented his native country at four consecutive Summer Olympics. (In 1976, I was in a 5,000-meter race at a U of N-hosted track meet. I don't recall my time but was happy that Tibaduiza, the race winner, did not lap me.)

WEST VALLEY TC ANNUAL CHRISTMAS RELAYS

Before leaving the subject of relay-races, the annual Christmas Relays in mid-December also drew top-flight relay teams. Some races provide opportunity to win unique, coveted awards. This West Valley Track Club-hosted event was one such. At the Christmas Relays, individuals each ran one 4.5-mile leg around Lake Merced (in the southwest corner of San Francisco) in teams of four to compete in various divisions. Since it's a scoring event for clubs, the race can be quite competitive. Teams and running clubs put their best 4-person teams together in many divisions.

Photo 6-2

Christmas Relays cup, and examples of race-associated long-sleeve t-shirts. Courtesy of Pat Buzbee

The awards for the Christmas Relay were cups, greatly sought after by participants. The number of cups to be given out was determined by the number of team entrants the previous year. For some divisions with many teams entered, there might be three awards—cups for the four individuals on each of the top three teams. For divisions with fewer entries, there might only be a single award. For example, last year there may have been eleven teams entered in the Seniors division (age 50-59). If there were fifteen teams this year, only the members of the top team would receive cups, because only 10 percent of the number of entries the previous year could receive an award. (This is likely a meet management tool, allowing the ordering of cups based on team participation the previous year, without the necessity to wait for the end of the race entry period.)

The good news is that all paid participants received very nice long-sleeved shirts printed with the Christmas Relays logo. In 2019, stocking caps replaced the shirts.

BUZBEE BREAKS OLYMPIC TRIALS STANDARD

On September 30, 1973, Mike Buzbee dipped below the qualifying standard necessary to compete in the marathon at the U.S. Olympic trials, a time of two hours and thirty minutes. This mark required a marathoner to average a 5:43 per mile pace for 26.2 miles. A brief description of the race (below left) from the *Enterprise-Record*, noted that Chico State professor Don Fridshal also participated in the race. Mark and I were also there, as shown in snippets from the *Northern California Running Review*. Mike was just 21 years old. Mark and I, who had just begun our junior year and were age 17 and 16, respectively, finished with a much more pedestrian 6:37 pace.

Bob Darling (5th) ran the 5,000- and 10,000-meter races for Chico State and qualified for the 1971 NCAA Division II Nationals in the 10K.

Chico's Buzbee Third at Napa

NAPA (E-R) — Chico's nationally-ranked marathon runner Mike Buzbee, representing the New-Ways Athletic Club, ran third in the Napa Champagne Marathon here Sunday.

Buzbee ran 2:29.55, just under the 2:30.0 time limit which qualifies a runner for the Olympic trials.

Don Fridshal, a Chico State University instructor competing in his first race, finished 90th in the field of 181.

```
 1 - George Stewart (US Army/WVTC) 2:21:29
 2 - Daryl Zapata (WVTC)            2:28:37
 3 - Mike Buzbee (NewWays AC)       2:29:55
 4 - Homer Latimer (Un)             2:34:25
 5 - Bob Darling (Excelsior TC)     2:34:40
 6 - Mike Conroy (Excelsior TC)     2:35:24
 7 - Frank Krebs (Golden West TC)   2:38:25
 8 - Harold DeMoss (WVTC)           2:38:45
 9 - Ross Smith (West Valley J&S)   2:39:36
10 - Bill Long (Pamakids)           2:41:03
11 - Jeff Wildfogel (Un)            2:41:40

21 - Jim Engle (NVRC)               2:47:40
22 - Charles Day (US Navy)          2:48:22
23 - Ed Daily (Naval Postgr. Sch)   2:48:55
24 - Gary Chilton (Stanford RC)     2:49:43
25 - Norm Simon                     2:50:57
26 - Michael Coke (Un)              2:51:00
27 - Dave Zumwalt (Un)              2:51:25
28 - Jack Hackmann (Un)             2:52:30
29 - Don Choi (Un)                  2:52:16
30 - Dave Bruhn                     2:53:26
31 - Mark Bureh                     2:53:45
```

The *Running Review* article nicely describes the race conditions that day, as well as how the race unfolded. Excerpts follow:

> West Valley TC's George Stewart, competing for the U.S. Army today, decided to try and go for a sub-2:20 marathon (sort of casual-like) on this newly certified course (pending on race day.) The temperatures had been around 90 all week, and even the day before, but someone must have realized that a few brain cells would fry while running a marathon in that heat…so, come race morn, you would never believe: OVERCAST & COOL. As a matter of fact, the sun didn't come out until just after the winner came through…in a PR by some 13 minutes, with a torrid 2:21:29.
>
> Fast-closing Daryl Zapata…[got] his first sub-2:30 effort, a fine 2:28:37…. Mike Buzbee just got under with a 2:29:55 in third.

LEGENDARY WALT STACK

It was cold and foggy at the start of the Napa Marathon. I believe the temperature was in the 40s. As we took off our sweats, and lined up behind the starting line, I happened to notice one participant preparing to race shirtless. He had a barrel chest, brawny arms like "Popeye" and sported a lot of tattoos. I immediately knew who he was, having just read an article about him in *Sports Illustrated* magazine.

I would have guessed Walt Stack to be in his 40s. I did not then know that he was born on September 28, 1908, had a birthday two days earlier, and was thus sixty-six years old. As I recall, the magazine article had reported that Walt was a former Merchant seaman and currently a hod carrier. A hod carrier was someone who assisted brickmasons, bricklayers, and stonemasons by bringing them bricks, stones, mortar, and other construction materials necessary for each project.

Walt passed away two decades later on January 19, 1995. Excepts from a tribute to him, posted by the Dolphin Club of San Francisco on its website, only give a hint of the uniqueness of this very colorful individual.

> Walt Stack was a Dolphin Club member and icon of the San Francisco running community in the 1960-90's. He ran approximately 62,000 miles in his lifetime. Even in his seventies and eighties, Stack ran many more marathons and 50-mile ultra-marathons than all but a few of his running peers.
>
> For 27 years, from 1966 until 1993, Stack maintained a grueling, daily, highly visible training routine that made him a San Francisco institution. Starting on his bike, he rode six hilly miles from his Potrero Hill home to Fisherman's Wharf. Once there, he'd strip off his shirt, displaying tattoos of peacocks, wild horses, and bathing beauties across his broad chest, and then proceed to run a 17-mile (27 km) route over the Golden Gate Bridge to Sausalito and back, after which he would take a one-mile (1.6 km) swim in the currents of the San Francisco Bay near Alcatraz Island.

Logo on outside of building

7

1973 Cross Country Season

Bill Gregg and Craig Larsen provided our senior leadership and look at the wonderful lives they have lived since then!

—Jim Walker commenting recently on two individuals who led Chico High School to its first-ever Varsity North Section Cross Country Championship. Our core group, which had previously won Freshman and JV championships, now had more power to lead us. Moreover, at Chico Junior High, Sheley, Noe, and Holzhey were developing even stronger runners to, in future years, move on to Chico High and up "into the line" so to speak.

Photo 7-1

Back row L-R: Chuck Sheley, Mark Burch, Tony Fasolino, Nathan Bunker, Brett Byers, Bill Gregg, Robert MacKay, Craig Larsen, and Ralph Patten.
Second row: Elise Ficarra, Steve Nicholson, Pat O'Connell, Jim Walker, Dave Bruhn, Brian Campbell, Jamie Starmer, Larry Day, Rich Gregg, Ron Caminada.
First row: Arnie Cervantes, Mike McCulley, John Patterson, Steve Zicker, Kent Pease, Duane Brock, and Mario Lemos.

The grainy photograph on the preceding page of Chico High varsity and jayvee athletes is significant because it includes: Elise Ficarra, the first girl to run cross country for Chico High School (girls hadn't previously been allowed to participate in this sport); and quarter-miler/half-miler Robert MacKay, and sprinter/hurdlers Jamie Starmer and Brian Campbell. MacKay, Starmer and Campbell may have been on the team because they secretly wanted to be distance runners. It's more likely that Chuck had drafted them to run cross country to develop strength for their respective track events. Having much greater percentages of quick-twitch muscle fibers necessary for leg speed than slow-twitch ones for endurance, they weren't scoring members of the team. Chuck once remarked to Jamie Starmer, "It's great if you can outkick ten people at the end of the race, but if that moves you from 100th to 90th place, you're not helping us."

Also in the photograph are assistant coaches Ralph Patten and Ron Caminada. We benefited greatly from former Chico State athletes or and/or student teachers at Chico Junior assisting with the program. Ralph ran with us, and regaled us with tales of Roy Kissin from San Ramon, one of the very best prep distance runners in California. Ralph was also from San Ramon and had previously coached Kissin.

As the Cross Country Season opened in fall 1973, we were confident. We were used to winning. Because Chuck had not shared with us by how little we had beaten Lassen in our previous North Section victories, we had cocky youthful optimism. That's not to say we took Lassen lightly. It was always a "dog fight" between Chico and Lassen. We had a slight advantage when competing against them on our home course, and they on theirs.

BEST CROSS COUNTRY RUNNERS IN THE 1970s

Before going further, it's worth identifying the best times run by Chico High's top seventeen boys and ten girls, 1970 through 1978. The courses changed in 1979, so those previous times and what they represent have been scrubbed from public knowledge. (The boys course changed to 3.0 miles, and the girls to 2.16 miles.) In running their best times, Doug Avrit averaged 4:53 per mile pace over the 2.55-mile course, and Darcy Burleson 5:36 over the 1.87-mile one.

Top Panthers on Chico High School Home Course, 1970-1978
Varsity Boys 2.55-Mile Course   Varsity Girls 1.87- Mile Course

Name	Time	Name	Time
Doug Avrit	12:29	Darcy Burleson	10:30
Greg Williams	12:40	Suzanne Richter	10:50
Kurt Graves	12:45	Jill Symons	11:03
Santos Cervantes	12:48	Luanne Park	11:41
Chris Johnson	13:03	Julie Selchau	11:55
Steve Growdon	13:05	Stacey Shols	12:02
Dave Bruhn	13:07	Joan Gregg	12:05
Bruce Eggleston	13:14	Kathy Jo Bernadett	12:09
Kent Pease	13:20	Vicki Whitburn	12:16
Mark Burch	13:23	Tammy Denny	12:29
Kevin Boone	13:24		
Bill Gregg	13:29		
Craig Larson	13:35		
Britt Brewer	13:40		
Josh Strong	13:47		
Pat O'Connell	13:53		
Chris Shols	13:58		

The girls in the table highlighted by grey shading comprised the "Charlie's Angels," Chico High School 1976 and 1977 Girls XC teams. The 1977 team was ranked second in the nation by *Harrier* magazine. A year later, Greg Williams was the 1978 North Section champion (beating Central Valley High School's John Frank) and the *Sacramento Bee* Boy Runner of the Year (1978).

The top six boys on the list, then still junior high students, would constitute the best Chico High Panthers of the 1970s. The future "Charlie's Angels" were also still in junior high.

LASSEN HIGH GRIZZLES NOT "ROLLING OVER"

> *The jinx continues. Chico High School's cross country team—touted as the best in the North Section—is still having trouble beating Lassen High School.*
>
> —Leading sentences in an *E-R* article titled, "Panthers Fall to Grizzlies Again" reporting on the results of a dual meet at Susanville on October 25, 1973.

Regarding the 1973 Season, it was not "smooth sledding" owing to the toughness of Lassen's XC team. We lost to them on their home course by two points (27-29) on October 25th. I remember thinking at the time, "it looks like they designed the toughest course possible." There were lots of steep hills; we were running in the cold at 4,186 feet; and competition followed a long 101-mile van ride on winding canyon roads. Of course, the Grizzles had the same travel when they came to Chico to compete on our course; and they probably groused about the absence of hills and too much oxygen in the air.

Lassen High School			Chico High School		
Name	Place	Time	Name	Place	Time
Bill Dyer	1st	16:17	Bill Gregg	3rd	16:54
Tim Patterson	2nd	16:36	Mark Burch	5th	17:41
Al Harris	4th	17:21	Dave Bruhn	6th	17:53
Scott Mieras	9th	17:58	Arnie Cervantes	7th	17:55
John Trujillo	11th	18:08	Jim Walker	8th	17:57

Following this defeat, we had only two weeks remaining until the Eastern Athletic League (EAL) Championships, which were followed nine days later by the North Section Championships.

EAL LEAGUE CHAMPIONSHIPS

I won't have to pull kids out of the choir to make a team for a change.

—Pleasant Valley High School coach Denny Varley, quoted in the *E-R* Prep Parade section of the newspaper, regarding his biggest and potentially best team ever (11 varsity boys, 12 on the jayvees and three girls).

We won the Varsity League Championship held on Pleasant Valley High's cross country course on November 8th, with "a little help from our friends." PV Vikings John Barneson (2nd), Dave Scott (12th), Tim Holt (13th), and Dave Brown (18th) added points to the Grizzles' team score by finishing in front of individual Lassen runners. (Dave Scott went on to be an accomplished XC runner for Butte College, and he also became a multiple top five finisher in the Western States 100-miler.)

In simple terms, by finishing second, Barneson added one point to every runner that finished behind him including Lassen's other top four (Dyer was the winner), and all five of Chico's scoring runners. Since all of Chico's runners were in the top ten, PV's Dave Scott, Tim

Holt, and Dave Brown drove Lassen's Bill Fuller and John Trujillo down in the standings and added points to our chief rival's team score.

Chico, Lassen, and Pleasant Valley High's Top Five Runners

1	LHS: Bill Dyer	6	LHS: Al Harris	13	PV: Tim Holt
2	PV: John Barneson	7	CHS: Craig Larsen	18	PV: Dave Brown
3	CHS: Bill Gregg	8	CHS: Dave Bruhn	19	LHS: Bill Fuller
4	CHS: Mark Burch	10	CHS: Pat O'Connell	20	LHS: John Trujillo
5	LHS: Tim Patterson	12	PV: Dave Scott	26	PV: Matt Maderos

Readers knowledgeable about scoring cross country races will realize that other league teams and their athletes affected the outcome in minor ways. (Paradise's Rob Erb, who would give Chico High's Track Team fits in the spring, finished eleventh.) Regardless, Chico was League Champion by a good margin, Lassen second, and Pleasant Valley third. The top seven finishers comprised the All-League team.

1973 NORTH SECTION XC CHAMPIONSHIPS

> *From the varsity down to the frosh it was Chico and Chico Junior High winning each event. Add in a couple of unofficial section events, [catholic school] Notre Dame of Chico won the elementary boys race and Chico Junior High the girls high school race.*
>
> *Chico High's varsity became the first team in 10 years to wrestle the varsity title away from Lassen.*
>
> *The Panthers had to overcome adversity to win. Their top runner, Bill Gregg, was hampered by illness all week and finished 17th. Still, he managed a strong kick to edge a Del Oro runner and secure the victory.*
>
> —*Chico Enterprise-Record* article titled,
> "Chico Harriers Dominate Section."

The North Section Championships were held on the campus of Del Oro High School in the town of Loomis in Placer County, located twenty-three miles northeast of Sacramento, and eighty-three miles southeast of Chico. It was raining, the course was wet and muddy, and Chico High Varsity team members raced in track spikes.

Craig Larsen ran his best race of the season, finishing second to Bill Dyer after leading the race for two miles. Mark Burch was right behind him, taking third place. Jim Walker was tenth, Pat O'Connell twelfth, and Bill Gregg seventeenth. It turned out there was a very strong team in the section outside our league. Chico beat runner-up Del Oro by only a single point, 44 to 45, with Lassen in third with 64 points.

Rob Erb of Paradise finished seventh in the race. Pleasant Valley was unable to field a full team and, thus, was not scored. The finishing order among the four runners that toed the line for PV were: Dave Scott, John Barneson, Dave Brown, and Tom Dempsey.

Kent Pease of Chico won the Junior Varsity race to end his season undefeated, and Doug Avrit won the Freshman race.

CHICO JUNIOR HIGH GIRLS CHAMPIONSHIP TEAM

The Chico Junior High girls team winning the high school competition foreshadowed great future success. The top five girls order of finish: Jill Symons (2nd), Julie Selchau (11th), Elise Ficarro (13th), Luanne Park (16th), and Melanie Martin (18th). Bob Noe was the head coach for the Cougars boys and girls teams, assisted by John Hesse from Chico State.

Photo 7-2

Picture of our varsity cross country team following the EAL Championships.
Kneeling L-R: Dave Bruhn, Craig Larsen, Jim Walker, Larry Day, Bill Gregg, Arnie Cervantes, Pat O'Connell, Mark Burch. Standing: John Petterson, Brett Byers, Nate Bunker, Mike McCulley, Steve Nicholson.

8

1973 Wildcat Cross Country

Photo 8-1

Chico State 1973 Far Western Conference champion team members. L-R in back: Mark Shuman, Greg Griffin, Tom Brown, Calvin Lantrip, Toni Ruggle, Jim Price. In front, coach Larry Burleson and Pat Finn.
Courtesy of Toni Ruggle

Autumn 1973 was a banner season for Wildcat cross country, one that would prove to be the best of the decade for Chico State harriers.

FAR WESTERN CONFERENCE CHAMPIONSHIP
Chico State coach Larry Burleson had changed up the composition of the team that he ran against other conference opponents in dual meets throughout the season, never putting his best seven runners on the line in any of these competitions. As a result, Chico entered the Far Western Conference Championship—held at Coyote Hills Regional

Park overlooking the San Francisco Bay—as a dark horse. Humboldt State University was expected to win, with the biggest challenge coming from University of California at Davis (UCD).

In an upset victory, the Chico State Wildcats nosed out the Davis Aggies, 46-48, for the team victory. Sacramento State's Kevin Furey finished first over the 5-mile course, setting a course record of 25:05 in doing so. Behind him came four Wildcats in the top ten spots and three others in the next eleven. Calvin Lantrip, the team's seventh man, finished twenty-first in the race. The point totals of the other schools were: Humboldt, 59; Sacramento, 108; Sonoma, 135; Hayward, 164; and San Francisco, 178.

Top Finishers at the 1973 Far Western Conference Championship

#	Name	School	#	Name	School
1	Kevin Furey	Sacramento	12	Hersh Jenkins	Humboldt
2	Dwayne Harms	UCD	13	Mark Elias	Humboldt
3	Chuck Smead	Humboldt	14	Anthony Reynoso	UCD
4	Mark Shuman	Chico	15	Conrad Lowry	Humboldt
5	John Sheehan	UCD	16	Steve Owen	Humboldt
6	Dave Anderson	Hayward	17	Pat Finn	Chico
7	Greg Griffin	Chico	18	Donn Wells	Davis
8	Jim Price	Chico	19	Toni Ruggle	Chico
9	Angelo Martinez	UCD	20	Bob Bunwell	Sonoma
10	Tom Brown	Chico	21	Calvin Lantrip	Chico
11	Pete Flores	Sacramento	22	Michael McGrath	Davis

Particularly gratifying for sports fans in Oroville, only twenty-five miles from Chico, was the fact that three members of the team—Tom Brown, Toni Ruggle, and Calvin Lantrip—were natives. Toni recently described the conference race, including ten extra miles devoted to the Wildcats pre-race warm up, and post-race warm down.

> Coach Burleson dropped us off five miles out from the course near Fremont for our warm up. Other teams were driving past us as we ran to the course. I can only imagine what they were thinking. That's right, all races included a five-mile warm up. Burleson's plan for the conference meet was well thought out. In order to get our team to Nationals we needed to win the conference meet.

> Because he knew the course was very hilly, he trained us all season with lots of runs in the areas outside of Chico. Runs would start from Chico State and either go up to Cohasset, or up to Paradise via Butte Creek Canyon and Honey Run Road, or continue through Butte Creek Canyon up past Centerville to Helltown.

Additionally, we would run weekly hill charges on the Vilas dirt road in the town of Cohasset. We were given the name "The Goats" by Burley. We were ready for any hills put before us. (Another group of Wildcats, who were particularly good on flat courses, were termed "The Greyhounds.")

Race day conditions were cool and sunny that day. Coach's instructions were very explicit. Run together as a team for the first mile plus on the flat area of the hilly Coyote Park course. When we hit the first hill, we were to make our move up and through the hills. We did just that, passing runners from other teams along the way. The road to the finish line was relatively flat. Everyone was letting it "all hang out" (70s slang).

After the race concluded it took several minutes to tabulate the results (This was the 1970s with no chip timing). Everyone waited anxiously and then the results came over the bullhorn that Chico State was the winner with 46 points followed by Davis and Humboldt. We all went crazy, then Burley directed us to hike up a steep hill above the finish line, where our picture was taken while we celebrated. After receiving our award our day wasn't done yet as we had to retrace our warmup steps with a 5-mile warm down as other teams drove past us. All in all, it was an amazing day that our team will never forget.

By virtue of their team win, the Wildcats qualified to compete in the NCAA Division II National Championships the following Saturday, November 10th, in Wheaton, Illinois. The top ten finishers in the conference championship race, excluding Wildcats, earned the right to also make the trip to Illinois.

NATIONAL CHAMPIONSHIPS

The NCAA II Championship Meet was hosted by Wheaton College on November 10th in Wheaton, Illinois. Not unexpected at that time of year, it was cold, 30 degrees, but the sky was clear with only a hint of wind from the northwest. One hundred ninety-four competitors completed the race, with many in the front finishing seconds apart from one another. Gary Bentley of South Dakota State University was the individual winner with a time of 23:49. Mark Shuman, the top Wildcat, clocked in at 24:50—finishing 23rd and earning All-American honors.

Photo 8-2

Wildcat Mark Shuman running to a 23rd place finish at the 1973 NCAA Division II Cross Country Championships. He led the Chico State harriers to a sixth-place team finish and individually earned All-America honors.
Courtesy of Toni Ruggle

The finishes of the other Wildcats were: 50th, Jim Price (25:16); 55th, Toni Ruggle (25:18); 58th, Tom Brown (25:20); 59th, Pat Finn (25:21); 81st, Greg Griffin (25:40), and 138th, Calvin Lantrip (26:59). Five of the "Cats" came across the line within 24 seconds of one another. The top twenty-five individuals in the race made All-American. Only 26 seconds separate college freshman Toni Ruggle (55th) from this honor. Less than half a minute faster, and he would have crossed the finish line one second ahead of Ron Peters in 25th from the University of Northern Iowa.

VERY SPECIAL TEAM
The 1973 "Cats" were a very special team with, among its members: All-Americans Mark Shuman (Cross Country) and Tom Brown (the steeplechase in Track & Field). It wasn't until 1999 that another Wildcat team equaled the 1973 sixth-place team finish at the Nationals, and 2002 when it was bested with a fifth-place finish. Moreover, after Shuman, the Chico State Mens Cross Country program did not boast another All-American until two decades later when Wildcat Eric Ricketts earned these honors in 1995. (Jill Symons garnered All-American honors as a Lady Wildcat Cross Country team member in 1979.)

9

1974 Track Season

SAN MATEO MARATHON PRECURSOR

> *This day was perhaps the most important step ever for women's long distance running, as the fair sex proved to the world that they could handle 'officially', the classic marathon distance of 26 miles, 385 yards.*
>
> —From an article in the January/February 1974 issue of *Northern California Running Review*, titled, "Ikenberry Garners Women's National Title; [Jim] Dare Takes West Valley Race."

1973 San Mateo Marathon patch
Courtesy of Pat Buzbee

On February 19th, as winter waned before the start of the 1974 Track Season, Mark Burch ran in the San Mateo Marathon, which also served as the national championship for women. He finished with his best time to date, 2:43:39 (6:15 mile pace), and twenty-first overall.

Less than a month later, on March 16th, Rich Kimball of DeLaSalle High in Concord (San Francisco Bay Area) led his U.S. team to the title in the Junior International XC Championships in Monza, Italy. The

American's finished with a team score of 22 points (4 members score), with second place Morocco a distant 36 points back.

Mark and I knew of Kimball's high volume of training, over 100 miles a week, and his great success; and we, like high school and college runners all across the country, were emulating this training regimen. It seemed pretty simple: run lots of miles, and you will be a great runner. We didn't know that by June of that track season, Kimball would have bests of 4:02.2 and 8:46.6 in the mile and 2-mile. Talent counts!

Hundred-mile-weeks in the 1970s injured a lot of runners and truncated their competitive careers in either high school or college. The sophisticated knowledge of sports physiology that exists today didn't exist back then. Football coaches at Chico High still gave players salt tablets at practices. Locker rooms smelled like Bengay (then spelled Ben-Gay) a salve rubbed into the skin to relieve muscle soreness. For muscle injury, it was common for coaches to prescribe whirlpool treatment (immersion in hot water), instead of ice massage to minimize muscle damage and internal bleeding. Additionally, there was not the same appreciation then for the importance of lighter, recovery days.

In any case, Mark and I, and separately the Buzbees, continued high mileage training. Mark appeared able to handle it. Pat and Mike who maybe weighed 125 pounds each, with rocks in their pockets, had an associated light footfall with each stride and, therefore, less stress on their legs and knees. Knee injuries were the most common type of injury experienced by distance runners. In retrospect, I would have been much better off running about 50 miles a week.

DEALING WITH ROB ERB OF PARADISE

EAL Track Championship was determined by dual meet season plus final standing at League Meet. Erb would run 440, 880, mile and mile relay. We met Paradise twice during dual meet part of season. How do we counter Erb and offset his scoring? Take him to the max each event.

We had the original "animal" in Robert MacKay. 440-MacKay beat Erb twice in extremely close races.

Mile: Even though Erb won twice, Dave Bruhn pushed him all the way in each race.

880: MacKay and Erb split. First race, both with same time, 2nd race MacKay by a tenth.

Result: Erb not at his best by time Mile Relay came. Chico wins both races and both meets.

—Chuck Sheley describing to the author, the strategy he employed to reduce the 30 points (three 1st places) that Paradise's Rob Erb would otherwise score, as well as contributing to another 10 points (anchoring the mile relay) in varsity track meets against Chico High School.

There are not a lot of "great kickers" among distance runners. Those that are, like Kim Ellison at Chico State, run very fast 880 and mile times. Chico High's Robert MacKay had great leg speed. As such, he routinely ran the 440, 880, and mile relay. He ran the mile at least once, and had a best time of 4:40. Such a time might score some points for a team, but probably wouldn't result in a win, unless the pace was so slow that MacKay was with the leaders at the end, and could unleash a blistering kick.

Photo 9-1

Robert MacKay breaking the tape in the 440-yard dash.
Chico Enterprise-Record photograph by Oz Mallan

Because of his fierce competitiveness and toughness, MacKay was the inaugural recipient of the "animal award," an honor enacted by Chuck Sheley. MacKay's successor (after he graduated) was Kent Pease, who I don't believe ever lost when kicking against someone at the end of a race. Pease ran the mile, and 880, and often a leg on the mile-relay, as did Greg Williams, who was then three years behind Pease in school, and another great kicker. Erb was extremely fast in the 440, mile, 880, and mile relay. In order to score the most points for Paradise, he would try to run just hard enough to win in his first three events by "sitting on" the leader and outkicking them at the end—thereby preserving as much energy as possible to anchor his team's 4-man mile relay. Meets were often won or lost by the outcome of this final event of the day; and teams usually put their fastest runner on the final (anchor) leg.

Kent Pease recently described the importance of the mile relay to team success:

> The relay races were special events that brought out the grit in the team. The mile relay (4 x 440) was the last event (maybe with a high point differential) and was often the deciding race in close meets. True distance runners were generally not part of the relay races, but I often had a 440 leg. With the weight of the team, everyone always gave it their all. We generally won, influenced by team depth which was not just the quarter-milers but also middle-distance guys like me and an "unlucky" sprinter tapped to gut it out.

"PACERS" VERSUS "RACERS"

Erb could not hold back and conserve energy in a quarter-mile race against MacKay. He had to run as hard as possible. He could easily both run a faster time than I could in the mile (my best was 4:33 that season) and also outkick me at the end of a race. Because my fastest quarter-mile was only a snail-like 57 seconds, I had to lead every mile race I was capable of and hope that no one was still with me at the end. I was a pacer and not a racer (kicker).

Some observers of distance running speak of "pacers" and "racers" derisively, referring to the former as being too preoccupied with their (lap) "splits" and running even race pace, while the latter only concern themselves with actually winning races. However, genetics determine what camp you are in. Runners lucky enough to have been born with a cardio-vascular system supporting distance running, as well as sufficient leg muscle quick-twitch fibers to have great "kicks" dominate the racers category. Those lacking leg speed and who desire to win races must, from the start, go to the front of a field of runners, push the pace, and hope they can unglue kickers well before the finish line.

The Buzbees were pacers; I was a pacer; even Doug Avrit (then a freshman who would become Chico High's best prep distance runner ever) was a pacer. Doug's top times of 4:16.5 for the mile and 9:11.9 for the 2-mile resulted in part from hard work and competitiveness, but neither of these is enough. He had more talent than everyone else, and could thus, almost always, pace away from the kickers. When Avrit was a junior and Pease a senior, the latter could occasionally remain close enough to the former to outkick him at the end of a race.

Readers interested in the best 880, mile, and 2-mile times of Chico High's top runners in the 1970s may consult Appendices A and B.

Kent Pease was unique in that he was a champion athlete who did not run year-round. He (and also Craig Larsen who didn't participate in track) played soccer between cross country and track season. This provided fun, fitness, and a mental break from pure running. However, as a result, Kent would not reach top form until mid-season or later. When he did, no one could touch him. Kent would win the jayvee mile at the section championships later that 1974 season with a time of 4:30.2 (which would have been good enough for second place in the varsity race); win the varsity mile both his junior and senior years; and set a school record of 4:19.1 in the mile.

Photo 9-2

Kent Pease and I running repeat 440s barefoot on the grass inside the curb of Chico High's dirt track. I would lead such workouts and mile races until Kent worked into shape after playing soccer. Once this had occurred, he would ascend to North Section mile champion.
Chico High School 1974-75 yearbook

KICKERS

A renowned college coach once observed (I believe that it was [James F.] "Jumbo" Elliott of Villanova), "The problem with great kickers is that they often get outkicked by other great kickers." Few great kickers take the lead in a distance race and push the pace. They see no point in enduring needless pain. If they are within striking distance at the end, they believe that they will likely win. Because of this, in races on the track with more than one kicker among the competitors (there might be several in high-level championship races) kickers content to sit at the back of the front group of runners, rely on their speed and, failing to begin their finishing drives early enough, often get beaten.

The only kicker I have ever seen who would routinely lead races from the start in cross country and on the track, and make other athletes "hurt," was Brad Doering of Yuba City High School. Following a naval career, I taught high school for ten years and coached cross country and track during a portion of it. In 2006/2007, I was an assistant coach to Mike Buzbee at Yuba High. One day, Mike remarked to me, "Brad can roll [run] a 50-flat quarter. He's our fastest quarter-miler." Doering's best high school times were 1:56.48 (800 meters), 4:18.55 (1,600 meters) and 8:43.98 (3,000 meters).

NORTH SECTION CHAMPIONSHIPS

> *It was over almost before it started for Eastern Athletic League track and field champion Chico High in the North Section Meet held at Mitchell Field last evening.*
>
> *The Panthers, expected to give Northern Athletic League champion Shasta High a solid test, didn't and tied for second with ridge-rival Paradise. Both had 25 points. Surprise Pleasant Valley (20 points) finished fourth in the meet.*
>
> *The confrontation between the two schools ended in the first heat of the qualifying for the 120-yard hurdles. Panther Jamie Starmer, the real backbone of the Chico team this season, finished fifth in the heat and was dropped from further competition in the event. The junior Panther then complained of a pulled muscle in his left leg and withdrew from the other two events he had qualified for, the 180-low hurdles and the long jump. His withdrawal was the end of Chico's chance to up-end Shasta.*
>
> —*Chico Enterprise-Record* article describing the 1974 North Section Track & Field Championship Meet in Oroville.

Bill Gregg and I entered the 1974 North Section Championships with bests in the mile and 2-mile of 4:32.1 and 9:46.1, respectively. His mark had come in the preceding Sub-Section Championships; mine earlier in the season at the Chico Invitational Meet held at Chico State. Like Kent, Bill also did not get in top form until the later part of the track season. While Kent played soccer, Bill was on the ski team his junior and senior years, and was MVP his senior year.

Photo 9-3

Mile race at the 1974 Sub-Section (Division) Championships which took place at Wheatland High School. I am leading the race, followed by Paul Ryan of Paradise, and teammate Bill Gregg. Bill outkicked me to win in 4:32.1 to my 4:33.7.
Photo by Jim Gregg

The Section Championships were held at Mitchell Field in nearby Oroville. The distance events were run in the evening, when it was cool and windy. My actions that night embarrass me to this day but need to be recounted as an example of things not to do, should any young athletes stumble across this book and read it.

I was unaware that teammate Jamie Starmer had been hurt earlier in the meet, and thus unable to continue or contribute any team points. He was exceptional at every track & field event, except middle-distance and distance events, and those involving throwing heavy things. Distance runners typically do long warmups outside stadiums knowing at what time(s) to return to compete in their event(s).

I was inside to watch the mile race and Bill compete in it. Normally after the start of a race, should someone fall in the first 100 yards or so, the starter will fire a recall pistol, signaling to the competitors to return to the starting line for a restart of the race. On this occasion, meet officials allowed the race to proceed for an entire lap before halting and then restarting it. I remember feeling sorry for the runners, because such action causes, in addition to fatigue associated with running the first quarter of the race, the need to regroup (become mentally focused once again) for competition.

Tom Olson of Central Valley won the mile with a time of 4:27.5; Bill was fourth with a 4:32.7, nearly his best for the season.

In the 2-mile race I wasn't running particularly well and stepped off the track after a mile, voluntarily ending my race. I had entered the race with the best two-mile time in the Section and was the favorite. I wasn't thinking about team points when I took this action and how it would negatively affect our team effort. I wanted to win, I wasn't doing well, and I wasn't interested in finishing second or third.

I don't believe the phrase "a teachable moment" then existed, but when I read the sports page the following day, I was taught well, and very thoroughly. Chuck was quoted in the article concerning my performance, and he wasn't happy. My immediate thought after reading his comments was, "Well, I'm never going to do that again." That was an important moment for me, and I never again committed this sin in sports, or the equivalent in other life endeavors.

Steve Hensen of Big Valley won the 2-mile with a time of 9:50.4; John Barneson of Pleasant Valley was third in 10:10.3, and Bill Gregg fourth was a 10:11.3. Rob Erb won the 880 with a time of 1:56.6.

Chico High's Varsity team won only a single event: the mile-relay.

In Junior Varsity competition, Kent Pease prevailed in both the mile (4:30.2) and the 880 (2:01.9), as recounted in the same article:

> Pease was his incredible self again last night. The Chico sophomore took first in the mile, holding off a determined charge by Weed's Dave Dawson, and first in the 880, again holding off Dawson. In both races, the runners were clocked in identical times.

In the Freshman competition, Doug Avrit won the 1½-mile race with a time of 7:26.3 and, doubling back, finished third in the half-mile with a 2:12.1 effort. Fellow Chico Junior High Cougars Chris Shols and Gary Layman finished second and third in the 1,320 with times of 3:32.1 and 3:33.3, respectively.

Photo 9-4

Kent Pease winning the jayvee mile.
Chuck Sheley collection

Photo 9-5

Chico Junior High's Doug Avrit rounding the final turn in the Frosh 1½-mile run, which he easily won in 7:26.3.
Chico Enterprise-Record photograph by John Matthews

POLE VAULTER BECAME GREAT DISTANCE COACH

Separately at the North Section Championships, Las Plumas High's Scott Fairley won the varsity pole vault competition with a height of 13-8 ¼. Currently, and for many years past, Scott had taught high school and been the head track & field and cross country coach at West Valley High in Cottonwood (located about 57 miles to the NNW of Chico). Fairley is the representative of the North Section for these sports. Each year, West Valley hosts the North Section Championships for both track & field and cross country, owing to the school's outstanding facilities.

Coach Fairley had produced many championship teams and also individual athletes, several of which later competed in their events at the U.S. Olympic trials. At least one, Nichole Teeter, made the Olympic team and competed in the 800-meter race.

ROAD RACING

> *Buzbee Brothers Take Top Honors at Woodland Race*
>
> —Title of an article in the *Northern California Running Review*, March/April 1974 issue, describing the results of a 20.7-mile race at Woodland, located 15 miles northwest of Sacramento.

During our track season, the Buzbees and others, including former Chico State athletes, had been participating in road races. At the Cupertino Marathon on April 7, 1974, Mike and Pat Buzbee finished second and fourth with times of 2:34.22 and 2:35.26. They were competing for the Gold Spike Track Club, and not the New Ways AC.

Three weeks later, on April 27th, Pat and Mike ran a 20.7-mile race in Woodland, California, trading places in finishing first and second while logging times of 2:01:30 and 2:04:04. An article describing the race noted that it was, "…held on a fairly pleasant morning, except that the runners were going into a fairly stiff breeze for the entire distance. This resulted in considerably slower times than in previous years. Chico's Dr. Don Richey finished fourteenth in the race with a 2:35.52 effort.

10

1974 Wildcat Track & Field

Wildcat Track & Field

Team Results

**Far Western Conference Championships:
2nd Place**

In the early season, Chico State participated in the Sacramento Relays, hosted by Sac State on April 6th. Wildcats teaming up for the distance medley relay (880, 440, 1320, mile), won it with a time of 10:10.4. In the 3-mile, Chico's Pat Stordahl ran 14:25.2 to finish third.

Photo 10-1

Wildcat Pat Stordahl following a University of Pacific runner in a race on the track. Stordahl's best times for the 3-mile and 6-mile were 14:06 and 30:15, respectively. Courtesy of Pat Stordahl

FAR WESTERN CONFERENCE CHAMPIONSHIPS

Near season's end, the FWC championships were held on May 17th-18th at Cal State Hayward. In a remarkable performance, Chuck Smead of Humboldt State won all three distance events: the mile (4:15.7), 3-mile (14:06.6), and 6-mile (time not known). Wildcat Tom Brown raced to victory in the 3,000-meter steeplechase with a time of 9:01. Chico State also had three other Conference champions:

- Stan Urmann in the long jump (24' 8½")
- Dave Faeth in the 440-yard intermediate hurdles (54.0)
- Mark Jones in the pole vault (15' 0")

Tom Brown was a great runner and he was tough. (Along with Chico State 4:06 miler Gene Meyers, Toni Ruggle, and Calvin Lantrip, he was from Oroville.) We liked to watch him compete in home meets at Chico State. The 7 ½-lap steeplechase is a very hard race, run over obstacles which for the men are 36 inches high, and for women 30 inches. These barriers are heavy and don't move. If athletes hit one, they go down, not the massive hurdle. At one of the home meets, I watched Tom catch his trail foot on a barrier while leading the race. This contact threw him sideways and, as he fell, his inside knee came down on the concrete curb inside lane 1, leaving him able only to painfully crawl off the track—and not continue the race.

Photo 10-2

Tom Brown clearing a steeplechase barrier.
Chico Enterprise-Record photograph

Competitors are required to clear 28 fixed barriers and seven water jumps during the race. The water jump includes a hurdle with a water pit directly behind it, which slopes upwards. The purpose of the slope is so that runners encounter less water if utilizing the correct technique. This requires them to spring off the track, land on the top of the hurdle with their lead foot, swing the other leg through and land as far as possible beyond the hurdle in the shallowest water. Runners too tired to do this, or who choose to hurdle the barrier, land in the deepest part of the pit—requiring more effort from fatigued legs to get clear of the water and continue the race.

1974 NCAA DIVISION II CHAMPIONSHIPS

The NCAA Division II and III Championships were hosted by Eastern Illinois University, May 27th-31st and June 1st, in Lincoln Stadium at Charleston, Illinois. Competing in the steeplechase, Tom Brown finished fourth with a time of 9:06.6, earning All-American honors for a second time in this event. (The top six in each event achieved this laudable recognition.)

Brown had become an All-American in the steeplechase for the first time a year earlier at the 1973 National Championships, May 31st-June 2nd, at Wabash College, Crawfordsville, Indiana. In that competition he finished sixth with a time of 9:18.5.

Tom Brown was the only two-time All-American among Chico State Wildcat distance runners in the 1970s.

CALVIN LANTRIP

A low point of the 1974 Season was the loss of Calvin Lantrip to injuries. These ailments and other responsibilities during Calvin's freshman year of track at Chico State ended his competitive running career. Previously while attending Oroville High School, he'd had a storied prep career, albeit one also accompanied by injuries. Between his freshman year until halfway through his senior year of cross country, he was the North Section's best 2-miler and the top-ranked cross country runner his junior year. Calvin won the section 2-mile as a junior and represented Oroville High in the 1972 State Meet. Unfortunately, injuries plagued him his senior year of cross country and track. He did however go on to be a member of the 1973 Chico State Cross Country team which placed sixth at the NCAA II Cross Country Championships.

Photo 10-3

Calvin Lantrip, at far right, running for the finish of the Nevada Union Invitational in 1972 with Dave Taylor (Merced) and Steve Martin (Davis). Courtesy of Calvin Lantrip

11

Second Chico North Section Varsity Cross Country Title

Photo 11-1

Chico High Panthers spread across the starting line before a cross country race, with Coach Chuck Sheley standing in front of the competitors providing instructions. Chico High School 1974-75 yearbook

On the eve of the 1974 Cross Country Season, the northern California year-round road racing schedule offered opportunity to compete in a 10-mile race at Lake Wildwood. This lake lay seventy miles by road southeast of Chico, and eleven miles due west of Grass Valley.

LAKE WILDWOOD TEN-MILE ROAD RACE

On September 14, 1974, several individuals now familiar to readers, and others well-known in the Chico running community, toed the mark at Lake Wildwood. Chico State Wildcat Pat Finn finished second in the tough 10-mile race, sponsored by the Gold Spike TC, with a time of 55.02. Eight other Wildcats finished in the top twenty. Mike and Pat Buzbee, running for the Gold Spike TC were 4th and 7th overall.

An article in the *Northern California Running Review* noted that, "Darcy Burleson (85:00, 56th) was the first of only two women finishers." Much more impressive than this informative plaudit was the fact that Darcy was just beginning her eighth-grade year at Chico Junior High School. When in high school, she would run the fastest time ever by a Panther on the Chico girls home cross country course.

```
 1 - Ron Zarate/Nevada TC         54:32    11 - Jack West/Chico St.           58:48
 2 - Pat Finn/Chico St.           55:02    12 - Nick Vogt/Gold Spike TC       59:39
 3 - Greg Griffin/Chico St.       55:42    13 - Tim Stone/Chico St.           59:39
 4 - Michael Buzbee/Gold Spike TC 56:17    14 - Mike Funntciaki/Chico St.     60:00
 5 - Tim Jordan/Golden West TC    56:47    15 - Gordon Vredenburg/GWTC        61:32
 6 - Tom Brown/Chico St.          57:27    16 - Mark Nygart/Gold Spike TC     62:05
 7 - Pat Buzbee/Gold Spike TC     57:28    17 - Tony Webb/Chico St.           62:13
 8 - George Raseas/Chico St.      57:43    18 - Norman Simon/Un               62:18
 9 - Tony Ruggel/Chico St.        57:44    19 - Doug Rennie/Buffalo Chips     62:32
10 - Humberto Hernandez/WVTC      58:00    20 - Dan Davinson/Golden West TC   63:38
```

CHICO HIGH / CHICO JUNIOR TEAMS ROLL ON

North Section Boys Cross Country Championship Teams

Varsity	JV	Freshman	Varsity	JV	Freshman
1971			**1976**		
Lassen	Lassen	Chico Jr.	Chico	Chico	Chico Jr.
1972			**1977**		
Lassen	Chico	Chico Jr.	PVHS	Paradise	Chico Jr.
1973			**1978**		
Chico	Chico	Chico Jr.	Chico	Lassen	Chico Jr.
1974			**1979**		
Chico	Chico	Chico Jr.	Paradise	Anderson	Nova
1975					
Chico	Chico	Chico Jr.			

In autumn 1974, like the preceding Cross Country season, Chico High and Chico Junior High XC teams would prevail in the North Section Championship Meet. As shown in the table, each year like clockwork from 1971 through 1978, Chuck Sheley, Bob Noe and Al Holzhey identified talented Cougars at the junior high and developed them. The resultant teams won Freshman championships, then moved on to high school. Chico High boys dominance would begin to wane following Doug Avrit and teammates' final cross country season in 1976. Its last varsity team victory of the decade came in 1978.

This chapter will recount a little of what transpired with the boys teams that 1974 season and introduce the girls moving up who, as a team in 1977, would be ranked second in the nation.

DEPTH COUNTS

Bill Gregg and Craig Larsen had graduated high school and moved on with their lives. Bill would run for Butte College and later UC Davis. Today, he is a legendary high school coach. Coach of the "Blue Devil" cross country teams and track distance runners since 1997, he has led teams and individual runners to great success, including 22 Sac-Joaquin Section Cross Country titles, multiple top finishes at California State Championships, and national meets. Bill also coached three athletes, which included his two children Brendan and Kaitlin, who competed in the U.S. Olympic Track & Field Trials.

Craig, as detailed in Chapter 20, titled "What Came Later," rides for Monta Vista Velo and has achieved great success in cycling at the senior division level.

Bill and Craig were gone, but there was a talented sophomore to move up to varsity at season's end and fill out our team.

SHENANIGANS IN OROVILLE

> *They did it again in later years. Established a course for the league meet that they only knew. All teams had to meet at LPHS and bus out to the course which only LP was familiar with.*
>
> —Chuck Sheley remarking on the below episode.

The Eastern Athletic League, of which Chico High was a member, consisted of six high schools. These were Chico and Pleasant Valley high schools in Chico; Oroville and Las Plumas in Oroville, 25 miles away; Paradise High, located 16 miles away in Paradise, a town on a wide ridge between deep canyons formed by the west branch of the Feather River and Butte Creek; and Lassen High in Susanville, 101 miles distant.

During that school year (1974-1975), Las Plumas High School and another league rival, both tried to concoct ways to beat us as a team (cross country) or individuals on our team (track & field).

The Chico High Boys Varsity team went undefeated that season, except for losing one league meet to Las Plumas, hosted by Las Plumas. We arrived at their high school where we were to warm up, because they would not let us see the course until race time. I led and won the race, but trying to figure out where to go caused me some concern. There is nothing worse than leading a race, then no longer so, because you took a wrong turn and, doubling back, ending up back in the pack. This did not happen to me, but I was frustrated by markers that were supposed to indicate to competitors where turns were in grassy areas through which the course passed. The rocks were painted green.

Paradise also competed against Las Plumas at Las Plumas in a dual meet that season. It is unclear whether it was the same "secret course" we had experienced, or another one known only to the LP team before the race. In any case, when the gun went off, LP's top five runners bolted off the line and separated from the field quickly. This was done so that they could be the first competitors to reach a tree by which the trail passed closely, hosting a large hornet's nest. The last one in this group to pass the tree, stopped, picked up a stick and hit the nest, then ran off. This left angry, stinging, flying insects for the field to encounter.

NORTH SECTION CHAMPIONSHIPS

The Panthers got an outstanding effort out of sophomore Doug Avrit just when they needed it most. Avrit came through with a school record performance over the 2.55-mile course finishing second to Lassen's Al Harris. Harris was timed in 12:57, Avrit, in 12:58. The school record was 13:07.

According to head coach Chuck Sheley, "[Jim] Walker is making a comeback from shoulder surgery in September and he arrived at the right time."

—*Chico Enterprise-Record* recapping the North Section Meet.

Photo 11-2

Doug Avrit at the 1974 EAL Championships.
Chico Enterprise-Record photograph

At the North Section Championship Meet, we beat Lassen by two points to win our second varsity title. In addition to praising the performance of sophomore Doug Avrit and senior Jim Walker, the article also noted that senior Mark Burch and junior Josh Strong "had been bitten by the flu earlier in the week," and thus not performed up to their normal standards.

Top Five Finishers of Top Three Teams

Chico High		Lassen High		Pleasant Valley High	
Doug Avrit	2nd	Al Harris	1st	Dave Scott	10th
Kent Pease	4th	Tim Patterson	6th	Don Rawlins	11th
Dave Bruhn	9th	Jim Holt	14th	Bruce Lodge	22nd
Steve Zicker	17th	Ted Fuller	15th	Tim Surminsky	36th
Jim Walker	18th	Jim Bunnell	16th	Scott Fogarty	58th

We finished first with a score of 50 points, Lassen was second with 52 points, and Pleasant Valley third in the team competition. Jim Walker and I were greatly aided by juniors Kent Pease and Steve Zicker and, of course, sophomore Doug Avrit.

In the Junior Varsity competition, Chico's Dana White was 4th, Kevin Boone 5th, Gary Layman 7th, Kurt Graves 8th, and Brian Maynard 11th to also garner a team championship.

GIRLS CROSS COUNTRY CHAMPIONSHIP MEETS

Chico Junior High School general athletic patch at left and cross country specific one at right

In the 1974 EAL (Eastern Athletic League) Varsity Girls competition, Lassen High School finished first with 24 points and Chico Junior High School with 31 points. Lassen's Pam Allen and Vicky Monroe went 1-2, and Darcy Burleson, Luanne Park, and Stacey Shols finished 3rd, 6th, and 7th respectively.

The finish for the top two Lassen runners was similar at the 1974 inaugural North Section Girls Championship Meet in which there were forty-eight competitors. Vicky Monroe and Pam Allen went 1-2 in the varsity race. Team scores were: Enterprise 25, Lassen 44, Shasta 68, and Central Valley 111. Chico Junior High only fielded four runners and, accordingly, did not score as a team. These individuals were: Kathy Jo Bernadette (3rd), Luanne Park (9th), Stacy Shols (17th), and Tammy Price (39th).

Darcy Burleson finished second to Jeannette Anderson (Durham) in the Elementary Girls Division.

The 1974 through 1979 North Section Girls Championship teams are identified in the table. Junior Varsity Championship Meets were not conducted until 1977.

Year	Girls Varsity	Girls Junior Varsity
1974	Enterprise High	
1975	Lassen High	
1976	Chico High	
1977	Chico High	Chico High
1978	Shasta High	Lassen High
1979	Shasta High	Chico Junior High

BUZBEES AT PEPSI 20-MILER

As the 1974 high school and college cross country seasons were coming to an end, the 9th Annual Pepsi 20-miler road race was being staged at Kennedy High School in Sacramento. On November 24th, running in a record field of 586 runners from four states, Mike Buzbee finished 18th in 1:54:48 and brother Pat, 39th, with a time of 1:58:15. New records were set in the High School Juniors and Seniors divisions. Following the race, only five of the existing records stood. One of them was Walt Stack's mark of 2:40:02 for the age 60-69 division.

12

1975 Track Season

Photo 12-1

Kent Pease winning the mile with a time of 4:27.6,
at the 1975 North Section Track & Field Championships.
Chico Enterprise-Record photograph

ROAD RACING PRECEDING TRACK SEASON

On January 26, 1975, Pat and Mike Buzbee, Mark and I, and someone we didn't then know, Professor Walt Schafer, competed in the First Annual Peach Bowl Pacers 10K race in Yuba City. In the field of 114 finishers, Pat and Mike were sixth and eighth. The professor (more about him in the following chapter), Mark, and I were farther back. The times for the first thirty finishers were not particularly fast; I recall that at least part of the course was run through loose, orchard dirt.

Since in the results, "New Ways AC" follows my name, the Buzbees must have drafted me to augment their team. (I'm not sure why Mark has Chico after his name; he also would have been conscripted.)

```
 1 - Jim Birnbaum (West Valley TC)    32:30    16 - Walter Schafer (NorCal Str.)   37:00
 2 - Henry Perez (Big Valley Harr)    33:49    17 - Dennis Capello (NorCal Str.)   37:07
 3 - Richard Flores (BV Harriers)     34:21    18 - Peter Hanson (Colfax RC)       37:21
 4 - Jon Higley (PB Pacers)           34:35    19 - Mark Burch (Chico)             37:39
tie  Keith Jacobson (BV Harriers)     34:35    20 - David Zunwalt (Unat.)          37:40
 6 - Pat Buzbee (New Ways TC)         34:41    21 - Craig Wells (Unat.)            37:41
 7 - Nick Vogt (Gold Spike TC)        34:52    22 - Jim Williams (PB Pacers)       37:43
 8 - Mike Buzbee (New Ways AC)        35:19    23 - Jeff Jahn (VMTC)               37:48
 9 - Mark Dawson (VMTC)               35:23    24 - Rich Vasquez (Diablo Vly TC)   37:52
10 - Keith White (Aggie TC)           35:58    25 - Frank Lemus (Unat.)            37:59
11 - Bruce Jones (Unat.)              36:14    26 - Barry Rounds (PB Pacers)       38:14
12 - Ray Batz (Pamakids)              36:36    27 - Doran Pedri (Unat.)            38:21
13 - Ross Smith (West Valley J&S)     36:39    28 - Kevin Daw (Napa Valley RC)     38:40
14 - Dave Bruhn (New Ways AC)         36:40    29 - Mary Nygaard (Gold Spike TC)   39:03
15 - Richard Stiller (TRAC)           36:46    30 - Jack Dixon (Lincoln)           39:07
```

The following month, Mike, Pat, and Walt Schafer ran the Trail's End Marathon in Seaside, Oregon, on February 22nd. Representing Chico well, Mike finished in sixteenth (2:30:52), followed closely by Pat in nineteenth (2:31:20), and Walt in thirty-ninth (2:41:56). Betty Best of Chico ran a 3:30:30 to finish 235th in the race.

The Buzbees had graduated from Chico State at year's end in 1973, then did their student teaching, and would begin teaching the fall of 1975. Mike was hired in Yuba City and Pat in Turlock, both smaller and more rural towns than Chico. During a visit by Pat back to Chico, we were standing by his car when I noticed a bumper sticker on it and started laughing. His response was, "Hey, you need to be able to get along with the locals." The sticker depicted a cowboy pushing a stroller, with a baby inside wearing a cowboy hat. The accompanying message said, "Marry a cowboy. We need more of them."

Photo 12-2

Pat Buzbee running the Trail's End Marathon in Seaside, Oregon.
Courtesy of Pat Buzbee

TRACK SEASON

If you were a track & field fan, Jamie Starmer provided a lot of excitement during the 1975 Season. It wasn't unusual for him to win four events at a meet, even at invitationals in which his 40 points for four wins would have put him, individually, near the top of final team point totals. Since this book is about distance runners, that venue is the focus of this chapter.

In the mile and half-mile (880) races, Kent Pease never failed to excite and to deliver wins—at least once he had gained top form after playing soccer for Chico High during the winter sports season. Teammate Doug Avrit loped along like a light-footed deer. Former teammate Bill Gregg, with his mane of long blond hair trailing behind, had resembled a horse—cantering during most of a race, then increasing to a gallop near the end. Kent Pease was more of a mountain lion. He stalked his prey and, like any of the cat species, his movements were most fluid when running very fast.

Two of the schools in our league also had milers who were very good kickers, but they couldn't prevail against Kent. At a meet hosted by one, we found the starting line at the beginning of the home stretch. This was very unusual. On every other track, as was customary, the finish line was, and still is, at the end of the home stretch. This provides great excitement for the fans, as competitors fight it out down the "home stretch" in front of the stands. This aberration was apparently intended to deny Pease his "killing ground." It didn't matter; he blew by their best on the backstretch, led around the curve, and won coming off it.

Kent understood geometry very well. After spending his first one and one-half years of college at Chico State, he transferred to UC Berkeley and earned a degree in Civil Engineering before moving on to Cornell University for a masters in CE.

THREE-WAY MEET IN EUGENE, OREGON

> *I remember the articles that coach Sheley would post on the cork board above the large bottle of salt pills in the locker room. I would devour these articles and the great pictures that accompanied them and it became a connection with a world I otherwise knew little about. The articles on South Eugene cross country and track & field brought us into their accomplishments and just how outstanding a team they were. Our distance squad took to calling each other Mc and our last name so, McBruhn, McPease etc. as we approached our trip north to Eugene. We all had a healthy respect for South Eugene track & field before we ever stepped on the track in Eugene.*
>
> —Doug Avrit recalling first learning that Chico High's Track team was going to venture north to Oregon to compete against powerful South Eugene High School.

One day, Mark and I were in the locker room at Chico High School and glanced up at a bulletin board on which Chuck affixed newspaper articles and other informative material. There was a new posting with a headline something like, "McChesneys will try to meet Olympic Trials qualifying standard for the 5,000 meters in race." Bill McChesney— who would later set school records at the University of Oregon for the 5,000 (13:14.80) and 10,000 meters (27:50.82)—was then a sophomore and fastest high schooler in the state of Oregon. His brother Steve, a senior, was the second fastest. Their older brother, Tom, and Steve Prefontaine had been teammates at Oregon.

What was particularly interesting about this article was that it indicated that the date of this attempt was to coincide with a scheduled three-way meet on April 11th between Chico High, Willamette High, and South Eugene High in Eugene, Oregon. The McChesneys attended the latter high school. Realizing that South Eugene was going to put on a 5,000-meter race in lieu of the 2-mile and that we were going to be participants in it, Mark and I were probably both thinking, "We're going to get killed in that race." The article included a photograph of the McChesneys. We couldn't tell much from it showing only the faces of the two runners, distorted by pain, finishing a race.

Chico High's Track team arrived in Eugene the day preceding the meet, and we were hosted by South Eugene High counterparts in their homes that night. Doug Avrit and I stayed with the McChesneys. Upon meeting them, I was shocked. Expecting formidable "distance running gods," we were instead greeted by two blond-haired, blue-eyed, angelic looking individuals each appearing to be at most 5 feet, 6 inches tall. The following day, we heard a story about at least one of our weight men (shot put or discus throwers) being "taken drinking" by their hosts. Our evening was much tamer. The McChesney parents took us out to dinner and a movie, *Young Frankenstein*.

We took the opportunity while staying with Bill and Steve to ask them about Prefontaine, since we thought they would have insider information about our idol gleaned from their brother Tom. The only thing I remember them telling us was that, reportedly, he could eat an awful lot of food—apparently much more than other, always hungry, hard-training runners.

The following day was cold and very windy, standard Eugene weather at that time of year. I finished third in the mile with a time of 4:36.0; Kent Pease, not yet in shape, was fourth in 4:38.2. Later in the meet, we ran the 2-mile (the 5,000-meter race having been cancelled). Bill won the race with a time of 9:16.6, followed by brother Steve, and a third South Eugene teammate (Harter). I led Chico's three entries (Doug, Mark, and me) with a fourth-place finish. We finished nearly a half lap behind the South Eugene-threesome. Doug recently noted about this race, "the McChesney's just ran away from us."

Photo 12-3

Doug Avrit (on the curb) and I (outside him) running the 2-mile; the McChesneys and their teammate are somewhere ahead in the distance.
Courtesy of Doug Avrit

At meet completion, South Eugene High had amassed 89 points, Chico High 54, and Willamette High 19 points.

DAY FOLLOWING THE MEET

The Chico High Track team did not immediately leave for home following the meet, it being such a long trip south to Chico. The next day was very memorable for our distance runners as explained by Avrit:

> We ran a workout at South Eugene with the South Eugene team and basically just ran their workout. Our workout with the distance squad was as follows: 1320 at South Eugene, run to Hayward Field and run a 1320 on the track, run back to South Eugene and run a final 1320 at South Eugene. While running at Hayward Field someone told me they saw Pre and I spent the rest of our run there trying to locate him. They knew how big a fan I was of Pre and knew that saying Pre was somewhere would totally mess with me, fun times. After the workout we were in the locker room and I and some others bought bright orange training shoes from Finland from no other than Mac Wilkins. Wilkins would go on to become the Olympic champion in the 1976 Montreal Olympics in the discus. Little did we know until later just who we were interacting with and buying shoes from.

INFLUENCE OF EUGENE ON CHICO TRACK & FIELD

The following section was penned by legendary coach Chuck Sheley, regarding his association with, and the importance of Eugene, Oregon:

Eugene Oregon is the capitol of Track & Field. I found that out early when, as a USFS (U.S. Forest Service) Smokejumper at Cave Junction, Oregon, I learned early in the '60s that Hayward Field is where you go to see the best in T&F. At least three times, while coaching the boys' team at CHS, I loaded my van with athletes and headed north after Friday's practice to catch the UCLA/Oregon dual meet on Saturday. Duals were big at that time, and this was the biggest. To see big-time T&F inspired my athletes in a high school world where football was the sport pushed by the coaches and Athletic Directors.

A close friend of mine from smokejumping days was Ed Sullivan, one of the top Ducks fans and personal friend of then Oregon coach Bill Dellinger, who had succeeded Bill Bowerman. We always got into the meets free of charge and one time they had a big "Welcome Chico High Track Team" on the display board.

Track & Field News ranked teams, and legendary coach Harry Johnson's South Eugene High was deemed the top team in the U.S. Johnson had won six Oregon State Championships in a row. He had Dirk Lakeman and Bill McChesney who both ran 4:08 miles plus a bunch of others. I wanted to run against South and wrote Harry thinking there would be no way we would get invited north. Wrong—Harry invited us to Eugene for the April 11th home meet.

This was very big at the time as inter-state competition was not common and required paperwork and agreements between the CIF (California Interscholastic Federation) and the Oregon high school administration. We would be at a big disadvantage, and we would only be able to take a very limited number of athletes in our three vans.

Bob Noe and I were hosted by Harry. This would pay off later as Eugene hosted the 1976 Olympic Trials. Harry was a big shot in the field event area, and he allowed Bob to sit right next to the high jump pit and take some excellent photos of Dwight Stones. (Stones had won the bronze medal at the 1972 Olympic Games, and would do so again in 1976.) Bob was there right next to the *Sports Illustrated* reporter.

The day of the meet we had crummy weather, but typical for Eugene. I could see right off the bat that I clicked mentally with Harry on how to run a track meet—like a 50s-disc jockey—no dead time. We were short on numbers to start with. Then the first event, the triple jump, which I will remember forever. South jumper, Mike Yoeman, started the meet with an Oregon State Record 48-0 leap. In Oregon you could set state records at a 3-way meet if you were

Harry Johnson. I looked over at the best all-around T&F athlete I've ever coached—Jamie Starmer. He was so blown away with Yoeman's jump, that he forgot how to triple jump. Bob Noe had him on the infield saying, "hop, step, and jump." Jamie came back to earth and took 2nd and went on to win the pole vault, the long jump, and, running it for the first time ever, the 330-hurdle race. I think that even Harry was amazed by Jamie's performance.

Bruhn and Pease got 3-4 in the mile; Rick Starkey got a 4th in the long jump; Charley Veronda, my kid from Korea, won the 100 and got 2nd in the 220; Bruhn came back in the 2-mile with a 4th against the McChesney brothers; and Joe Altman got 2nd in the 120 high hurdles. For a travel squad with one-quarter the numbers of South, does it get any better?

There are postscripts to this story. A year later Jamie and I were sitting in the office of Oregon Track Coach Bill Dellinger. Jamie had gone to Hawaii on a Track Scholarship and found out the situation was a complete con-job. He was considering running for Bill. Bill called the Pac-10 commissioner and learned, as we thought, that Jamie would have to sit out a year. I remember Dellinger's words very distinctly: "OK, I just want to make sure we aren't running against this guy (Jamie) this spring." Eugene is where T&F and running was—period. The trips to Eugene with my athletes set a mental attitude that carried them on to success in track and life.

NORTH SECTION CHAMPIONSHIPS

At the section championships on May 31st at Mitchell Field in Oroville, Jamie Starmer won both the 100-meter dash (10.1) and 330 low hurdles (38.7), and finished fourth in the long jump (20-7). The only other Chico High winner was Kent Pease. He won the mile (4:27.6), outkicking Dave Dawson from Weed, who finished second (4:28.7), just as he had a year earlier. Dawson was no slouch regarding leg speed. He came back in the 880 later in the meet, and finished second to Shasta's Elwell (1:56.7) with a time of 1:58.0.

Steve Henson from Big Valley repeated as North Section champion in the 2-mile with a time of 9:57.2. I was second in 9:59.9 and Doug fourth in 10:11.6. The times were relatively slow, because I sat back in the pack, instead of leading the race as I normally would have. The meet day was marked by 100-degree heat. By the time of this race, it had cooled off a little and the wind had picked up. On a calm night, I would have led from the start in an attempt to draw far enough ahead of Henson to prevent being outkicked by him, and hope that I didn't "die" by going out too fast and get picked off by Avrit.

At the League Championships, I had tried to break the Chico High School 2-mile record of 9:24 set by Jack Forrester in 1966. The pace I set was too ambitious, and I went into oxygen debt (which happens when your leg muscles are starved of oxygen). This phenomenon was commonly referred to, at that time, as "hitting the wall," or "the bear jumping on your back." As I slowed, Doug easily beat me.

The next week, I beat him in the Sub-Section Championships with a time of 9:45.4. When Chico's future best prep distance runner ever (Doug) was a sophomore (this season), I could prevail over him in a kick at the end of a race but not if I led into the wind the entire race and he stayed tucked in behind me, conserving energy.

Such practice (drafting) is analogous to sprinters in the famous Tour de France cycling race staying back in the peloton (main body of cyclists) until near the end of a stage race, letting other competitors do the work and drafting off them until time to kick. Drafting is not nearly as important in running because runners are much slower than cyclists, but on a windy day tucking in behind someone can pay big dividends. In this case, kicking was a relative term. Neither of us were kickers; we were pacers, but I could pace faster than Doug if I ran smart.

Henson was a kicker, and I really did not want him tucked in behind me if I was leading and running as hard as possible. So, I decided to sit in the pack, keep an eye on Avrit and Henson, and start an extended drive to the tape with two laps to go. This plan failed miserably, as evidenced by him beating me by nearly three seconds over the latter part of the race from when I began "my kick." Even then, I did not know how good Henson's leg speed was. Because he attended Big Valley High School in Bieber, I never saw him nor competed against him until season's end. Bieber was a census-designated place in Lassen County, located on the Pit River, 55 miles north-northwest of Susanville, at an elevation of 4,124 feet. I don't know what its population was then, but recently it boasted 266 residents in 2020.

A year later, I ran the 5,000 meters at the 1976 California Junior College Small School Championships. The meet was held in Porterville, a city in the San Joaquin Valley, 324 miles south of Chico. I was competing for Butte College and Henson, also in the race, for the College of the Siskiyous. I don't remember the number of athletes in the field, but there were medals for the first five finishers. They were on display, quite large and impressive, and I vowed that I would earn one "if it killed me." It was cold and windy that night; for some reason this seemed always to be the case during evening-time championships.

After the gun went off, I didn't see Henson for nearly the entire race. On the final lap, it was clear who would win and finish second. I was battling someone for third place. I passed the 3-mile mark with a split of 14:43, recall being tired, and finished in 15:15. A 5K race is 3 miles, 180 yards long. Current or former competitive distance runners reading this, probably note that I wasn't exactly "picking them up and putting them down" in covering the final 180 yards in 32 seconds. On the stretch run, Henson came blasting by us, finishing third. The other overtaken runner was fourth and myself fifth. I was happy with this result. After the race, coach Gene Meyers told me that Henson had been 40-yards behind us with a half lap to go.

JEFF STOVER OF CORNING HIGH SCHOOL

As disappointed as I was to finish second at the North Section Finals and, accordingly, fail to qualify to run in the 1975 State Championships, I suspect Corning's Jeff Stover was even more so. He was certainly much more deserving than I. At the Section Meet, Steve Montgomery of Lassen and Stover produced the longest shot-put throws in North Section history. I don't know what the final national rankings were, but at one point that season they were 1-2 in the country. Montgomery propelled "the rock" 61-9½ that day, and Stover 59-5.

Following his senior year, Stover received a track scholarship to the University of Oregon. He finished third place in the NCAA shot put competition in 1979. Following college, Stover played professional football for the San Francisco 49ers in the 1980s as a defensive end and earned two Superbowl rings.

At the 1975 California State Track & Field Championship Meet, Steve Montgomery won the shot put and set a new meet record of 68 feet. One half hour later, he threw discus 188-5 to finish second. Jeff Stover's best of 65-2¼, stands twenty-first of all-time state marks.

The following year, Montgomery went on to set what was then the State Record in the shot put, throwing 69-9 at the State Meet. He later attended USC on a full ride (athletic scholarship).

OTHER SECTION MEET RESULTS

In the Junior Varsity boys competition: Chico High's Kurt Graves won the 2-mile (10:29.0) with two teammates trailing close behind—Dana White in second (10:35.6) and Kevin Boone fourth (10:46.2)—and Chris Shols won the 880 with a time of 2:02.9. Dave Meyers from Oroville (Gene Meyers younger brother) won the mile in 4:41.0, and Chico's Jim Grubbs was fifth in 4:58.2.

Photo 12-4

Kurt Graves finishing a JV race on the track, 1975.
Courtesy of Kurt Graves

In Freshman competition, Tino Nava of Chico Junior finished second in the 1½-mile with a time of 7:47.1; and teammates Jackson and Escamilla were second and fourth in the 1,320 with 3:29.4 and 3:30.6. respectively. Chico Junior's Brad Marzolf won the 880 with a time of 2:08.4 and Jackson was third with a 2:10.1.

The final scores of the top three varsity teams were: Chico 36, Shasta 30, Pleasant Valley 20. Chico High and Chico Junior High won the Junior Varsity and Freshman team competitions.

STEVE PREFONTAINE KILLED IN CAR CRASH

On May 31st, contained in the local *Chico Enterprise-Record* sports page, below the leading article with the headline, "Starmer Wins Twice Panthers Capture North Section Track Crown," was a smaller article about the death of Steve Prefontaine. Excerpts follow:

> Steve Prefontaine, the United States' premier distance runner and the holder of seven American records was drunk when he died in the crash of his sports car [an MG], an autopsy showed today.
>
> The colorful and controversial Prefontaine, 24, was alone in his convertible Friday when it veered over the center line of a Eugene street, jumped a curb, smashed into a stone embankment and flipped over, pinning him beneath the vehicle.
>
> His death created shock throughout the sports world.

Prefontaine's death came only a few hours after a track meet featuring his 5,000-meter victory over Frank Shorter, his friend and Olympic marathon gold medal winner. It was a time when "Pre" as the Oregon star was known, liked to meet in good fellowship and drink a few beers with competitors.

This news caused sadness among runners and track fans all across America. Doug Avrit recently described his reaction to learning of Prefontaine's death, "I can remember coming on campus at Chico that Monday morning, the accident occurred on Saturday night in Eugene, and just the pall that we felt in losing a hero of the sport and someone who inspired greatness in a young athlete like myself."

TIME TO GET OFF THE STAGE

Following track season, Jim Walker, Mark Burch, and I graduated from Chico High with our classmates. We then, figuratively speaking, passed the baton to our much faster heirs. Our legacy of four successive North Section Cross Country Championships—1971 (Frosh), 1972 (JV), 1973 (V), and 1974 (V)—was in good hands.

1975 Wildcat Track & Field

Wildcat Track & Field

Team Results

Far Western Conference
Championships:
2nd Place

NCAA III Championships:
3rd Place

FAR WESTERN CONFERENCE CHAMPIONSHIPS

Humboldt State hosted the 1975 Far Western Conference (FWC) Track & Field Championships, May 15th-17th, at Arcata, California. In the team competition, Cal State Hayward came out on top with 142 points, followed by Chico State (126), UC Davis (117), Sacramento State (112), Humboldt State (83), and San Francisco State (68).

Tom Brown led Chico's middle-distance and distance runners with a second place-finish in the steeplechase, followed by Dennis Butler (3rd) in the 880 and Toni Ruggle (3rd) in the mile. Tim Stone, a transfer from Yuba College, finished behind Ruggle in the mile, and Charlie Griffin garnered a sixth-place finish in the 3-mile race.

Middle-Distance and Distance Races

Event	Name	Place	Mark
880-yard run	Dennis Butler	3rd	1:55.2
mile	Toni Ruggle	3rd	4:13.1
mile	Tim Stone	4th	4:15.8
3,000-meter steeplechase	Tom Brown	2nd	9:09.9
3-mile run	Charlie Griffin	6th	14:19.0

The results of top Wildcats in other track & field events gave proof of the strength of the team, and foreshadowed great success in the forthcoming National Championship Meet.

Hurdles, Dashes, and Team Relays

120-yard high hurdles	Mike Stokes	1st	14.8
440-yard intermediate hurdles	Mike Stokes	2nd	54.7
440-yard dash	Steve Porter	3rd	48.6
mile relay	Chico State	4th	3:18.7

Jumps

high jump	Paul Sullivan	3rd	6' 6"
long jump	Stan Urmann	1st	23' 11"
long jump	Carl Knox	2nd	22' 11¾"
triple jump	Herman Blake	2nd	48' 1¼"

Throws and Decathlon

discus throw	Steve Frankienich	1st	169' 0"
javelin throw	Doug Ladd	3rd	211' 4"
decathlon	Bob Myers	2nd	6,319 points

NCAA DIVISION III CHAMPIONSHIPS

In 1975, Chico State and Humboldt State competed in the NCAA III Championships; during the remainder of the decade, the Wildcats were in Division II. In team competition at the national championships held at Baldwin-Wallace College in Berea, Ohio, the "Cats" were third overall of the sixty-two schools participating in the meet.

Wildcats who had finished in the top three places in their events at the FWC championships were named to the All-Conference team, and qualified for the Nationals if they had met the standard. These included Toni Ruggle in the mile and Tom Brown in the steeplechase. In his heat at the Nationals, Ruggle ran 4:13 in his marque event, but missed qualifying for the final by one spot.

Chico's third place in the team competition resulted from points accumulated by five Wildcats in throwing and jumping events and the decathlon. All five of these individuals made All-American and two were national champions.

Chico State Track & Field All-Americans

Name	Place	Event	Mark
Steve Frankienich	1st	discus throw	164' 0"
Stan Urmann	1st	long jump	24' 3"
Doug Ladd	3rd	javelin throw	220' 10"
Bob Myers	5th	decathlon	6,404 points
Herman Blake	6th	triple jump	47' 6¾"

14

Chico Running Club, and Visit of Peter Snell to Chico

Photo 14-1

vintage t-shirt

Walt Schafer running the Trail's End Marathon in Seaside, Oregon, 1976; he finished with a very laudable time of 2:37:51—6:01 per mile pace for the 26.2 mile race.

The Chico Running Club, which champions running generally, supports local high school programs, and puts on two races annually—the Almond Bowl in autumn and Bidwell Classic in spring. The registration fee at the first Almond Bowl Run in November 1975—at which there were 175 participants in the 3 and 6-mile races—was $2.50. The race was given this name to bring attention to it on a weekend near the pre-existing PVHS-CHS Almond Bowl football game. Maximum participation in the Bidwell Classic was 2,400 in 1984, with 1,600 in the half-marathon, 400 in the marathon, and 400 in the 3-mile fun run.

The Chico Running Club was formed in summer 1975. At that time, summer weekly all-comers evening track meets were held at Chico State, put on by the university's head track coach, Larry Burleson, and Chuck Sheley. College and high school athletes, and anyone else who desired, could compete for ribbons against one another at these meets (which took place on mostly very hot nights).

Following one of these meets, Walt Schafer hosted a meeting at his home for anyone interested in attending and discussing forming a local running club. Several individuals showed up—Chuck Sheley,

Don Richey, Frank Burk, Larry Dion, Jim Remillard, Mike Andrews, and Suzie Alexander—becoming collectively, along with Walt, the founders of the club. At this gathering, they agreed upon three things:
- They would form a club
- They would find a notable speaker to mark its establishment
- They would host the first Almond Bowl race in November

Walt was a Professor of Sociology, who had previously taught at the University of Oregon, and just arrived in Chico to take up a faculty position at Chico State. He was then 36 years old, and an accomplished athlete. He had run bests of 4:16 in the mile and 1:54 in the ½-mile at the University of Michigan prior to graduation in 1961; and went on to earn his Master's Degree and PhD in 1962 and 1965, respectively, at the same school. In 1976, Walt would run 2:37.51 for a marathon in Seaside, Oregon. (As an indication of how good this time was, in 1972, the qualifying time to participate in the U.S. Olympic Trials Marathon had been two hours and thirty minutes.)

Photo 14-2

Walt Schafer finishing a cross country race at Ludington High School in Michigan in 1956.

Olympic Champion and World Record Holder New Zealander Peter Snell was the notable speaker for the first gathering of club members and potential club members in September 1975. First, a little about Snell, whose story is well-known to runners of a particular generation. He was a quarter-finalist in the New Zealand National Junior Tennis Championships when he came to the notice of famed New

Zealand Track Coach Arthur Lydiard. Less than a year later, Snell won the Gold Medal for the 800 meters at the Olympic Games in Rome. He was so new to the sport, that announcers of the Olympic final race, knew nothing about him. Four years later, Snell won Gold Medals for both the 800 meters and 1,500 meters at the Olympic Games in Tokyo.

Snell began his talk in Chico, by saying something to the effect, "In America, when someone introduces me by saying, this is Peter Snell, he won at the Olympics, I can see that I go up in their eyes. In New Zealand, a countryman might say, well, so you can run a little, what else can you do?" He then explained how he happened to be with us that night. Following his athletic career, he had accepted a position as a spokesperson for the Reynolds Tobacco Company, but came to feel bad about this choice, partially because both of his parents had been educators. So, he had come to the United States to pursue a bachelor's degree in exercise physiology at U.C. Davis.

Walt, learning of this, had called the Department Office at U.C. Davis and asked the person answering the phone if he could speak with Snell, to which the reply was, he is standing right here. (Snell ultimately obtained his Bachelor and Master degrees at Davis, his PhD at Washington State, and became a scholar at the University of Texas.)

Having agreed to speak, Snell journeyed 100 miles north to Chico, and gave a very inspiring talk to some 175 captivated attendees in the university auditorium. At completion, he invited those interested to show up the following morning at Sycamore Pool (a nearby public swimming area on Big Chico Creek), for a fun run with him. Some 100 people did so and ran a loop in lower Bidwell Park with the champion.

Walt had been kind enough the previous evening to invite me to go out with him and Snell for drinks after the presentation. I accompanied them; being only 18, did not partake of the favorite beverage of most runners, beer; said very little, and enjoyed listening to the conversation. My recollection of the run the following morning was that when Snell, who was then in his late 30's took off his sweat pants, it was obvious from his chiseled legs why he was renowned for having a great kick.

Previously, while Professor Schafer was teaching at the University of Oregon, he had continued a vigorous training program and ran workouts with great runners, including Steve Prefontaine, Kenny Moore, and visiting Jim Ryun. I knew none of this, nor did I know then that he was a former 4:16 miler. (I learned of this only a few years ago when he showed me a photograph of him with his teammates taken during a recent U of M reunion, and explained his background.)

I did know that Walt had run a very good time for a marathon but, in January 1976, on the eve of the Peach Bowl 10K race in nearby Yuba

City, I was shocked that some of his buddies in the Chico Running Club, all adults, opined, unsolicited, that he was going to beat me. My thought at that time, there was no way I was going to lose to this old professor. (Age eighteen can easily believe that thirty-six is old.) For whatever reason, youth prevailed in that race.

Walt Schafer taught at Chico State University from 1975 to 2004. He competed in seventeen marathons in the 1970s and 1980s, and ran for decades at high age-group levels before finally switching to cycling. A national age-group championship title followed in this new sport, as well as world competitions. Today, he continues a vigorous cycling regimen in his early 80s.

Photo 14-3

Walt Schafer running on the Great Wall of China in 1983, wearing a Chico Running Club jersey.

Moreover, athletic prowess prevails in succeeding family members; Walt's granddaughter Linnea Mack set seven school swimming records at UCLA whence she graduated in 2017. She continues as a professional swimmer and hopes to make the 2024 U.S. Olympic team.

15

1975 Cross Country Season

These assistant coaches are a story in and of themselves. One of the legacies of Chuck's leadership was his willingness to enroll and empower assistant coaches such as the Buzbees, Pat Haley, Pat Finn, and Karl Schaechterle. To this day I use his example with the people I work with constantly.

—Kurt Graves remarking on Chuck Sheley's practice of allowing former Chico State athletes (who were student teaching for him) to assist with and add richness to the Chico High and Chico Junior running programs.

We were the beneficiaries of these young knowledgeable coaches. All came with different personalities and intensity.

—Doug Avrit echoing this sentiment.

Photo 15-1

1975 Chico High School Boys Varsity and Junior Varsity Cross Country teams.
Back row L-R: assistant coach Pat Finn, Kent Pease, Steve Zicker, Chris Lambert, Doug Avrit, head coach Chuck Sheley. Middle row: Chuck Veronda, Steve Lewis, Kevin Boone, Chris Shols, Rich Gregg. Front row: Dana White, Kurt Graves, Mike Byrne, Brian Maynard, Mark Prouty.

PAT BUZBEE BREAKS 1972 TRIALS STANDARD

The next three finishers broke 2:30 for their first time: Jim Barker (2:28:11), Pat Buzbee (2:28:22), and Ron Johnson (2:28:37).

—*Northern California Running Review* May/June issue describing highlights of the Avenue of the Giants Marathon.

Photo 15-2

L-R: Mike and Pat Buzbee after completing the Avenue of the Giants marathon. Courtesy of Pat Buzbee

Four months before the start of the 1975 Cross Country Season, during the latter part of the preceding track season, Pat Buzbee, one of Chico's former assistant coaches mentioned in the quoted material at chapter's head, had his best race to date on May 11th at the Avenue of the Giants Marathon in Humboldt Redwoods State Park. He broke the existing 1972 Olympic Trials qualifying standard of 2:30 for the marathon with a 2:28:22 effort; joining brother Mike, who had accomplished this earlier with a 2:29:55 on September 30, 1973.

Mike Buzbee and Walt Schafer finished the race in twelfth and fifteenth place, respectively.

1 - Wayne Badgley/Un	2:18:06	9 - Brian Chapman/Ore	2:34:51
2 - Reid Harter/WVTC	2:20:55	10 - Conrad Lowry/HSU	2:35:46
3 - Jim Barker/WVTC	2:28:11	11 - Thomas Brant/Ore	2:37:48
4 - Pat Buzbee/NCS	2:28:22	12 - Mike Buzbee/NCS	2:39:09
5 - Ron Johnson/Ore	2:28:37	13 - Kevin Kirby	2:39:38
6 - Bob Bunnell/MAC	2:32:00	14 - Hersh Jenkins/HSU	2:39:55
7 - Fred Emerling/WVTC	2:32:36	15 - Walt Shafer	2:40:28
8 - Roger Gerard/Colo	2:33:28	16 - Raymond Bonner	2:40:33

Unfortunately, Mike and Pat would fall victim to the continuing migration of former national-caliber track athletes (who had competed at very high levels in the 5,000 and 10,000 meters) to the longest race associated with the Olympic Games, the 26.2-mile marathon. Such possibility had been highlighted by Frank Shorter at the 1972 Olympic Games in Munich, Germany, when he won the marathon. Shorter had previously excelled as a track athlete and continued to do so even after moving up to the marathon. As more and more runners with great leg speed moved up to the marathon, times dropped and the 1976 Olympic trials committee lowered the qualifying standard to a time of 2:23. The Buzbees, early leaders in the marathon-running community, fell victim to this phenomenon—and were unable to meet the new standard. Had they been three years older, they would likely have competed in the 1972 trials.

CHICO HIGH PRESEASON TRAINING CAMP

> *Our basis for creating a program starts with the seventh, eighth and ninth grade students. I've heard from many coaches that the kids will burn out—at least they will lose interest—but the results are there or at least I think they are. Our coaching staff works together (Bob Noe at Chico Junior and Karen Sinor with the Chico Junior and Chico Senior girls) regardless of the level or grade of the athlete. The success is a product of all and not any one person.*
>
> —Chuck Sheley quoted in a 1975 *Enterprise-Record* Paging the Preps article by Skip Reager.

In early fall, coach Sheley put on a training camp at Eagle Lake—located at 5,098 feet, 125 miles northeast of Chico in Lassen National Forest—to kick off the cross country season. Panthers in attendance stayed in a vacation home, bunking on the floor in sleeping bags. Each day, the athletes trained at elevation, went swimming, and played hearts (a card game) in the evening. The camp, which promoted team building, in additional to training and relaxation, culminated in a race between teammates on the final day.

CROSS COUNTRY SEASON HIGHS AND LOWS

Photo 15-3

1975 Chico High Boys Cross Country team members toeing the line at the start of a cross country race. Kent Pease and, to his left, Doug Avrit are on the starting line in the center of the photograph. At the left of the photo, are Kurt Graves, with Rich Gregg (wearing glasses) behind him, and Steve Zicker and Chris Shols to his left. Courtesy of Doug Avrit

EARLY SEASON LOSS TO PARADISE HIGH SCHOOL

> *We train through the [weekly] Thursday duals [dual meets] and do not put emphasis there. We start very slowly to avoid injury. We do want to win the duals but will not alter our final objectives to do so.*
>
> *Even if we had started earlier and trained harder it would probably not have changed the outcome of the Paradise meet. They (the Bobcats) have a great bunch of athletes and they were ready for us.*
>
> —Chuck Sheley quoted in the same 1975 *Enterprise-Record* Paging the Preps article by Skip Reager.

As the 1975 Cross Country Season broke, Chico High's Varsity Cross Country team had been on top for a few seasons, and it appeared this was going to be another banner season. Kent Pease was a senior and leader of the team assisted by Doug Avrit and, with many up-and-coming runners, Chico looked to be strong once again. Enter Paradise, which appeared seemingly out of nowhere as perhaps the most powerful team in the North Section. Doug Avrit recently recounted the first meeting of the two teams that season:

> Paradise had a talented and creative young coach in Kim Ellison and he was determined to lead the Bobcats in an upset of Chico. [Mike Genga was the XC coach. Ellison who helped out was the track coach.] The first big test of their ability to challenge Chico came in a dual meet at Hooker Oak, our home course. We did not know a lot about their team but knew that they wanted a piece of us and were going to be tough.
>
> Paradise had recruited a young runner, I don't recall his grade, who they determined could challenge Kent and I at the front. As we were gathering before the race, they pointed myself and Kent out to this individual so that he would know who he had to follow once the race began. Follow he did! At one point in the race, he was staring at me as though to try and intimidate me or something. It was strange. I had never experienced that before in a race and just basically ignored him and kept running.
>
> This individual, I don't know his name, eventually fell off the pace but that opened up the gates for the emergence of a great runner in Larry Greer. He moved to the front and would go on to win, beating both Kent and I and leading Paradise to a narrow victory. The challenge had come and it was successful.

Following this loss to Paradise, Chico won all its other dual meets with league opponents; the most satisfying, perhaps, coming against longtime rival Lassen.

DUAL MEET AT LASSEN

When the gun went off in the autumn 1975 dual meet at Susanville, the Chico Panthers (comprising the best Chico Boys Cross Country team fielded to date) sprinted to the lead and never relinquished it. As the trail necked down after the tough uphill portions of the course, it was the chasing Grizzles that were hindered in any attempt to catch and overtake fleet Panthers, and not, Panthers chasing them.

Photo 15-4

Doug Avrit leading Kent Pease during the race at Lassen in Susanville.
Chuck Sheley collection

> *This is the year after you graduated. We said before the race that we wanted to put a punctuation mark on the end of their dynasty and this is a continuation of the one you all began.*
>
> —Kurt Graves in correspondence to the author, explaining the motivation behind Panthers sweeping the first seven places in a cross country race against Lassen High School.

Photo 15-5

L-R: Kurt Graves, Kevin Boone, Chris Shols, Ted Kutz, Kent Pease, Steve Zicker, and Doug Avrit.
Courtesy of Kurt Graves

MCKINLEYVILLE BEACH RUN

At this meet, Chicoans made a clean sweep, winning three of four divisions. Only the Varsity boys team lost, because seniors Kent Pease and Steve Zicker had been left behind to take a college entrance examination. As it was, the team led by Doug Avrit lost by only one point to Brookings (43-44), the defending Oregon II champions.

| \multicolumn{3}{l}{Chico High Varsity Boys Team} |||
No.	Name	Time
2	Doug Avrit	15:30
6	Kurt Graves	15:37
8	Ted Kutz	16:07
9	Chris Shols	16:10
19	Kevin Boone	16:26

Chico High Jayvee Boys Team		
No.	Name	Time
1	Chris Johnson	10:52
3	Tina Nava	10:53
16	Jim Krajerik	11:05
17	Dave Carroll	11:06
28	Jeff Gustafik	11:16

Chico Junior High Boys Team		
No.	Name	Time
1	Greg Williams	10:31
3	Steve Growdon	10:51
16	Scott Lape	11:18
27	John Rayl	11:37
28	Dave Girimonte	11:38

Chico Junior High Girls Team		
No.	Name	Time
1	Tammy Denny	12:31
5	Julie Lorente	12:50
6	Julie Mattoon	12:51
7	Vickie Whitburn	12:53
9	Robin Cushman	13:25

LEAGUE CHAMPIONSHIPS

> *There's a psychological component in that a race is more than who's the fastest — it's person vs person. The "kicker" can get psychologically drug along by the "runner," knowing that he just needs to stay in contact to win the race. Although the tactic can win some races, it doesn't promote confidence and independence of the "kicker" to set a fast pace and run good times as he's always tied to another runner(s). I also recall the "runners" who of course were distasteful of the tactic and expressed their pleasure when a "runner" outran a "kicker" by creating enough distance before the finish.*

—Kent Pease explaining recently, regarding the subject of "kickers" versus "runners," that while tactics commonly employed by kickers enable them to expend less energy during a race, there were weaknesses associated with their use.

Chico's success continued at the League Championships, at which the Panthers narrowly prevailed over Paradise to take the team title. It was not easy, as Doug Avrit's vivid description of Larry Greer, Kent Pease, and he contending for individual honors, demonstrates:

Paradise and Chico next met at the EAL Finals hosted by Las Plumas High School. This was going to be a barn burner and it did not disappoint! Throughout most of the race Larry was attached to my right hip, as he had obviously been instructed to stick to me like glue. He was successful in this and as we closed in on the final 200-300 meters, we were together. All of a sudden, the pounding feet of Kent Pease came charging down the hill as we approached the finish. Kent went right past Larry and I and was pulling away to victory.

Larry detached from me and began to chase after Kent. This would be a futile attempt as no one chased down Kent late in a race! He didn't have the title "animal" for no reason. As Larry began his kick, I did one of the most team-oriented things I ever did in a race, I yelled, "He's coming Kent." Not that Kent needed my warning, but I thought it prudent at the time. Kent won, Larry was second and I third.

In the chute Larry curled up into a ball as he was cramping up from his hard effort throughout the race and then topped off by his attempt to chase down Kent. People asked me to hold him up but I was spent also. We and everybody that day were giving it their all in an attempt to win our league. Larry eventually came back to life after being given some coffee and maybe some massaging to get his cramped muscles to loosen up.

NORTH SECTION CHAMPIONSHIPS

> *Since 1971 the Panthers have won three section titles and three EAL [League] championships; the li'l panthers four section titles and four EAL championships; and the Cougars have taken five section championships and four EAL championships.*
>
> —1975 *Enterprise-Record* Paging the Preps article by Skip Reager.

One week later, at the North Section Championships held at Enterprise High School in Redding, junior Doug Avrit and senior Kent Pease finished 1-2 to spark a nine-point victory over Paradise (37-46). The Chico High Jayvee and Chico Junior Freshman teams also captured their respective titles. The varsity race was once again hard-fought; Avrit explains:

Chico was going in as the favorites if we ran well as a team. Kent and I along with Larry Greer of Paradise and a runner or two from the Redding area were in the hunt for an individual championship. There was heavy rain during the week of the finals, which meant the course would be muddy in places and possibly slippery. Kent had gone to a local shoe store and had waffle bottoms put on his shoes so as to help him with the muddy conditions. The Tiger Jayhawks that we raced in had slick soles and were thus not the best for racing in slippery conditions. I can remember this kind of psyching me out because I thought Kent had an advantage with these new soles.

This concern was offset by coach Noe coming up to me at some time during a practice and advising, "There is not a 16-17 year old boy alive that will put themselves through what Larry experienced at the league final, two weeks in a row. If you push the pace in the middle of the race he will not respond!" I was surprised to hear this and would have never thought of it on my own.

On the day of the meet, there was bright sunshine after a rainy week. Before the race, during warm up and our meeting right before the race, I was extremely focused and envisioned a challenging race but one I invited and was excited to be a part of. Just like Noe had predicted, when I pushed the pace near the midway mark, Larry did not respond and it was Kent and I. I knew that I did not want to tangle with him late in the race, continued to push the pace, and eventually was able to open a gap. We finished 1-2 and led Chico to another section title.

ROAD RACING IN AUTUMN 1975

As the cross country-season was winding down, the newly established Chico Running Club hosted three- and six-mile races at the first annual Almond Bowl Run. As can be seen from the results published in the *Northern California Running Review*, there were among the top finishers in these races, present and former Wildcats, as well as other local runners and competitors from out of town.

3-Mile Race

1 - Lee Ferrero	14:10	9 - Harry Ellis/ChicoSt	15:39
2 - Tim Stone/Chico St.	14:37	10 - Steve Coronado/WVTC	15:48
3 - Pat Finn/Chico St.	14:43	11 - Steve Harvey	16:05
4 - Karl Schaecterle	14:49	12 - Dave Callnon	16:09
5 - Wayne Barth	15:05	13 - Scott Ellis	16:10
6 - Michael Hovar	15:08	14 - Wayne Moss	16:34
7 - Jack Betschart	15:26	15 - Eric Peterson	16:40
8 - Kent Mulkey	15:28	16 - Dale Booth	16:43

```
17 - Stephen Broderick    17:16    25 - James Cavanaugh      18:36
18 - Mark Morgan          17:32    26 - Mike Gregg           18:45
19 - Robert Chavez        17:36    27 - Brandon Muncy        18:47
20 - Floyd Harden         17:45    ***WOMEN***
21 - Ken Long             17:47    35 - Cindy Claiborne      20:00
22 - Thomas Grady         18:30    36 - Jeanette Anderson    20:01
23 - Paul Fuller          18:35    44 - Betsy Petersen       21:25
24 - Charles Engle        18:35    48 - Danae Luper          22:42
```

6-Mile Race

```
 1 - Dennis Swart/WVTC    29:17     9 - Pat Buzbee           32:27
 2 - Wayne Badgley/SUTC   29:22    10 - Mike Buzbee          32:32
 3 - Gary Singer/SUTC     30:09    11 - Steven Cain          32:50
 4 - Jack West/WVTC       30:34    12 - Doug Rennie          33:35
 5 - Chris DeFazio        30:43    13 - David Wood           33:46
 6 - Rodger Stordahl      31:34    14 - Paul Holmes/BCTC     34:05
 7 - Tony Webb            31:49    15 - Tom Olsen            34:16
 8 - George Rogers        32:00    16 - Mark Shumen          34:22

17 - Dan Ralston          34:35    25 - Michael Huwaldt      35:39
18 - Jim Middleton        34:38    26 - John Moran           35:46
19 - Jim Engle            34:39    27 - Stan Edwards         35:59
20 - Walt Betschart/BCTC  34:57    28 - Roger Herndon        36:23
21 - Tom Hannickel        34:58    29 - Brian Newell         36:32
22 - Gary Kohl            35:08    ***WOMEN***
23 - Harry Daniell        35:14    60 - Merrill Cray         40:47
24 - Mark Glenesk         35:22    67 - Betty Best           42:01
```

On November 30, 1975, the annual Pepsi 20-Miler was held in Clarksburg. This tiny town, located on the Sacramento River fourteen miles south of Sacramento, was the hub of the Delta's wine country. Among the finishers in the race, won in a very fast time, was Chico Running Club cofounder Walt Schafer (39th in 1:57:57).

```
 1 - Steve Dean/GWTC        1:43:44    31 - Kevin Kirby            1:55:49
 2 - Benton Hart/BYU        1:46:52    32 - Jim Shettler/WVJS      1:56:24
 3 - Ron Wayne/WVTC         1:47:41    33 - Dave Himmelberger      1:56:28
 4 - Dale Fuller            1:48:15    34 - Tim Farrell            1:56:52
 5 - Bill Seaver/WVTC       1:48:35    35 - Frank Krebs/GWTC       1:57:05
 6 - Jan Sershen/ETC        1:48:57    36 - Jan Markowski          1:57:10
 7 - Howard Labrie/SRRC     1:49:34    37 - Clark Rosen/PAMA       1:57:34
 8 - Gene Fitzgerald/PK     1:49:41    38 - Chris Cole             1:57:53
 9 - Rich Langford          1:50:18    39 - Walt Schafer/Chico     1:57:57
10 - Dennis Rinde           1:50:28    40 - John Finch/NCSTC       1:58:04
11 - Jim Sane/BCTC          1:50:56    41 - Bob Bourbeau           1:58:06
12 - Tom O'Neil/Jesuit      1:51:36    42 - Ernie Rivas            1:58:08
13 - Ed Schelegle/AGTC      1:51:52    43 - John Thomas            1:58:11
14 - Mike Smith/PAMA        1:52:10    44 - Jim Simpson/WVJS       1:58:24
15 - Bob Darling/ETC        1:52:28    45 - Stephen Bird           1:58:25
16 - Mike Conroy/ETC        1:52:57    46 - Armando Lagunas        1:59:05
```

16

1976 Track Season

Photo 16-1

Panther distance runners training on Chico High School's dirt track.
Left photo L-R: Doug Avrit, Dana White, Kurt Graves, Chris Shols, and Steve Zicker.
Right photo L-R: Steve Zicker, Kurt Graves, Dana White, and Kevin Boone.
Chico State University's Butte Hall is in the background.
Courtesy of Kurt Graves

ROAD RACING PRECEDING TRACK SEASON
Kicking off the new year, on January 25, 1976, 148 runners participated in the Peach Bowl 10K race in Marysville, California. Among them were Chico Running Club's Dave Bruhn (10th, 34:32), Walt Schafer (15th, 35:17), and Frank Burk (44th, 38:32).

A month later, Walt Schafer and 575 other finishers battled cold rain on February 28th, during the 26.2-mile Trail's End Marathon in Seaside, Oregon. Despite these conditions, Walt ran a lifetime best of 2:37:45 to garner fifty-seventh place overall.

BIDWELL CLASSIC RACES IN CHICO
On March 6, 1976, the Chico Running Club, formed just a little over six months earlier, hosted three- and twelve-mile races in Bidwell Park in Chico. Pat Finn finished second in the 3-mile, followed by several

young Chico High athletes which the book visits in later chapters. These were Greg Williams (8th, 16:38), Kevin Boone (10th, 17:09), and Steve Growdon (19th, 17:53). Dick Symons, father of Jill Symons, won the masters division with a time of 18:33.

In the longer 12-mile race, Pat and Mike Buzbee (now teachers in Turlock and Yuba City, and visiting Chico) finished second and sixth with times of 67:37 and 70:03. Recently, Pat reminisced about changes associated with post-college employment and the resultant breakup of the Buzbees by virtue of their living in different geographic locations:

> After getting our first real job out of college, we could now afford purchasing a new pair of running shoes. We no longer got our shoes from the lost and found bin.
>
> Leaving Chico in the mid-70's was both welcome and sad. Here I was losing what was familiar, Bidwell Park trails, friends, training partners, hill runs at Forest Ranch, Cohasset, and Paradise, and fond memories. I also lost my training partner of many years, my twin brother Mike, when we took different teaching jobs. I was now gaining a new dimension. New races, new faces, new places to run, new training partners, and a new outlook, "New Ways."

Other locals in the Bidwell Classic 12-mile race included Butte College track coach John Lanzavecchia (17th, 76:11) and Chico Running Club co-founder Jim Remillard (18th, 77:04).

TRACK SEASON SUB-SECTION MEET

At the Sub-Section Meet late in the 1976 Track Season, Kent Pease won the mile; Doug Avrit, Santos Cervantes, and Kurt Graves finished 1-2-3 in the two-mile; and Chico's pole vaulters, Jerry Mulligan and David Marler finished first and second in that event. Mulligan and Marler had gone higher than anyone else in the North Section. A Paging the Preps article by Skip Reager, published in the *Enterprise-Record* on the eve of the subsequent North Section Track & Field Championships, suggested that Chico's hopes for a team title could rest on the performances of the Panthers pole vaulters and distance runners. Excerpts from the article follow:

> One thing that most coaches agree on is that if Chico gets a 1-2 in the vault and a 1-2-3 in the two mile, it's all over for everyone else.
>
> The trio [Avrit, Cervantes, and Graves] could do that again in the [section] finals although Jon Schmidt of Anderson and Riley of

Shasta could break up the Panther stranglehold. Even three of the first five places could greatly enhance the Panther title hopes.

The Panthers' Kent Pease won the mile [at the sub-section meet] and is favored to do so in the section meet despite the fact Schmidt ran four seconds faster in qualifying. Pease runs only to win and has not worried about time. He is the defending champion in that event and has a 4:20 to his credit this season.

NORTH SECTION BOYS T&F CHAMPIONSHIPS

On May 28th, at the North Section Championships held at Mitchell Field in Oroville, Kent Pease defended his title from the previous year, winning the mile in 4:23.6 with a stretch kick over Riley from Shasta (4:23.7). Dave Meyers (younger brother of Gene Meyers) of Oroville was third in 4:28.2.

Shasta's Mark Elwell won the 880 (1:56.2), followed by Ellsworth of Paradise (2:00.1); Chico's Chris Shols (2:01.0) and Kent Pease (2:01.6); and Bob Hastings (2:02.7) of Las Plumas High School.

Chico High took the top three spots in the 2-mile, and would likely have had another Panther in the top four, if rules did not limit the number of competitors from any one high school, participating in a track or field event, to three individuals. As a result of this regulation, Kevin Boone, who had a best of 9:53.6 that season, was left home. Chico's Doug Avrit (9:42.3) won the race, with Santos Cervantes (9:46.8) and Kurt Graves (9:56.3) completing the Chico sweep.

Chico won the overall team title (47 points), with Pleasant Valley (26), Paradise (26), Yreka (18), Shasta (17), and Lassen (15) rounding out the other top teams.

NO PANTHER WINNERS IN JV DISTANCE RACES

Seemingly ominous for Chico High's future Boys Cross Country team hopes, there was only a single Panther in the top five places of the 880, mile, and 2-mile in Junior Varsity competition at the Section Meet. Mike Brand and Seth Roberts of Paradise won the mile and 880 with times of 4:36.0 and 2:03.3, respectively. Chico's Brad Marzolf ran 2:08.7 to finish fifth in the latter race. There were no Panthers or Bobcats among the top five finishers in the 2-mile race. Without its normal hefty distance event points to augment those earned from the sprints, jumps, throws, and relays, the Chico jayvee squad finished sixth in the overall team competition with 12 ½ points, well behind winner Enterprise with 41.

GIRLS NORTH SECTION CHAMPIONSHIPS

The Girls North Championships, held a day earlier on May 27th at Sutter High School, had included the 2-mile race for the first time. Among the meet competitors were elements of the future "Charlie's Angels" spread across events ranging from the 100-yard dash to the 2-mile run. Chico's Stacy Shols and Luanne Park, both possessing good leg speed, finished second in the 100 and 440-yard dashes with 11.9 and 60.1, respectively.

Vicky Monroe of Lassen easily won the mile in 5:13.1; Chico's Darcy Burleson (5:19.5) and Joan Gregg (5:36.6) finished second and fifth in the race. Separating the Panthers were Debbie Rudolph of Lassen in third (5:28.5) and Red Bluff's Lean Knedler (5:34.6) with a fourth-place finish.

Debbie Rudolph doubled back to win the inaugural 2-mile with a time of 12:00.6. Cindy Claiborne of Bidwell Junior High (Chico Junior High's rival in Chico) finished fourth (12:43.2), followed by Chico High's Julia Sabin in fifth (12:56.3).

Lassen High School won the team competition with 43 points. Chico Senior High School was second (36), and Chico Junior High fourth (17) overall.

1976 U.S. TRACK & FIELD OLYMPIC TRIALS

Photo 16-2

Ticket to the 1976 U.S. Olympic Track & Field Trials.
Courtesy of Kurt Graves

In early summer, Chuck Sheley arranged for present and former Panthers to attend the U.S. Olympic Track & Field Trials held June 19th-27th in Eugene, Oregon. We brought tents and stayed in a KOA campground in Coburg, just north of Eugene. Each day we car-pooled to the stadium to enjoy, as spectators, the excitement of watching athletes compete in the trials and finals of various events. While running very fast, the distance runners appeared to be out for a stroll, their body mechanics being so good. Red and white, and blue and white vertically-stripped "dolphin running shorts" made famous by 1972 Olympic Marathon champion Frank Shorter were in abundance at the trials, and Shorter was in attendance competing in the 10,000-meter run.

Doug Avrit recently described his memories of this race:

> The 10,000 at the Trials was one of the most exciting races I have ever witnessed. First you had Craig Virgin challenging Frank Shorter at the front and at one point when Virgin had surged to the lead Frank just extended his arm as though to say, "here he is!", this brought a good response from the crowd. Then the race climaxed in the final lap with Gary Bjorklund, who had lost one of his spikes earlier in the race, chasing down and passing Bill Rodgers and garnering the coveted last spot on the Olympic team. You couldn't hear yourself scream during that last lap as Gary chased down Bill. For an aspiring young athlete to witness this was truly inspiring.
>
> Also in that 10,000 field were two high school athletes, Rudy Chapa from Indiana and Eric Hulst from Laguna Beach. This was an amazing accomplishment for a high school athlete and especially in an event that usually was a more mature distance runner's domain. I had just competed against Hulst, well I was on the same track and in the same event, at the California State Meet just a month earlier. He was a specimen and a very strong runner who pounded the ground in aggressive fashion as he surged away from most. Chapa would attend the University of Oregon in the fall of that year and Hulst would attend UC Irvine.

As might be expected, some athletes at the trials experienced great joy and others great sorrow. I have a vivid memory of watching Marty Liquori, in frustration, kick a chain link fence surrounding the track after a hamstring injury suffered in his 5,000 meters heat forced him to quit the race, ending his quest to make a second Olympic team. Liquori, known as a fierce competitor, rose to fame when he became the third American high schooler to break the four-minute mile by running a 3:59.8 in 1967. A year later, he made the 1968 U.S. Olympic team as a nineteen-year-old freshman at Villanova University coached by Jumbo Elliott. Liquori reached the finals of the 1,500 meters but suffered a stress fracture and finished twelfth.

Frank Shorter had already made the team by winning the marathon trials held earlier on May 22, 1976; he earned another spot by finishing first in the 10,000-meter race as well. (The three Americans to make the marathon team were: Shorter, 2:11:51; Bill Rogers, 2:11:58; and Don

Kardong, 2:13:54. The temperature at that race was 70 degrees at the start, then cooled off somewhat with a slight wind.)

For readers who followed running in those days, the following lists of men's and women's Olympic team qualifiers at Eugene in the middle-distance and distance races may offer a nice trip down memory lane.

1976 Men's Olympic Team Members in Middle-Distance/Distance Races

	800 Meters			5,000 Meters	
1	Rick Wohlhuter	1:44.78	1	Dick Buerkle	13:26.60
2	James Robinson	1:45.86	2	Duncan MacDonald	13:29.46
3	Mark Enyeart	1:46.28	3	Paul Geis	13:38.46

	1,500 Meters			10,000 Meters	
1	Rick Wohlhuter	3:36.47	1	Frank Shorter	27:55.45
2	Matt Centrowitz	3:36.70	2	Craig Virgin	27:59.43
3	Mike Durkin	3:36.72	3	Gary Bjorklund	28:03.74

	3,000m Steeplechase			Marathon	
1	Doug Brown	8:27.39	1	Frank Shorter	2:11:51
2	Henry Marsh	8:27.42	2	Bill Rodgers	2:11:58
3	Mike Roche	8:32.70	3	Don Kardong	2:13:54

Women were not yet allowed to run the steeplechase, 5,000 meter, or marathon races. In these trials, Madeline Jackson set an American record in the 800 meters, and Cyndy Poor in the 1,500 meters race.

1976 Women's Olympic Team Members in Middle-Distance/Distance Races

	800 Meters			1,500 Meters	
1	Madeline Jackson	1:59.81 AR	1	Cyndy Poor	4:07.32 AR
2	Cyndy Poor	2:00.55	2	Jan Merrill	4:07.35
3	Kim Weston	2:00.73	3	Francie Larrieu	4:08.08

RUNNING DURING FREE TIME IN EUGENE

During breaks in the athletic competition, we would venture outside the stadium for training runs, to eat meals, or to shop for souvenirs. The Prefontaine Memorial Trail was nearby and enjoyable to run on. You could also train on the streets of Eugene. On one such run we passed a rocky outcrop at a turn in the road, identified by painted lettering as the protuberance Steve Prefontaine's MGB had struck at speed, before overturning and killing him. A very sad sight, particularly when viewed during the trials at which he would have been participating and, almost certainly, making the team.

Nineteen years later, *The Running Times* published an article in its May 1995 issue, describing the importance of "Pre" and his loss to the running community. Excerpts follow:

> Pre lost the 5,000m at the '72 Olympics. He was outkicked for a medal, but he made the race great.... He gave everything he had.... He finished fourth. He was young; there was still time.
>
> Some say that Pre wasn't the same after Munich, that he was more human. He didn't lose often, but when he did, he bounced back. He grew from his defeats.
>
> He was always talking about his future, the life he'd lead after he'd retire from running. He was getting faster, his best running still ahead. But, for all of us, there's a finish line.
>
> Pre drank. Pre drove. Pre didn't wear his seat belt.
>
> Steve Prefontaine died on May 30, 1975, at age 24, on a road he knew every inch of, the metal of his gold MGB convertible pressing on his chest, his powerful lungs unable to expand. And in a way, the future of track and field in this country died with him.
>
> Transcending the sport, he was by far the most popular runner of his era. Like James Dean, ahead of his time, never replaced.
>
> Pre died believing he would win an Olympic gold medal. Pre's People will die believing it, too.
>
> We miss him still.

SUMMARY OF VISIT TO THE TRIALS

Recently Pat Buzbee nicely summarized the time we spent at the Olympic Trials as spectators, the atmosphere that surrounded them, and some of our activities in the local community:

> I recall Marty Liquori's frustration, the runs we did on the winding road where Prefontaine crashed, Pre's trail in the chips ["easy on the legs" memorial running trail cushioned with wood chips].
>
> One thing we noted in particular, was that everyone in Eugene, particularly the young gals, were wearing running shoes. We thought that was pretty neat. We also ate at Track House Pizza, which was a famous hangout for U of O Track athletes.

[At the stadium] they still had the old GREEN bleachers and the place was packed. Unlike a Giants or Oakland A's game, people were in their seats and were paying attention to details. This is as good as T&F gets in this country! It was a premier event, and nice hearing people discuss performances and athletes we didn't know.

It was also nice to walk around and look at what was going on and get glimpses of famous runners. We also enjoyed some nice short runs around the community when we could squeeze them in between all of the excitement.

Pat also dug into his running diary from that period, which revealed details about training runs with his brother Mike, Chico High athletes, and members of the Chico Running Club—all present in Eugene to enjoy the trials and "laid back" but, at the same time, competitively "electric" atmosphere.

Thursday, June 24th:
Morning. Ran Fredericks Park (Eugene) loop with the Chico High School runners. A nice new loop to run. Ran at fairly decent pace. There's a pretty good hill in this loop also.
Evening. Same - tried to follow the same route from this morning. I think we were successful.
Total miles today: 12 miles
Special Notes: We saw George Wright, Joe McNally, and Tom Castro [from Chico] out for a run on this loop also. Nice to see them.

Sunday, June 20th:
Morning. Ran about 6 miles from KOA Campground N of Eugene near Coburg and the McKenzie River. Mike, Ron Caminada, and Doug Avrit.
Evening. With Mike and Dave Bruhn. Ran from (Lane?) college after meet today to Alton Baker Park (a large city park in Eugene). Ran from this park to Autzen Stadium area and bike paths onto Pre's Trail. After running on these trails for a while, we turned around and returned.
Total miles today: about 18 miles

17

1976 Wildcat Track & Field

Wildcat Track & Field

Team Results

Far Western Conference
Championships:
2nd Place

The highlight of the 1976 Track & Field Season among the Chico State distance running corps was Wildcat steeplechaser Karl Schaechterle earning All-American honors at the national championships.

WOODY WILSON RELAYS

Throughout the season, Schaechterle progressively improved in his marque event. At the Woody Wilson Relays, hosted by UC Davis on April 17th, he finished second in the 3,000-meter steeplechase with a time of 9:18.2. Wildcats Kent Mulkey (880), Ron Teague (440), Toni Ruggle (1,320) and Tim Stone (mile) won the distance medley with a time of 10:05.6. (Competing separately in the Junior College Division were two former Chico High athletes. Butte's Jamie Starmer won the 440-yard intermediate hurdles in 55.3, and Dave Bruhn the 2-mile in 9:38.6.)

FAR WESTERN CONFERENCE CHAMPIONSHIPS

The 1976 Far West Conference Championships were hosted by San Francisco State, May 13th-15th. Cal State Hayward won the team title (189 points), followed by Chico State (133) in second; then UC Davis

(120), Sacramento State (86), San Francisco State (57), Humboldt State (51), and Stanislaus State (12).

The best performance among Wildcat middle-distance and distance runners was by Karl Schaechterle who finished second in the 3,000-meter steeplechase with a time of 9:05.0. Tim Stone was third in the 1,500 meters (3:53.6) and teammate Toni Ruggle fourth. Chico's Kent Mulkey ran 1:53.7 in the 800 meters to finish third, and Charlie Griffin garnered third and fourth place in the 10,000 and 5,000-meter races with times of 31:04.2 and 14:46.8, respectively.

NCAA DIVISION II TRACK & FIELD CHAMPIONSHIPS

At the national championship, held at Slippery Rock, Pennsylvania, May 25-29, 1976, Karl ran the race of his life, coming from behind to finish third in the steeplechase (8:57). Chico State's Bob Myers was fifth in the decathlon, earning All-American honors for a second year in a row. Tim Stone and Toni Ruggle ran in separate 1,500-meter heats at the meet, and both missed making the final by one place.

18

CHS Boys Strongest Ever; Charlie's Angels More So!

A team like this comes along once in a person's coaching career. We have the top three finishers from last year's two-mile in the section track meet plus two others of similar caliber.

We have five runners who can run two miles under 10 minutes and in seasons past we have been lucky to have one right at 10 minutes.

—Chuck Sheley commenting on the strength of the 1976 Chico High School Varsity Boys Cross Country team in a *Chico Enterprise-Record* Paging the Preps article in late autumn that year.

Photo 18-1

Top five runners of Chico High's strongest-ever Varsity Boys Cross Country team. L-R: Doug Avrit, Santos Cervantes, Kurt Graves, Chris Johnson, and Kevin Boone. All were seniors in autumn 1976 with the exception of Chris Johnson.
Chico Enterprise-Record photograph

CHICO INVITATIONAL CROSS COUNTRY MEET

"Chico High Harriers Dominate Invitational" proclaimed the headline of an article in the *Enterprise-Record*, describing the results of the previous Saturday's well-attended cross country meet hosted by the Panthers on their home course in Chico.

In the varsity boys race alone, there were 134 runners—the largest field ever to compete in the annual event. Paradise's Larry Greer won the 2.55-mile race in a time of 12:35; eight seconds ahead of Doug

Avrit, who finished second in 12:43. Rounding out Chico's top five finishers were Chris Johnson (9th), Santos Cervantes (11th), Kurt Graves (12th), and Kevin Boone (19th). Their combined team score of 52 points (the individual places of the five Panthers added together), resulted in a win over Paradise in second (66 points).

Photo 18-2

Paradise's Larry Greer, the winner of the Varsity boys race at the 1976 Chico Invitational Cross Country Meet. *Chico Enterprise-Record* photograph by Ray Kirk

Chico's Varsity girls did even better as a team than the boys. Darcy Burleson won the shorter 1.87-mile race in 10:50, followed closely by teammates Julie Selchau, Suzanne Richter, Luanne Park, and Joan Gregg, in fourth, fifth, sixth, and ninth place finishes, respectively. The Chico girls totaled 25 points to easily beat Shasta's sixty-six.

DARCY BURLESON

> *If you saw him on the street, you probably wouldn't think of him as being an athlete. Well, a 5-7, 115-pound frame doesn't exactly project the image of super star does it?*

Matter of fact, this athlete is not even a "he." "He" is a girl and she's a sophomore at Chico High School. Her name is Darcy Burleson. In relation to what she does—cross country—Darcy has no equal in the North State and that's not just idle chatter. She's proved it.

—Excerpt from an *Enterprise-Record* Paging the Preps full-page article devoted to the 1976 Panther Girls and Boys Cross Country teams.

Photo 18-3

"Charlie's Angels" from left to right: Luanne Park, Jill Symons, Joan Gregg, Darcy Burleson, Julie Selchau, Stacy Shols, and Suzanne Richter.

In the 1976 season, Darcy was leading a team known, or soon to be known, as "Charlie's Angels"—so named after their coach Chuck (Charles) Sheley and a popular television show in the 1970s. Sheley said in the article, which included the preceding quoted material and photograph, that he believed that "several of the girls on the CHS [team] rival Burleson in sheer ability but Darcy's background in running gives her the edge."

Darcy was engaged in a very demanding training regime. She worked out with teammates on Monday and Tuesday, and with the Chico State Men's Cross Country team the remainder of the week. (There was then no women's college team.) Head coach Larry Burleson said in this piece about his daughter:

> Darcy has been running since she was in the seventh grade but only decided last summer that she would pursue it seriously. She works out twice a day, the first time at 5 a.m. She is running between 95 and 105 miles a week.

REMAINING GIRLS TEAM MEMBERS

Several of the other girls also trained in the morning, including Joan Gregg, the only senior on the team, who ran to school to log more miles. Sheley highlighted her pivotal role, noting:

> Gregg deserves a lot of credit because she helped get the program off the ground. Joan was one of the first girls to turn out for cross country just before women's athletics became the "in" thing. It was her stick-to-itiveness which showed other girls that cross country was, indeed, a sport for women.

The Paging the Preps article provided a little additional information about the team's composition and relative strengths of some members:

> Gregg usually runs in the No. 2 position depending on the type of course it is. Jill Symons, a junior, who is better known for her exploits in the swimming pool, has come on strong in the flat land races to finish second a couple of times. Joan has more endurance on a hilly course.
>
> The remainder of the varsity team includes sophomore Julie Selchau, and Luanne Park, Stacy Shols, and Suzanne Richter.

In early summer, prior to the cross country season, Jill Symons had swum in the U.S. Olympic Swimming Trials, June 16th-21st, at Long Beach, California. By time, she finished 13th (5:05.74) in the 400-meter individual medley, and 16th (1:04.68) in the 100-meter butterfly. Remarkable accomplishments for a sixteen-year-old from Chico.

More about the 1976 Girls team success in a bit. Highlights from both Panther varsity teams at invitationals follow.

NEVADA UNION INVITATIONAL, GRASS VALLEY

At the Nevada Union Invitational on October 2nd, the Chico Boys faced off against some very strong Sac-Joaquin Section teams, and finished third with 72 points behind Jesuit (41) and Mira Loma (49). Readers who followed running in northern California in that era will appreciate the talent it took to push Doug Avrit back to fourth (15:25). Finishing ahead of him were the winner, Tim Holmes from Downey (15:17), Nick Breuer from Mira Loma (15:18), and Tom O'Neil from Jesuit (15:24)—the number one runners of the other top-flight teams.

In the Varsity girls race, Darcy Burleson (12:00) won, followed by Vardell (12:18) of Yuba City, Debbie Rudolph (12:39) of Lassen, and Chico teammate Julie Selchau (13:04) in fourth place.

SAN RAMON INVITATIONAL, OCTOBER 9TH

Photo 18-4

Varsity Boys team with team and individual trophies from the San Ramon Invitational.
Back row: Kevin Boone, Doug Avrit, and Santos Cervantes.
Front row: Kurt Graves and Chris Johnson.
Courtesy of Kurt Graves

In early October, the Panthers traveled to Danville (located 23 miles east of Oakland in the San Francisco Bay Area) to compete in the San Ramon Invitational. Arriving on October 8th, they spent the night in a high school gym before racing the following day.

In their race, the Chico Varsity girls won the team competition with a score of 34 points, to Granada's 63 and Pleasant Hill's 83. Darcy Burleson sped to victory in 7.54, and three other Panthers also finished in the top ten places: Luanne Park (6th, 8:22), Joan Gregg (7th, 8:22), and Julie Selchau (8th, 8:28). Stacy Shols won the JV girls race in 8:52.

In the Varsity boys medium-size category, Chico (50) prevailed over Tamalpais (89) and Mission San Jose (106). Aaron Collier from Tamalpais won the race with a time of 8:18, followed by Doug Avrit (8:26). This race gave Avrit an introduction into aggressive running techniques. The runner leading Doug in making a turn around a chain-link fence on the course, grabbed a pole to assist himself in whipping around the corner. Avrit, turning a little wider without this assistance, caught a forearm, propelling him in the opposite direction of the intended turn.

MCKINLEYVILLE INVITATIONAL "BEACH RUN"

Following sequential Chico, Nevada Union, San Ramon, and Rio Linda Invitationals, and intervening dual meets with league opponents, it was "beach time" for hardworking Panthers.

Photo 18-5

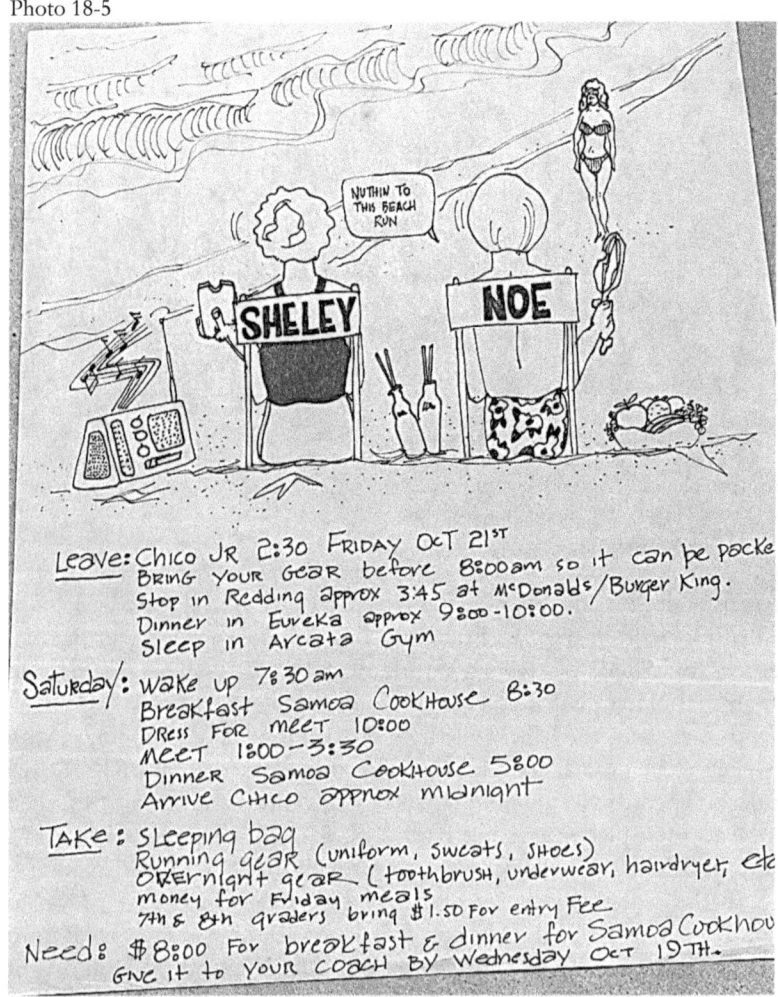

Humorous drawing by Bob Noe alludes to time demands levied on coaches associated with creating and sustaining outstanding athletic programs.

As in years past, coaches Sheley and Noe took Chico High Panthers to the McKinleyville Invitational, 212 miles northwest of Chico on the California coast, and 69 miles south of the Oregon border. As was the convention, the trip included dining at the Samoa Cookhouse. But lodging now consisted of sleeping bags in the gym at nearby Arcata High School, instead of spending the night before the race in the bunkhouse at the Cave Junction smokejumper camp, located about thirty miles south-southwest of Grants Pass, Oregon.

This change resulted, at least in part, from how coach Sheley's green van came to be known as, "the chuck wagon." This moniker was not related to his first name, but instead to a particularly awful nausea-inducing stretch of highway 101, coming down the coast from Oregon. An athlete in the back, trying desperately to project vomit outside the van through the small opening in a hinged, vented window, had failed miserably in this endeavor—spurring a new route to the meet.

At this year's meet, the Chico girls took five of the top six spots in their race on Clam Beach, chalking up a nearly perfect score of 16 points, and winning their fifth invitational meet. In each race, Darcy had led the team to victory.

Cross Country Meet	Individual Winner	Team Champion	Team Points
Chico Invitational	Darcy Burleson	Chico High	25
Nevada Union Invitational	Darcy Burleson	Chico High	31
San Ramon Invitational	Darcy Burleson	Chico High	34
Rio Linda Invitational	Darcy Burleson	Chico High	17
McKinleyville Beach Run	Darcy Burleson	Chico High	16

LEAGUE CHAMPIONSHIPS AT SUSANVILLE

It was a bear of a race. It was a great course. Bob Wall (Lassen's head coach) did a great job of laying it out. A course like that is a credit to the sport.

—Remarks by Chuck Sheley in a *Chico Enterprise-Record* article titled, "EAL Cross Country CHS Takes 4th Title," about the Lassen High School-hosted league championships.

At the League Championship, there were only 34 seconds between the first and fifth finishers of the Chico High Varsity Boys team. The top seven competitors across the line in both the boys and girls races were named to the All-League team and ten of them were Panthers. The Chico Varsity boys finished the season 13-0 in dual meet competition.

In addition, they won the Chico Invitational, medium school division at San Ramon, Rio Linda Invitational, the McKinleyville Beach Run, and were second at the Nevada Union Invitational.

	Varsity Boys Race (2.7-mile course)				Varsity Girls Race (2.2-mile course)		
No.	Name		Time	No.	Name		Time
1	Doug Avrit		14:18	1	Darcy Burleson		13:45
2	Kurt Graves		14:28	2	Joan Gregg		14:19
3	David Crabb Paradise		14:29	3	Luanne Park		14:29
4	Santos Cervantes		14:38	4	Julie Selchau		14:32
5	Chris Johnson		14:41	5	Cindy Claiborne PV		
6	Dave Meyers Oroville		14:46	6	Deb Rudolph Lassen		15:01
7	Kevin Boone		14:52	7	Stacy Shols		15:19

19 points team score
PV: Pleasant Valley High School

16 points team score

The Chico girls scored a near perfect 16 points at the League Championship Meet at Susanville. Pleasant Valley High's Cindy Claiborne finished fifth in the varsity race but, since she was not part of a full team, Rudolph and Shols moved up one spot to the fifth and sixth positions, respectively, for team-scoring purposes.

In the boys competition, the Bobcats top runner, Larry Greer, did not run for Paradise owing to a foot injury. Pleasant Valley High School was third behind Chico and Paradise in team composition, led by Jim Scott (future ultramarathoner) with a 15:33 and fourteenth place finish.

NORTH SECTION CHAMPIONSHIPS

Avrit, Burleson Top Runners
CHS Teams Sweep NS Meet

The headline of an article in the *Chico Enterprise-Record* following the North Section Championships held at Shasta College, summarized nicely the dominance of Chico teams and individuals in the meet.

> Chico High produced three champions: varsity, junior varsity and girls division while Chico Junior took the frosh title. For the Panther varsity, it was its fourth straight championship while the jayvees took their fifth consecutive title and the frosh captured their sixth in a row.

The Panthergals were capturing their first-ever championship but it might not be their last as only Joan Gregg graduates from a team which were unbeaten this season.

The strength of the varsity teams was evidenced by the top five runners of each, finishing in the top ten spots in their respective races. The CHS Varsity boys team score was 20 points and the girls 24 points.

CHS Varsity Boys			**CHS Varsity Girls**		
No.	Name	Time	No.	Name	Time
1	Doug Avrit	16:09	1	Darcy Burleson	14:18
2	Santos Cervantes	16:34	4	Julie Selchau	14:32
3	Kurt Graves	16:48	5	Joan Gregg	14:53
5	Chris Johnson	17:05	7	Jill Symons	15:07
9	Kevin Boone	17:18	10	Luanne Park	15:19
16	Jim Krajcirik	17:51	11	Stacy Shols	15:37
20	Randy Lamb	18:04	13	Suzanne Richter	15:51

CHS Jayvee Boys		
No.	Name	Time
2	Greg Williams	12:21
4	Steve Growdon	13:05
5	Rob Sylvester	13:10
9	Howie Waugh	13:19
20	Walt Lucio	13:45

JUNIOR OLYMPICS CROSS COUNTRY

Photo 18-6

Chico High runners Greg Williams (seated left) and Doug Avrit (seated right) won their age divisions at Fresno, qualifying to compete in the National Junior Cross Country Olympics at St. Louis, Missouri. Looking over travel plans with the two athletes are Neal Williams (standing left) and coach Chuck Sheley.
Chico Enterprise-Record photograph by Oz Mallan

As the winter sports of basketball and wrestling were just beginning, the cross country seasons of Doug Avrit and Greg Williams were extended beyond the North Section Championships by their participation on November 27, 1976 in the Region 13 Junior Olympics Cross Country Championships in Fresno, California.

The two Panthers won their respective age divisions, which is quite a feat, coming from the same high school and because the region takes in all of California and Nevada. Competing at different distances as well as age groups, Doug Avrit captured the Boys 16-17 Division by running 15:05 over the hilly 3-mile course. Greg Williams did the same in the Boys 14-15 Division with a 10:08 over the shorter 2-mile course. The Boys 9-and-under age group winner was Mike Wall, son of Lassen High School coach Bob Wall, with a time of 5:55. (Years later, during the 1986 Track Season, Mike Wall clocked a best of 9:15.1 for the 3,200 meters.)

At the National Junior Olympics held in St. Louis, Missouri, on December 11, 1976, it was cold (21 degrees) and windy. Avrit finished fourteenth, Williams sixth in 10:00, and Wall eighth in 5:54, respectively.

FIVE PANTHERS HONORED POST-SEASON

Sophomore Darcy Burleson went unbeaten in cross country and, following completion of the 1976 Season, was named the All-Northern California Girl Runner of the Year, and to the All-Girls first team. Luanne Park and Joan Gregg received Honorable Mention. Doug Avrit was named to the All-Northern California Boys First Team, and Kurt Graves to the Second Team.

The area represented by these Boys and Girls "All-Star" Teams included the North, North Coast, Central Coast, Sac-Joaquin, San Francisco, and Oakland sections; stretching from Merced north to the Oregon border. The following assessments and summaries related to top Girls team standings, and selectees to the All-Star teams are from the *Northern California Running Review* November/December 1976 issue.

```
TEAMS: - Chico's girls defeated Granada (Livermore), the North
Coast Section champs, by 29 points at the San Ramon Invit.
They were undefeated in prep competition and won the Northern
Section with a phenominal score of 24 points. Rio Americano
won the Sac-Joaquin Section. Pleasant Hill placed third to
Chico and Granada at the San Ramon Invit., and finished second
in the North Coast Meet. Miramonte took third at the North
Coast Section.

    #1--CHICO;    #2--RIO AMERICANO (Sacramento);
    #3--GRANADA (Livermore);    #4--PLEASANT HILL;
    #5--MIRAMONTE (Orinda)
```

TOP TEN INDIVIDUAL GIRLS

#1--DARCY BURLESON (Chico--a soph!)--Firsts at Chico, Nevada Union, San Ramon, Rio Linda, League, Northern Section; Third at Women's State AAU X-C Championships.

#2--LINDA ROBINSON (Pleasant Hill)--Firsts at Antioch, League, North Coast Section; Seconds at College Park, Pleasant Hill, NCS Central Region; Fourth at San Ramon.

#3--MICHELLE STEVENSON (Castro Valley--junior)--Firsts at Hayward Area Invit., Pleasant Hill, League, NCS Southern Area; Seconds at San Ramon, North Coast Section.

#4--SARAH SWEENY (Marin Catholic, Kentfield)--Firsts at Sonoma St., League, NCS Redwood Empire; Thirds at Pleasant Hill, North Coast Section.

#5--DEBBIE RUDOLPH (Lassen, Susanville--junior)--First at Walnut Festival; Second at Northern Section; Third at Nevada Union; Fifth at State AAU (14-18 Div.) Champs.

#6--KAREN BAIN (Rio Americano, Sacramento)--Firsts at Nevada X-C Carnival, League, S-J Section; Second at Rio Linda; 14th at State Women's AAU X-C Champs.

#7--ANN TRASON (Pacific Grove)--First at Aptos Invit. -- The Central Coast Section doesn't have a section meet yet so she saw limited competition at big meets too.

#8--MICKY VARDELL (Yuba City)--Firsts at Bella Vista, League, S-J Sub-Section; Seconds at Nevada Union, S-J Section; 16th at State Women's AAU X-C Champs.

#9--REBECCA SCHMIDT (Half Moon Bay--soph)--Firsts at Soquel, 2-Mile Postal...No Section meets in CCS for girls.

#10--TONI TAYLOR (Sunnyvale)--Firsts at Stanford & Del Mar Invits...No Section meets in CCS for girls.

TOP TEN INDIVIDUAL BOYS

#1--TIM HOLMES (Downey, Modesto)--Firsts at Livermore, Center Meet, Nevada Union, Matador Relays, Conference, S-J Dist. 4, S-J Section, 3-Mile Postal, PA-AAU Jr. 10K (top prep); Third at Mt. SAC Invit.

#2--ROD BERRY (Redwood, Larkspur--junior)--Firsts at San Ramon, Soquel, Pleasant Hill, NCS Redwood Empire, NCS; Seconds at Marin County AL, 3-Mile Postal.

#3--ARAN COLLIER (Tamalpais, Mill Valley)--Firsts at San Ramon, Pleasant Hill, Marin County AL; Seconds at Soquel, NCS Redwood Empire, NCS.

#4--CARLOS CARRASCO (Mt. Pleasant, San Jose)--Firsts at Alum Rock, Stanford Invit., Soquel, Lynbrook, 2-Mile Postal, CCS Region III, CCS...only a soph!

#5--GREG HITCHCOCK (South Tahoe)--Firsts at Alum Rock, South Tahoe, League, Sub-Section; Second at S-J Section.

#6--DOUG AVRIT (Chico) Firsts at Chico, Rio Linda, League, Northern Section, Jr. Olympic Meet; Second at San Ramon; Fourth at Nevada Union (fell at start).

#7--MARK STILLMAN (Willow Glen, San Jose)--Firsts at Serra, Del Mar, League, his heat of 3-Mile Postal; Second at Central Coast Section; 22nd at 2-Mile Postal.

#8--NICK BREUER (Mira Loma, Sac'to)--First at League; Seconds at Alum Rock, Nevada Union; Third at S-J Sec.

#9--GLEN BORLAND (Del Norte, Crescent City)--Thirds at NCS Redwood Empire and North Coast Section.

#10--BOB LOVE (Carlmont, Belmont--junior)--First in League; Second at Stanford Invit.; Thirds at 2-Mile Postal, Central Coast Section, 3-Mile Postal, third prep at PA Jr. 10-Kilo; 27th at CCS Region Meet.

132   Chapter 18

Photo 18-7

Members of Chico High School's 1976 North Section Cross Country Championship teams honored on an awards night held in Chico High's Lincoln Hall.

Bottom row, L-R: Lisa Terrell, Vickie Snyder, Christie Denn, Rosemary Taylor, Tammy Denny, Robin Cushman, Rena Thompson.

Second row: Andy Park, Clint Simic, Mike Sherman, Scott Crosby, Estaban Nava, Leon Gillett, Herb Bladorn.

Third row: Chris Johnson, Stacey Shols, Jill Symons, Julie Selchau, Suzanne Richter, Darcy Burleson.

Forth row: Tino Nava, Jim Zicker, Frankie Alvarez, Scott Sheley, Robbie Sylvester, Greg Williams, Joan Gregg.

Top row: Jim Krajcirik, Kevin Boone, Kurt Graves, Doug Avrit, and Santo Cervantes.

Arguably (little argument), individuals in the upper three rows comprised the strongest Varsity girls and boys teams ever produced by a single school in a single season in the North Section.

Photo 18-8

Final look at the top five runners of the 1976 Chico High Boys Cross Country team—the strongest team ever produced in the Chico area.
L-R: Chris Johnson, Kurt Graves, Santos Cervantes, Kevin Boone, and Doug Avrit.
Courtesy of Kurt Graves

As the Panthers were closing out their season, taking place on the same day in Chico, November 6th, were the Far West Conference Cross Country Championships, and road races open to all in Bidwell Park.

FAR WESTERN CONFERENCE CHAMPIONSHIPS

On November 6th, Chico State hosted the 1976 Far Western Conference Cross Country Championships in Chico. The highlight for the "Cats" was Mark Shuman finishing in twelfth place with a 25:51. Chico State was fourth in team competition at the meet. The top fifteen individuals were All-Conference, Toni Ruggle was 15th.

ALMOND BOWL CLASSIC IN BIDWELL PARK

Nearly two-hundred & fifty runners finished both races in the Almond Bowl Classic, showing just how much running has grown in and around Chico recently.

Lee Ferrero of Weed opted for the short race and bounced Chico's Jim Price over 3 miles, 14:18 to 14:28. Peanut Harms and teammate Pete Sweeney paired up at the finish line in a good 29:20 for double that distance.

—Excepts from a *Northern California Running Review* article in the November/December 1976 issue, covering the results of Almond Bowl Classic-road races in Bidwell Park.

Among the top twenty finishers in the three and six-mile races were ex-Wildcats Jim Price, Dave Wood and Pat Stordahl; marathoners Pat and Mike Buzbee and at least one other former Panther, Josh Strong.

1-Lee Ferrero/SWEAT	14:18	11-David Callnon	15:43
2-Jim Price/Chico	14:28	12-Michael Hovas	16:00
3-Dennis Rinde	14:33	13-Bill Anderson	16:05
4-John Clary/TRAC	14:56	14-Nelson Cobb	16:11
5-Mike Sweeny	15:03	15-Joshua Strong	16:12
6-David Leopold	15:08	16-Brian Newell/NVRC	16:56
7-Brian Farrell	15:23	17-Vincent Soto	16:58
8-Richard Stiller/TRAC	15:24	18-Roberto Chavez	17:16
9-Tom Burns	15:25	19-Lisa Foy	17:19
10-Stan Edwards	15:33	20-Jerry Arnat	17:32

1-Peanut Harms/AGRC	29:20	16-Rodger Stordahl	31:25
-Pete Sweeney/AGRC	29:20	17-Michael Garrett	31:31
3-Robert Deis	29:40	18-David Mineau	31:32
4-David Wood	29:57	19-DeWayne Little	31:40
5-Dennis Swart	30:15	20-Mike Buzbee	31:45
6-John Flores	30:32	21-Steve Ellis	31:53
7-Ray Darwin	30:33	22-Bob Meyers	31:57
8-Russell Black/TRAC	30:35	23-Robert Ricketts	31:59
9-Dave Boyet	30:36	24-Joe Ferreiro	32:06
10-Bruce Caputo	30:43	25-Guy Ealey	32:17
11-Pat Stordahl/WVTC	30:45	26-Chris Haner	32:21
12-Jim Bowles/WVTC	30:51	27-Edwin Jerome/TRAC	32:30
13-Steve Barr	30:57	28-Robert Felsch	32:38
14-Ross Smith/WVJS	31:12*	29-Tom Hayes	33:00
15-Pat Buzbee	31:18	30-Paul Holmes/BC	34:22*

19

1977 Track & Field Season

As a new year broke, three of the North Section's finest runners had already begun their track seasons by participating in indoor track. Racing on short, banked wooden tracks between the end of cross country and start of the outdoor track season was very popular on the U.S. East Coast and other parts of the country, in which snow and ice drove runners indoors. In sunny California, such meets were scarce, and few counted athletes from the North Section among their competitors. This was because these contests attracted the very best from across the vast state, stretching from Mexico to the Oregon border.

On January 15, 1977, Chico High sophomore Darcy Burleson competed in the mile in the Sunkist Indoor Meet in Los Angeles. The winner, Sharon Hulse of Edison High School in Huntington Beach, crossed the finish line in 5:00.5. (Darcy's finish place and time are unknown to the author.)

A week earlier, on January 8th, Paradise's Larry Greer and Chico's Doug Avrit had run a 2-mile race in the *San Francisco Examiner* Games qualifying meet (on an outdoor track at San Mateo Junior College). Tim Holmes from Downey High School won the fast heat and had the best qualifying time of 9:13.6. Greer with the second-best (9:17.0) and Avrit fourth (9:19.0) finished 1-2 in the slow heat—placed there because of their "unknown" status.

Both qualified for the *Examiner* Indoor Games held at the Cow Palace in Daly City on January 21st. More about this arena in a subsequent chapter on the 1978 Wildcat Track & Field Season. It's sufficient to note here that it's challenging for almost all athletes to run top times on a small track—eleven laps to a mile—negotiating tight turns in the race while jostling with others in a large field of competitors.

Holmes prevailed over Greer (9:21 to 9:25.2) in the 2-mile race, with Tom O'Neil of Jesuit (9:28.8) and Avrit (9:35) finishing in third and fourth place. It was Doug's first and only indoor race in his running career—one in which he learned that running "on the boards" is an acquired skill.

BIDWELL CLASSIC PRELUDE TO OUTDOOR TRACK

Photo 19-1

Buzbee, Cray Capture Marathon Wins

Runners at the starting line waiting for the Bidwell Classic Marathon to begin. Also offered were both half-marathon and three-mile races; 118 competitors completed the marathon, 99 the half-marathon, and 167 the three-mile race. *Chico Enterprise-Record* photograph by Ray Kirk

On March 5th, the Chico Running Club staged its first marathon race (officially sanctioned) in Chico, held concurrently with a half-marathon and a three-mile. The event was managed by meet director Walt Schafer. In the marathon Pat Buzbee's 2:36:52 led the pack, as fairly warm temperatures (60s and low 70s) slowed the times somewhat, although much of the race was in the shade. Among the top finishers were Mike Buzbee; Chico Running Club members Frank Burk and Don Richey; and Panther Santos Cervantes. Merill Cray was the women's winner in 3:09:31.

1-Pat Buzbee/Turlock	2:36:52		14-Santos Cervantes	2:53:39
2-Jake White/TRAC	2:37:44		15-David Moss	2:54:48
3-Byron Richardson/WV	2:41:09		16-Fraser Rasmussen	2:57:29
4-Kerry Kilgore/SUND	2:43:14		17-Thomas Brown/Fresno	2:58:41
5-Frank Burk/Chico	2:47:16		18-Lenny Stein/S.F.	2:59:24
6-Ed Stromberg/Sacto	2:48:13		19-Hank Dickerson/Ore	2:59:52
7-Bob Myers/PMK	2:49:27		20-Erwin Forbes	2:59:57
8-Jeff Wall	2:50:42		21-Mike McLain/Madera	3:00:23
9-Clifford Stewart	2:51:21		22-Britt Brewer/Chico	3:01:34
10-Mike Buzbee/YubaCity	2:51:31		23-Steve Crescenti	3:02:56
11-Ross Rowley/Stktn	2:51:46		24-Phil Wilder/Okld	3:04:03
12-Gene Schaumberg/VMTC	2:51:50		25-Kent Ball/Chico	3:05:00
13-Larry Pugh	2:53:14		26-Don Richey/CRC	3:05:00

Photo 19-2

Marathoner Merill Cray.
Courtesy of Walt Schafer

WOMEN
34-Merill Cray/CRC   3:09:31
46-Sally Edwards/OPHIR   3:18:42
47-Caron Schaumberg/VM   3:19:32
49-Teri Hagerty/SUND   3:20:52
58-Karen Diekmeyer/SUND   3:27:09
65-Karen Gallagher   3:34:07
73-Bettina Brownstein   3:39:36

Among the top twenty-two finishers in the half-marathon were former Wildcat Dave Wood; Chico High senior Kurt Graves; Wildcat Roger Stordahl; and Joe Henderson, former prep track and cross country champion in Iowa, runner at Drake University, and currently, chief editor of *Runner's World* magazine.

1-Ted Quintana/WVTC	1:08:29	12-Mike Rowerdink	1:18:05
2-David Wood/Chico	1:10:33	13-Tom Thomas	1:18:13
3-Fred Veliz/FairOaks	1:12:22	14-Richard Stiller	1:18:32
4-Tom Burns	1:12:55	15-Dick Look/Redding	1:18:52
5-Kurt Graves	1:14:18	16-Tom Hayes/Redding	1:19:06
6-Frank Hagerty/SUND	1:14:39	17-Jeff Nicklaw	1:19:06
7-Dirk Feenstra/Sacto	1:15:02	18-Jerry Swartsley/SOS	1:21:13
8-Doug Rennie/BC	1:16:11	19-Lyle Lough	1:22:12
9-Roger Stordahl	1:16:21	20-Paul Holmes/BC	1:23:13*
10-Greg Durbin	1:17:15	21-Steve Daniels	1:23:36
11-David Mineau	1:17:55	22-Joe Henderson/R.W.	1:23:44

Victory in the three-mile race was fiercely contested between the winner Randy Sturgeon of the West Valley Track Club, and Butte College coach Gene Meyers (a former Wildcat 4:06 miler).

1-Randy Sturgeon/WVTC	14:25	19-Peter Castellanos	17:48
2-Gene Meyers/Chico	14:33	20-Gary Johnson	17:51
3-Michael Williams	15:19	21-Jeff Alaways/Chico	17:59
4-Lloyd Leighton	15:27	22-Mark Thomas/Chico	18:09
5-Peter Hallingsworth	15:54	23-Garrett Grant/Chico	18:22
6-Walt Schafer/CRC	16:10	24-John Rice/Chico	18:23
7-Wayne Moss/Weaverv'le	16:18	25-Jim Howard/Redding	18:24
8-Greg Williams/Chico	16:35	26-Kathleen Sullivan/CRC	18:29
9-Ken Takao/Lodi	16:59	27-Joshua McKinney	18:32
10-William Lionberger	17:10	28-Glen Bayley/Chico	18:32
11-Bryon Taylor/Chico	17:11	29-Tom Jennie/Redding	18:33*
12-Bill Willson/Chico	17:22	30-Steve Nicklow	18:35
13-Jim Myers/PMK	17:26	31-Richard Henneman	18:42
14-Jack Frost/Redding	17:30	32-Tim Morrison/Davis	18:43
15-Ivan Miller/Chico	17:35	33-Maurice Wiebelhous	18:48
16-Eric Iverson/Davis	17:36	34-Jamie Purganan	18:55
17-Glenn Reed/Redding	17:43	35-Joe Knox/Chico	18:56
18-Ron Harrison/Orland	17:44	36-Jim Nulty/Stktn	19:04

TRACK SEASON HIGHLIGHTS

Photo 19-3

Kurt Graves nipping teammate Doug Avrit at the finish line of the mile race during a three-way meet with Pleasant Valley and Las Plumas high schools at Chico.
Chico Enterprise-Record photograph

WOODLAND INVITATIONAL

> *This is one of the outstanding team performances that I've had in coaching 16 years of track and field.*
>
> *Doug Avrit gave a performance which earned him the title of "the greatest distance man in the history of CHS.*
>
> —Coach Chuck Sheley quoted in an *Enterprise-Record* article titled, "Woodland Invitational Arvit's 4:16.5 Mile Highlights CHS Win."

On May 7, 1977, the Chico High School Track team won the prestigious Woodland Invitational for the first time since the meet was begun in 1962. There were seventy-five schools involved in the Large School competition from five different sections. At the end, Chico was champion with 80 points, narrowly beating Grant of Sacramento

(78) by two points. Rounding out the top six places were DeAnza (59), Burbank of Sacramento (48), Sacramento (41) and Berkeley (40).

In light rain and a 20 mph-cross wind, Doug Avrit won the mile race in 4:16.5, beating the old school record of 4:19.1 held by Kent Pease. In an ensuing unbelievable performance, Avrit ran the mile distance a second take, this time in 4:19.7, to anchor the distance medley from third place to a win in 10:31.8. (The members of this relay team and the legs which each ran were Santos Cervantes, 880; Chris Lambert, 440; Greg Williams, 1,320; and Avrit.) Kurt Graves ran a personal best in the 2-mile with a 9:37.0, finishing in third place. In the two-mile relay, Cervantes, Brad Marzolf, Graves, and Williams each ran a half-mile leg, for a combined time of 8:15.5 and third place.

Altogether, Panthers garnered one school record set, six personal bests and eight marks in the all-time CHS top ten. Nevertheless, Chico thought it had lost the meet 78-76, and Grant had already taken home the team trophy. A points-check the next morning showed that Dave Weathers' late-meet, second place finish in the pole vault had earned Chico the team victory. Chuck Sheley recently described why he believes that the victory at Woodland was one of the top CHS performances of his coaching career:

> The Woodland Meet was divided into two divisions: Championship and "others." In the Championship Division the point totals were doubled in the sprints and relay events. That meant that a winner in those events got 20 points vs the normal 10 points. The same with the scoring for the top five places.
>
> Our strength was in the distance events. When I asked the meet director why we had a totally slanted scoring system he replied, "People come to meets to watch the sprinters." I then asked him if he had ever heard of Steve Prefontaine, turned and walked away. We were screwed as the large urban schools were loaded with sprinters.
>
> Last event of the evening, the mile relay, we had nothing to lose and I moved our team into the Championship Division. Gene Antone gave us a sub-50 second anchor and a 2nd place and those Championship points.
>
> We left the meet thinking we had lost by two points. I still remember unloading the van at 1:00 a.m. in front of the CHS locker room. Bob Noe was checking the scoring all the way home. He starts yelling we won! We won! He was right. The next day Rob Laxson, CHS grad and Woodland Coach drove the team trophy up to Chico.

In the girls competition, Luanne Park won the 440 with a time of 59.4. Darcy Burleson and Suzanne Richter ran 5:11.5 and 2:24.7 to finish second in the mile and 880, respectively. Attesting to their great leg speed, four Panthers combined to win the mile-relay in 4:06.8.

The Chico girls also won a team title by beating El Cerrito by seven points. Scores of the top teams were: Chico (33), El Cerrito (26), Lassen (18), Sacramento (17), Berkeley (13), Vallejo (13), and Summerville (12).

LEAGUE CHAMPIONSHIP MEET

At the League Championship Meet, Chico scored 71 points to easily outdistance crosstown rival Pleasant Valley with 49, Paradise with 48, Las Plumas with 44, Oroville at 23, and Lassen with 20 points. In addition to deciding league team standings, the meet also served as a qualifier for the North Section Championships a week later in Yreka. Unlike in previous years, there were no intervening Sub-Section (Division) Championships. The top five finishers in individual events, and relay races qualified to move on to the Section Meet.

A summary of the top five finishers, if known, in the varsity and jayvee middle-distance and distance races follows. Complete records are not available to the author.

Photo 19-4

Varsity Boys 880-Yard Race

#	Name	Time
1	Seth Roberts, Paradise	1:57.6
2	Larry Greer, Paradise	1:57.9
3	Dave Meyers, Oroville	2:01.3
4	Harvey, LP	2:03.7
5	Brad Marzolf, Chico	2:04.2

Varsity Boys Mile Race

#	Name	Time
1	Larry Greer, Paradise	4:18.4
2	Doug Avrit, Chico	4:27.7
3	Mike Brand, Paradise	4:28.4
4	Cote, Lassen	4:30.0
5	Santos Cervantes, Chico	4:30.8

Seth Roberts of Paradise edged teammate Larry Greer to win the 880, after Greer had already won the mile. *Chico Enterprise-Record* photograph

#	Varsity Boys 2-Mile Race		#	Jayvee Boys 2-Mile Race	
	Name	Time		Name	Time
1	Doug Avrit, Chico	9:20.37	1		
2	Kurt Graves, Chico	9:38.1	2	Steve Growdon, Chico	10:18.7
3	David Crabb, Paradise	10:04.1	3	Robbie Sylvester, Chico	10.30.4
4	Santos Cervantes, Chico	10:13.1	4		
5	Cote, Lassen	13:04	5		

#	Jayvee Boys Mile Race		#	Jayvee Boys 880-Yard Race	
	Name	Time		Name	Time
1	Greg Williams, Chico	4:34.3	1	Greg Williams, Chico	2:02.3
2			2		
3	Steve Growdon, Chico	4:43.7	3		
4			4	Scott Lape, Chico	2:10.9
5			5		

NORTH SECTION CHAMPIONSHIP MEET

Chico finished 1-2-5 in the two-mile behind Avrit's NSCIF-record time of 9:24.8 for 11 points.... Another NSCIF record-time of 3:24.3 for first [came] in the mile relay by Panthers Jim Bryant, Chris Lambert, Pete McKinnon and Gene Antone.

Gene Antone really did a good job. He had to be the key to the meet. You won't find Antone's name among the individual winners but he ran a 49.6 anchor leg in the mile relay to overcome Pleasant Valley on the last lap.

Antone also exemplified Chico's great depth with a second and third place against some top flight competition in the 120 high hurdles and 440, respectively.

—Excepts from an *Enterprise Record* article describing Chico's narrow victory over Enterprise at the North Section Championships coming only at meet's end.

The 1977 North Section Boys Track & Field Championships were held on May 27th at Yreka High on the school's all-weather track. This would be the last year there would be junior varsity and freshman championships. They were eliminated leaving only varsity championships thereafter.

A *Sacramento Bee* headline, "Chico Edges Enterprise for North T&F Crown" informed readers that the Chico High School Panthers totaled 43 points to edge Enterprise High, which earned 38 points.

Modoc High won the Junior Varsity title, while Las Plumas High was the victor in the Freshman division.

Photo 19-5

Varsity Boys 880-Yard Mile Race

1	Kevin Taft, WW	1:57.0
2	Dave Meyers, Oroville	1:58.9
3	Sanders, Enterprise	159.7
4	Seth Roberts, Paradise	1:59.9
5	Muir, Trinity	2:01.7

Varsity Boys Mile Race

1	Larry Greer, Paradise	4:21.5
2	Schmidt, Anderson	4:30.5
3	Mike Brand, Paradise	4:33.3
4	Muir, Trinity	4:34.4
5	Steve Hadley, Anderson	4:35.0

Varsity Boys 2-Mile Race

1	Doug Avrit, Chico	9:24.8
2	Kurt Graves, Chico	9:44.8
3	Schmidt, Anderson	9:52.5
4	Coplon, Willows	9:54.5
5	Santos Cervantes, Chico	9:59.0

Doug Avrit racing to victory.
Chico Enterprise-Record photograph

Larry Greer of Paradise and Chico's Doug Avrit both broke existing North Section Championship Meet records. Greer won the mile in 4:21.5, besting the 4:23.6 mark of Panther Kent Pease set the previous year. Avrit set the only individual meet record, with a quick 9:24.8 in winning the 2-mile. His mark was nearly 10 seconds better than the old record for the event and a full 20 seconds faster than the second-place finisher. (Chico had to leave its fourth sub-10 minute 2-miler Kevin Boone at home, because any one team can only put three athletes on the track in any particular event.)

In a particularly exciting, concluding race, the Chico Panthers set a new record of 3:24.3 in the mile relay (average of 51.075 per lap), cracking the old mark of 3:26.0 set by Del Oro in 1969.

Chico won the closely contested meet over Enterprise 43-38, with Pleasant Valley (27), Paradise (26), and Willows (19) finishing third, fourth and fifth, respectively, in the team competition.

VARSITY GIRLS NORTH SECTION CHAMPIONSHIPS

The Girls Section Meet had been held a day earlier, May 26th, at Sierra College in Rocklin, Placer County, eighty-six miles SSE of Chico. As expected, members of the Charlie's Angels did well, led by Darcy Burleson who won two events and finished second in a third race.

#	440-Yard Dash Name	Time	#	880-Yard Run Name	Time
1	Donna Kesterman, Wh	59.0	1	Shawn Hoose, Shasta	2:21.4
2	Luanne Park, Chico	59.9	2	Darcy Burleson, Chico	2:21.8
3	Nichole Stkins, Mt. Sha	61.2	3	Suzanne Richter, Chico	2:21.8
4	Georgia Pugh, Shasta	61.5	4	Tillie Peikert, Nova	2:23.9
5	Kathleen Richter, Chico	62.1	5	Donna Kesterman, Wh	2:26.0

#	Mile Run Name	Time	#	2-Mile Run Name	Time
1	Darcy Burleson, Chico	5:18.2	1	Darcy Burleson, Chico	11:42.2
2	Joan Gregg	5:22.2	2	Deb Rudolph, Lassen	11.57.1
3	Leann Knedler, RB	5:22.9	3	Leann Knedler, RB	12:06.0
4	Eda Thomason, CV	5:26.2	4	Joan Gregg, Chico	12:09.5
5	Cindy Claiborne, PV	5:34.0	5	Brenda Billson, Shasta	12:36.0

CV: Central Valley   Mt. Sha: Mount Shasta   PV: Pleasant Valley
RB: Red Bluff   Wh: Wheatland

In team competition, the Panthergals prevailed over twenty-nine schools. The scores of the top five were Chico 64, Red Bluff 36, Shasta 23, Lassen 18, and Colfax 17 points.

CALIFORNIA STATE MEET

The California State Meet was held June 3rd-4th in Westwood, 470 miles downstate from Chico in southern California. Located in Los Angeles, bordered by Beverly Hills to the east and Century City on the southeast, Westwood encompasses the sprawling UCLA campus and track stadium—the site of the meet—and Westwood Village. As shown in the photo, Drake stadium, only partially enclosed, offered fans in the bleachers a view of the surrounding area as well as action on the track.

It's unusual for athletes from the North Section, which is only able to send one competitor for each event, to make it into the finals at the California State Meet, a Track & Field powerhouse. The 2-mile is an exception; there are no qualifying heats, and all twenty-eight entrants toe the starting line. At this meet, Larry Greer finished fifth in the mile, and Doug Avrit tenth in the 2-mile. In doing so, each set a school record, at Paradise and Chico High, respectively, that remain today. Their times were also North Section records, since surpassed.

Top Ten Finishers in the Mile Race

#	Name	Time	#	Name	Time
1	Mark Stillman	4:06.87	6	Stan Ross	4:12.9
2	Mark Fricker	4:07.9	7	Jon Stormo	4:13.9
3	Charlie Christensen	4:08.5	8	Jesse Mitchell	4:17.3
4	Ron Cornell	4:10.0	9	Mike Galligan	4:17.3
5	Larry Greer	4:10.7	10	John Sup	4:17.7

Photo 19-6

Entrants in the 2-mile on the starting line at the State Meet.
Courtesy of Doug Avrit

Photo 19-7

2-mile race in progress.
Courtesy of Doug Avrit

Top Ten Finishers in the 2-Mile Race

#	Name	Time	#	Name	Time
1	Frank Assumma	8:52.9	6	Chuck Assumma	9:01.6
2	Rod Berry	8:53.4	7	Dave Daniels	9:04.0
3	Felix Elieff	8:55.7	8	Rick Perez	9:10.7
4	Steve Alvarez	8:56.4	9	Ken Holladay	9:11.6
5	Steve Ortiz	8:57.8	10	Doug Avrit	9:11.6

AVENUE OF THE GIANTS MARATHON

While high school and college track was still in progress, former Wildcats and others were participating in road racing. On a very wet day on May 1st, the Buzbees ran the Avenue of the Giants Marathon. Pat finished 9th in 2:28:43, and Mike ran a very respectable 2:33:01 for 18th. Bill Peck, their Chico High School Cross Country coach in 1966, ran a 2:45:36 to finish sixty-fourth.

Photo 19-8

Pat Buzbee finishing his race, and brother Mike being assisted by Keith Crowder. The two ran the race together and at the end, Buzbee faltered and Crowder lent support as they crossed the finish line.
Photographs courtesy of Pat Buzbee

A listing of the top finishers in the marathon and their times follows:

1-Ernie Rivas/PMK	2:23:35		25-Dick Ratliff/S.F.	2:36:55
2-Ed Strabel/Colorado	2:23:48		26-Frank Krebs/BC	2:37:13
3-Daryl Zapata/WVTC	2:24:18		27-Tom Lunne/Berk	2:37:43
4-Alan Kerr/B.C.	2:24:44		28-Kim Schaurer/TAM	2:37:45
5-Robert Cooper/WDS	2:26:11		29-David Mineau/Chico	2:37:47
6-Tom Lee/Pasadena	2:27:32		30-Thomas Robt. Kempf	2:37:48
7-Michael Merrell/Ore	2:27:45		31-Atkins Chun/S.F.	2:38:13
8-Ron Nabers/Colorado	2:28:39		32-Doug Rennie	2:38:50
9-Pat Buzbee/Turlock	2:28:43		33-Bryan Gieser/WDS	2:38:56
10-Mark Proteau/AGRC	2:28:58		34-Ed Almeida/SDTC	2:39:02*
11-Chris Cole/HSU	2:29:05		35-Joe Maher/TAM	2:39:13
12-Kevin Heaton/SD	2:30:43		36-Audun Endestad/M.L.	2:39:25
13-Keith Forman/Wash	2:30:54		37-Ed Stromberg/Sacto	2:39:38
14-Joe Burgasser/CCAC	2:31:08		38-Bundy Phillips/Arc.	2:39:47
15-Brian Bonner/LVRC	2:31:17		39-Howard Moody/S.D.	2:39:48
16-Jack Case/Portervle	2:32:29		40-Bruce Rider/WVJS	2:39:51
17-Keith Crowder	2:33:01		41-Scott Claypoole	2:41:02
18-Mike Buzbee/Y.C.	2:33:01		42-Ray Menzie/WVTC	2:41:28*
19-Stewart Fall/B.C.	2:33:54*		43-James Harper/Arcata	2:41:35
20-Geoff Pietsch/Miami	2:34:17		44-Rick Brown/Arcata	2:41:45
21-David Worthen/L.J.	2:36:11*		45-Ron Medel/Eureka	2:41:47
22-David Fuller/S.F.	2:36:29		46-Fred Forsberg/Sacto	2:42:38
23-Bob Coleman/Berk	2:36:33		47-Steve Cole/Wash	2:42:42
24-Greg Jewett/PMK	2:36:47		48-Dick Look/Redding	2:42:48

Photo 19-9

Folded vintage t-shirt.
Courtesy of Pat Buzbee

NORCAL 10-MILER

Four weeks after the Avenue of the Giants, former Wildcat Jim Price and ex-Panther Mark Burch finished 1-2 in a ten-mile race in Redding, seventy-three miles north-northwest of Chico. Price led the field of 72 runners from start to finish to establish a course record of 55:32 for this first annual event. The race replaced the 7.62-mile Lake Redding Run, which had been held for seven years previously.

Photo 19-10

Center: Jim Price while still a Wildcat, circa 1974. Teammate Jack West is running inside of him in lane 1, and a third Wildcat, Toni Ruggle, just outside of Price. Courtesy of Jack West

Readers may recall that it was Mark who led the start of Chico's prep running dynasty in the 1970s. In winning the 1971 Frosh and 1972 Jayvee North Section Cross Country Championship races, he first headed the victorious Chico Junior High Cougars, then led the Chico High Panther sophomore squad to a jayvee victory.

1-Jim Price/SWEAT   55:32
2-Mark Burch/CRC   59:19
3-Rick Martinez/SWEAT   60:00
4-Greg Nelson/Un   60:21
5-Gary Alderman/PMK   61:57
6-Bob Felsch/Un   62:08
7-Tom Olson/SWEAT   62:09
8-Bob Malain/NCS   62:58*
9-V.I. Wexner/SWEAT   64:22
10-Phil Harder/Ore   65:28*
11-Glenn Reed/SWEAT   65:43
12-Bill Flodberg/WVJS   65:59*
13-Harry Daniell/SWEAT 66:13*
14-Rick Elefant/Un   66:18
15-John Howard/Un   66:18
16-Mike Andrews/CRC   66:39
17-Jim Jackson/Ore   67:01
18-Dave Cargill/Un   67:18

19-Giles Marion/Un   67:46
20-Martin Cote/Ore   68:30
21-Dean Irvin/Ore   68:57
22-Jerry Ardnt/SWEAT   69:05
23-Lynn Aase/SWEAT   69:12
24-Gus Petras/SWEAT   69:12
25-Milt Shultz/SWEAT   69:27*
26-Mark Stinson/Un   69:39
27-Bob Milton/SWEAT   70:21*
28-Ken Stanley/Un   71:00
29-Lee Leonard/SWEAT   71:05*
30-Don Snow/Ore   71:19*
31-Glen Shook/Un   71:26
WOMEN
39-Merill Cray/CRC   73:07
51-Laurie Badley/Un   77:40
52-Jean Irvin/Ore   78:38*
56-Christiane Jackson/OR 79:57

1977 Wildcat Track & Field

Wildcat Track & Field

Team Results

Far Western Conference Championships: 4th Place

On April 30, 1977, San Francisco State and Chico State tied in a mid-season dual meet; each team scored 84 points. Wildcats prevailed in several events with Steve Porter and Brian Smith double winners.

Name	Event	Time or Mark
Steve Porter	200 meters	22.4
	400 meters	48.5
Kyle Crenshaw	400m intermediate hurdles	54.9
Kent Mulkey	800 meters	1:55.8
Toni Ruggle	1,500 meters	4:05.6
Tom Keller	5,000 meters	15:24.8
Dave Crum	Shot Put	46' 6"
Brian Smith	Discus throw	147' 9½"
	Hammer Throw	184' 8½"
Bob Myers	Javelin Throw	226' 10½"
Mike Franson	Pole Vault	14' 0"

FAR WESTERN CONFERENCE CHAMPIONSHIPS

Chico State hosted the Far Western Conference Track & Field Championships on May 14, 1977. The "Cats" finished fourth in team competition with 93 points; behind Cal State Hayward (156), UC Davis (101) and Humboldt State (95); and ahead of Stanislaus State (88), Sacramento State (86) and San Francisco State (32).

Chico's Steve Porter ran 48.0 to finish third in the 400 meters, and three Wildcat teammates finished in the top five in the 1,500 meters. Behind the race winner, Sac State's E. P. Richardson in 3:51.7, came Tom Keller (3:52.5), Lynn Ryan (3:54.0) and Toni Ruggle (3:57.2) in second, fourth and fifth place, respectively. Highlights of the meet for Chico were a Wildcat thrower and a decathlete emerging victorious in their events:

- Brian Smith in the discus throw (156' 1½")
- Bob Myers the decathlon (6,994 points)

NCAA DIVISION II TRACK & FIELD CHAMPIONSHIPS

The Nationals were held at Fargo, North Dakota, May 24th-28th. Bob Myers won the javelin throw with a toss of 243 feet—finishing the meet as both a national champion and an All-American.

21

Second in the Nation
1977 Charlie's Angels

Photo 21-1

1977 Chico High School Girls Cross Country team ranked by *Harrier* Magazine, a New York publication, behind Edison High School of Fresno. Suzanne Richter, Julie Selchau and Jill Symons were named to the All-Northern California team. Darcy Burleson, not pictured, received honorable mention

Standing L-R: Suzanne Lotti, Jill Symons, Julie Selchau, Suzanne Richter, Stacy Shols, and Luanne Park.

Kneeling: Joyce Lombard, Tammy Denny, Kathleen Richter, Rosemary Taylor, Vicki Whitburn, and Robin Cushman.
Chico Enterprise-Record photograph

Among the graduating seniors in the Chico High Class of 1977 were "Charlie's Angel" Joan Gregg; and from the Panthers strongest-ever boys team, Doug Avrit, Kurt Graves, Santos Cervantes, and Kevin Boone. The seniors had "left the building"—some would continue their competitive running, including Gregg at UC Davis, and Avrit and Graves at West Valley College in the San Francisco Bay Area. The concluding chapter of *Toe the Mark*, titled "What Came Later" provides

TOP-OF-THE-STATE 7-MILER

During the summer preceding the 1977 Cross Country Season, a group of Chico Running Club (CRC) members travelled 140 miles north to Weed, California. Located near the Oregon border and halfway between San Francisco and Portland, this small town is nestled at the base of Mt. Shasta in the Cascade Mountains.

In the second annual race, ex-Wildcat Pat Finn clocked a good 40:23 over the hilly route. Chico Junior High freshman Britt Brewer finished in seventh place with a time of 44:31.

1-Pat Finn/Chico RC	40:23	8-Mark Burch/CRC	44:57
2-Rick Martinez/SWEAT	40:41	9-Evan Quatse/Un	45:12
3-Tom Olson/SWEAT	43:16	10-Don Richey/CRC	45:43
4-Tom Hayes/SWEAT	43:52	11-Steve Daniels/SWEAT	46:05
5-Dick Look/SWEAT	44:14	12-Carl Martin/WVJS	46:40*
6-Walt Schafer/CRC	44:22	13-Glenn Reed/SWEAT	47:07
7-Britt Brewer/CRC	44:31	14-V.I. Wexner/SWEAT	47:18
15-John Lanzavecchia/CRC	48:26	22-Rich Emerson/Un	51:22
16-Marc Cullen/CRC	49:18	23-Bob Davis/CRC	51:31
17-Norm Spencer/SWEAT	49:44	***WOMEN***	
18-Ron Webb/Un	49:59	28-Barbra Becker/CRC	52:48
19-Scott London/Un	50:40	29-Kathy Sullivan/CRC	52:48
20-Harrison Smith/SWEAT	50:56*	30-Susan Prielipp/Un	53:20
21-Pete Larko/SWEAT	51:15	33-Susan Condon/CRC	58:05

CHICO INVITATIONAL CROSS COUNTRY MEET

Photo 21-2

Runners on the levee by Hooker Oak competing in the Chico Invitational XC Meet. *Chico Enterprise-Record* photograph by Jayne LaGrande

On September 24th, the Chico High Varsity Boys team tallied 116 points to finish fifth at the Chico Invitational Meet behind winner Petaluma (52), Oakmont (91), Del Oro (93), and Arcata (108).

The Chico boys had been decimated by the loss of Avrit, Graves, Cervantes, and Boone; but had senior Chris Johnson as well as two strong juniors, star Greg Williams and upcoming Steve Growdon. Williams finished fifth in the race with a time of 13:15.

The Chico girls easily won their competition with a low of 22 points, followed by Sunset from Beaverton, Oregon, with 68; Shasta, 87; Bishop (Southern Section), 135; and Del Oro, 142 points. Some girls teams had traveled great distances to compete in this meet, suggesting they wanted to face off with the "Charlie's Angels." Darcy Burleson won the race in 10:54, with teammates Suzanne Richter (2nd, 11:07), Julie Selchau (4th, 11:18), Jill Symons (6th, 11:23), and Luanne Park (9th, 11:41) all among the top ten finishers. Coach Sheley noted about the Panthers' win:

> They defeated a powerful CIF Southern Section Championship team from Bishop in addition to a strong AAA Championship team from Beaverton, Oregon.

NEVADA UNION INVITATIONAL, OCTOBER 1ST

A week later, the Chico High harriers travelled to Grass Valley on October 1st to compete in the Nevada Union Invitational. Foster of Jesuit High ran 15:56 to win the varsity boys race; Chico's Greg Williams was first among juniors with a time of 16:09.

In the girls competition, Chico continued to roll with a team score of 20 points, besting Bella Vista (93), Merced (100), Del Oro (108), and Foothill (138). Burleson won in 12:38, followed by Richter (3rd, 13:05), Selchau (4th, 13:16), Symons (5th, 13:21), and Park (10th, 13:40).

UC BERKELEY INVITATIONAL, OCTOBER 1ST

That same day, 133 miles to the southwest, the UC Berkeley Women's Cross Country team hosted a meet at Tilden Park. Located north of the campus, the course had dirt trails, grass, a little pavement, and was hilly, with a very long, steep grade about half way through the race.

UC Davis won the three-way meet with 35 points, followed closely by Chico State (37) and Cal (48). The top ten finishers included two Wildcats, as well as Joan Gregg (now a Davis Aggie).

#	Name	Time	#	Name	Time
1	Tina Aney, Davis	19:38	6	Joan Gregg, Davis	21:21
2	Sally Matteer, Cal	20:04	7	Eileen Burger, Davis	21:27
3	Julie Mastain, Chico	20:21	8	Carey, Cal	21:35
4	Aubuchan, Chico	20:45	9	Brandt, Davis	21:47
5	Barb Sprague, Chico	21:17	10	Jill Campbell, Cal	22:15

SAN RAMON INVITATIONAL, OCTOBER 8TH

In the medium school competition at Danville, the Chico High Varsity Boys team scored 108 points, finishing second to Pleasant Hill (82). Greg Williams was third in the race with a time of 8:21. The Chico High Panthergals were tops in the large school division with a low 40 points, followed by Shasta (105), Miramonte (112), Granada (120), and Pleasant Hill (144). Suzanne Richter won the 1.5-mile race with a time of 7:55. On her heels came Jill Symons (8:00) in second, and Julie Selchau (8:01) in third, with Luanne Park finishing in eighth (8:14) and Stacy Shols (8:35) in twenty-sixth place. (Coach Sheley moved the Chico Girls team up to the large school, more competitive division.)

CHICO VERSUS PLEASANT VALLEY LEAGUE MEET

Chico High School's Cross Country team rallied in the last 600 yards to overtake Pleasant Valley's Vikings 26-30 and capture their 22nd dual meet win over a three-year period.

The come from behind victory was held before the largest crowd Chico coach Chuck Sheley had ever seen at the Hooker Oak Complex.

—From an *Enterprise-Record* article titled, "Defeats PV Runners It's Chico Again" by Rob Donoho.

At a dual meet on October 13th between Chico and Pleasant Valley high schools at home, the majority of the fans were for Pleasant Valley, hoping to see the Vikings defeat Chico in cross country for the first time. For the first two miles of the Varsity boys race, it appeared that these fans were going to have their way. Greg Williams led as usual, but the next three runners wore Pleasant Valley's blue and white.

However, Chris Johnson and Steve Growdon dashed Viking hopes by overtaking Chris Hood, Jim Scott, and Mark Cyr in the last half mile to assure the Panthers of victory. The first four finishers in the race all ran their best times ever at Hooker Oak Park. Williams became the second fastest Panther ever on the 2.55-mile course with an outstanding time of 12:40.3. (Doug Avrit's course record of 12:29 remained intact.) Johnson (13:03) and Growdon (13:05) shaved twenty seconds off their previous best times. Hood set a PV best for the course with a 13:10. A summary of best times by Panthers in the 70s may be found on the following page, and also in Appendix C.

Photo 21-3

Chico's Greg Williams pictured at left, with teammates Chris Johnson and Steve Growdon finishing second and third behind the race winner. *Enterprise Record* photographs

Top Chico High Finishers			Top Pleasant Valley Finishers		
Place	Name	Time	Place	Name	Time
1	Greg Williams	12:40.3	4	Chris Hood	13:10
2	Chris Johnson	13:03	5	Jim Scott	13:19
3	Steve Growdon	13:05	6	Mark Cyr	13:30
9	Rob Sylvester		7	Rob Bannon	13:41
11	Tino Nava		8	Rich Stensrud	13:45

Readers wondering how hard the Panthers ran to beat the Vikings need only look at the table on the following page, which identifies the best times ever of the top seventeen Panthers on Chico's 2.55-mile course. This day, Williams, Johnson, and Growdon ran their best times for both this season, and remaining time as Panthers.

Chico Boys 2.55-Mile Cross Country Course
(Course changed in 1979 to 3.0 miles)

Name	Time	Name	Time
Doug Avrit	12:29	Mark Burch	13:23
Greg Williams	12:40	Kevin Boone	13:24
Kurt Graves	12:45	Bill Gregg	13:29
Santos Cervantes	12:48	Craig Larson	13:35
Chris Johnson	13:03	Britt Brewer	13:40
Steve Growdon	13:05	Josh Strong	13:47
Dave Bruhn	13:07	Pat O'Connell	13:53
Bruce Eggleston	13:14	Chris Shols	13:58
Kent Pease	13:20		

There was no such drama in the Varsity girls race. Chico easily beat Pleasant Valley 23-33 and collected their fifteenth straight dual meet win. Suzanne Richter led her teammates with a time of 10:50 on the 1.87-mile course.

Chico Girls 1.87-Mile Cross Country Course
(Course changed in 1979 to 2.16 miles)

Name	Time	Name	Time
Darcy Burleson	10:30	Stacey Shols	12:02
Suzanne Richter	10:50	Joan Gregg	12:05
Jill Symons	11:03	Kathy Jo Bernadett	12:09
Luanne Park	11:41	Vicki Whitburn	12:16
Julie Selchau	11:55	Tammy Denny	12:29

Individuals highlighted by shading were all members of the 1977 Charlie's Angels

In the Freshman boys competition, Britt Brewer led Chico Junior to a perfect 15-44 margin over Bidwell Junior High School. Brewer's time of 10:07 was the fifth fastest ever on the 1.87-mile course.

RIO LINDA INVITATIONAL, OCTOBER 15TH

A week after traveling to San Ramon in the San Francisco Bay Area, the Panthers were in Sacramento for the Rio Linda Invitational. In the Boys Junior competition (teams comprised of high-school juniors), Greg Williams raced to a win in 15:59. The Chico High girls were second in team competition to Rio Americano (41-55), with Bella Vista (112), Merced (126), and Downey (136) the other top participants. Darcy Burleson finished second in the race with a time of 11:28, with teammates Suzanne Richter (3rd, 11:31) and Julie Selchau (6th, 11:51) also among the top ten across the line.

The Charlie's Angels were without Jill Symons and Stacey Shols that day, as both were taking the SAT (Scholastic Aptitude Test) for college admission. The *Nor-Cal Running Review* staff was aware of their absence, it did not affect Chico's seasonal ranking.

MCKINLEYVILLE BEACH RUN, OCTOBER 22ND

That autumn, only the Chico Boys made the annual Panther migration to McKinleyville (like cliff swallows to San Juan Capistrano), for the race on Clam Beach. Chico (64) narrowly beat Oregon high schools Brookings (71) and Marshfield (75) to prevail in the team competition. Eight years earlier in 1969, Steve Prefontaine had graduated from Marshfield High School in Coos Bay, following cross country and track seasons his junior and senior years in which he never lost a race.

Greg Williams won the race on the beach in 15:23, with teammate Steve Growdon finishing in eighth place (15:49).

LEAGUE CHAMPIONSHIPS

At the League Championships on October 27th in Oroville, Chico's Varsity Boys and Girls teams prevailed over second place Pleasant Valley High. Team scores were as follows:
- Varsity Boys: Chico 38, Pleasant Valley 44, Lassen 72, Paradise 105, Las Plumas 106, Oroville 149
- Varsity Girls: Chico 18, Pleasant Valley 60, Lassen 70, Paradise 84, Las Plumas 119

NORTH SECTION CHAMPIONSHIPS

The North Section Cross Country Championships were held on November 5th at Susanville. As expected, the Charlie's Angels prevailed. However, as good as the Chico girls were individually and as a team, they did not have a monopoly on community talent. Joining five Panthers in the top twenty were Vikings Cindy Claiborne (5th), Dunwoody (10th), and Jan Lodge (19th) from crosstown rival, PVHS.

Varsity Girls Top Ten Finishers

#	Name	Time	#	Name	Time
1	Suzanne Richter, Chico	13:29	11	Smith, Lassen	14:38
2	Shanks, Quincy	13:42	12	Foster, Lassen	14:41
3	Julie Selchau, Chico	13:54	13	Thompson, Colusa	14.44
4	Jill Symons, Chico	14:00	14	Hoose, Shasta	14:48
5	Cindy Claiborne, PV	14:11	15	Bagley, Shasta	14:51
6	Denise Weaver, Paradise	14:18	16	Peikert, Shasta	14:51
7	Prince, Anderson	14:26	17	Luanne Park, Chico	14:55
8	Knedler, Red Bluff	14:29	18	Deb Rudolph, Lassen	15:00
9	Billson, Shasta	14:35	19	Jan Lodge, PV	15:15
10	Dunwoody, PV	14:35	20	Stacy Shols, Chico	15:21

Photo 21-4

L-R: Jill Symons, Julie Selchau, Suzanne Richter, Stacy Shols, and Luanne Park with coach Chuck Sheley.
Northern California Running Review Winter 1977 (photograph by K. Conning)

Comprising the Varsity Boys Championships were both large school and small school divisions. The Panther boys finished third in the large school category with 77 points, behind the winner Pleasant Valley (48) and second-place Lassen (58), and ahead of Shasta (93), Enterprise (134), Anderson (145), Paradise (180), Central Valley (181), and Oroville (217). Pleasant Valley placed four of their top five runners in the first twenty finishers. Chico's Greg Williams was fourth in the race, and Tino Nava twelfth.

Varsity Boys Top Ten Finishers

#	Name	Time	#	Name	Time
1	Frank Turner, Colfax	16:42	11	Cote, Lassen	18:09
2	Martinez, Shasta	17:10	12	Tino Nava, Chico	18:19
3	Stout, Lassen	17:23	13	Manuel, Truckee	18:21
4	Greg Williams, Chico	17:25	14	James, Colfax	18:25
5	Ellison, North Tahoe	17:34	15	Mark Cyr, PV	18:26
6	Chris Hood, PV	17:37	16	Schmidt, Anderson	18:28
7	Spears, North Tahoe	17:41	17	Wingate, Shasta	18:32
8	Stokes, Lassen	17:45	18	Miles, Mike LP	18:37
9	Rich Stensrud, PV	17:55	19	Jim Scott, PV	18:39
10	Lahr, Portola	18:04	20	Bob Ingram, Paradise	18:43

Chico's number two runner Chris Johnson was unable to compete due to illness. Running behind Greg Williams and Tino Nava were Steve Growdon (22nd, 18:47), Rob Sylvester (24th, 18:55), and Jim Antone (43rd, 19:46). The PV Vikings earned their Section title.

POST-SEASON HONORS

The *Northern California Running Review* Winter 1977/1978 issue published the rankings of the top prep Cross Country teams and individuals in northern California. The Chico Girls team was ranked number one, and Suzanne Richter the number three girl in all of northern California.

TOP GIRLS' TEAMS: #1--CHICO; #2--RIO AMERICANO (Sacramento); #3--HALF MOON BAY; #4--MISSION SAN JOSE (Fremont); #5--CARLMONT (Belmont); #6--SHASTA; #7--SOUTH TAHOE; #8--MIRAMONTE (Orinda); #9--PLEASANT HILL; #10--SAN CARLOS.

GIRLS

#1--IRENE CROWLEY (Overfelt, San Jose)--Firsts at Alum Rock, Leigh-Lynbrook, 2-Mile Postal, League, Regional Qualifying, Region III, Central Coast Section; Third at Artichoke Invit.

#2--LAURIE CRISP (Downey, Modesto)--A junior; Firsts at Cordova, Bella Vista, Rio Linda, League, District IV & Sac-Joaquin Section; Second at 2-Mile Postal.

#3--SUZANNE RICHTER (Chico)--Firsts at San Ramon, Matador Relays, League, Northern Section; Second at Chico; Thirds at Nevada Union and Rio Linda.

#4--ARLENE DALEY (Granada, Livermore)--Firsts at League, Central Area NCS and North Coast Section; Fourths at Artichoke and San Ramon.

#5--ANN TRASON (Pacific Grove)--Firsts at Artichoke, Aptos, Soquel, Pacific Grove & League; Seconds at Region IV and Central Coast Section.

#6--DIANE KENNY (Novato)--Firsts at McAteer & Redwood Empire Area Meet; Seconds at San Ramon, League & North Coast Section; Third at Stinson Beach Relays.

#7--STACEY DENNISON (El Camino, Sacramento)--A freshman; Firsts at League, District 3 & NorCal Jr. Olympics (12-13 Division); Seconds at Cordova and Sac-Joaquin Section.

#8--NANCY HUYCK (Aptos)--A soph; Firsts at Center Meet (10/13), Peninsula Invit., League & Region IV; Seconds at Artichoke, Aptos, Soquel, Pacific Grove; Third at Central Coast Section.

#9--DIANA BUBANJA (Piedmont)--Firsts at OAL Invit., San Ramon, Pleasant Hill, League & Southern Area NCS; Ninth at North Coast Section.

#10--SHELLY NIETO (Merced)--A freshman; Firsts at Frogtown and 2-Mile Postal; Seconds at Nevada Union, League & District IV; Third at Sac-Joaquin Section; Fifth at Rio Linda Invit.

Julie Selchau and Jill Symons were named to the All-Northern California Second Team, and Darcy Burleson received Honorable Mention.

NATIONAL JUNIOR OLYMPICS XC CHAMPIONSHIPS

The 1977 National Junior Olympics Cross Country Championships were held on December 10th at Longview, Washington. In the girls race, four of the top thirty finishers were from the North Section's Eastern Athletic League of which Chico High, Lassen High, and Pleasant Valley High were members and had athletes competing. The race winner clocked a 17:09. Spread between 21st and 29th place were the following four runners:

- Suzanne Richter, Chico High School (21st, 18:41)
- Debbie Rudolph, Lassen High School (23rd, 18:47)
- Jill Symons, Chico High School (27th, 18:55)
- Cindy Claiborne, Pleasant Valley High School (29th, 18:59)

Photo 21-5

The boys competition was divided into age groups. In the Boys 16-17 category, Chico's Greg Williams finished 45th (15:43) and Pleasant Valley's Chris Hood 74th (16:29). Chico Junior freshman Britt Brewer raced to an 8th place (10:28) among the 12 to 13-year-old boys. Mike Wall of Susanville (son of Lassen High coach Bob Wall) was 13th in the age 9-and-under division with a time of 8:59.4.

Freshman Britt Brewer leading another runner in his race.
Courtesy of Britt Brewer

WEST VALLEY'S DOUG AVRIT ALL-CONFERENCE

Photo 21-6

1977 All-Golden Gate Conference team: L-R, bottom to top (finish order in the CGC Meet): Paul Mello, Rich Pincombe, Bob Paulin, Joe Fabris, Doug Avrit, Joe Green, Paul Sechrist, Dave Parish, Joe Salazar, Kevin Searls, Ron Criner, Giovanni Cassara, Mike McQueeney, Danny Grimes, Matt Dowling.
Northern California Running Review Winter 1977

During his freshman cross country season at West Valley College after graduating from Chico High School, Doug Avrit made the All-Golden Gate Conference team. More about Doug, and other former Panthers, in the "What Came Later" concluding chapter of the book.

ROAD RACING IN LATE AUTUMN

FERRERO AND WOOD ARE EASY ALMOND BOWL VICTORS

On November 5th, almost 500 runners showed up for the most successful Almond Bowl race staged to date in Chico. Lee Ferrero of Weed clipped off a quick 14:30 to win the 3-mile race, and ex-Wildcat Dave Wood took the 6-miler in 29:21, just four seconds off Dennis Swart's 1975 course record. Merill Cray led a strong field of women in the 6-mile with a fine 35:42, and Kathy Spence raced to a 17:42 in the 3-mile, nearly two minutes ahead of the next woman finisher.

Former Panthers Pat and Mike Buzbee, and recent Chico High graduate Joan Gregg, toed the line in the 6-mile race.

```
***3-MILE***
1-Lee Ferrero/SWEAT      14:30    12-V.I. Wexner          17:27    24-Doug Riggle         18:04
2-Jim Price              15:04    13-Mike Andrews         17:27    25-Sean Alles          18:10
3-Paul Resignato         15:39    14-Steven Caudle        17:35    26-Rich Gobey          18:22
4-Walt Schafer/CRC       15:46    15-Erik Ferry           17:36    27-Gary La Pado        18:34
5-Bob Gordon             16:27    16-Jim Horner           17:40    28-Mason Nichols       18:35
6-Gary Crangle           16:37    17-Roberto Chavas       17:41    29-Charlie Main        18:38
7-Rolf Himpler           16:42    18-Kathy Spence         17:42    30-Bill Steinbrook     18:40
8-Glenn Reed             16:44    19-Don Fridshal         17:43*   31-Jeff Johnson        18:40
9-Mike Lambert           17:11    20-Estiban Nava         17:45    ***WOMEN***
10-Sam Wilson            17:20    21-Jerry L. Lilly       17:47    18-Kathy Spence        17:42
11-Mac Forbes            17:24    22-John Lanzavecchhia   17:48    46-Sabrina Schreder    19:36
                                  23-Richard Henneman     17:49    56-Barbara Davis       19:52

***6-MILE***
1-Dave Wood/Chico        29:21    19-Bob Hedges           32:57    38-J.K. Pedrotti       34:43
2-Daryl Zapata/WVTC      29:57    20-David Swayne         33:10    39-James Claesgens     34:45
3-Pat Buzbee/Un          30:58    21-Ed Shomvere          33:15    40-Bob Rusk            34:59
4-Mike Buzbee/Un         30:58    22-Jim Middleton        33:17    41-Dave Cargill        35:02
5-Dan Smolich            30:59    23-Roland Chell         33:22    42-Dave Nyquist        35:09
6-Lyle Freeman           31:01    24-Larry Duke           33:26    43-Bill Blackburn      35:13
7-Arvid Kretz/WVTC       31:41    25-Don Richey/CRC       33:45    44-Rob Rusk            35:14
8-Mike Souza             31:47    26-B. Fricke            33:50    45-E.J. Rusk           35:17
9-Perry Linn             31:49    27-Joe Sloan            33:52*   46-Sam Simmons         35:19
10-Paul Holmes/BC        32:05*   28-Walt Betschart/BC    34:01*   47-P.J. Downey         35:20
11 Larry Sumner          32:13    29-Nick Look            34:05    48-Richard Doty        35:25
12-Lloyd Sampson         32:20    30-Mike Bradley         34:20    49-Richard Hanna       35:29
13-Tom Hannickel         32:29    31-Robert Felsch        34:31    ***WOMEN***
14-Jim Holben/WVTC       32:31    32-Robert Seals         34:32    50-Merill Cray/CRC     35:42
15-Larry Pugh            32:34    33-Charles Hansell      34:32    56-Sally Edwards/OPHIR 36:19
16-Tom Hayes             32:41    34-David Blue           34:33    62-Diane Williams/PBP  36:57
17-Steve Daniels         32:49    35-James Davis          34:37    86-Kathy Kaiser        38:56
18-David Haubert         32:56    36-John Lundquist       34:39    96-Barbro Lauri-Beckett 39:36
                                  37-Herb Bladorn         34:42    101-Joan Gregg         39:56
```

PEPSI 20-MILER

Britt Brewer of Chico was an easy victor in the age 12 to ninth grade division.

—From an article in the *Northern California Running Review* Winter 1977 issue, titled "Maxwell is Surprise Winner at Pepsi 20-Miler."

The annual Pepsi 20-mile road race took place at Clarksburg, south of Sacramento, on November 27th. (This race was later renamed the Clarksburg Country Run.) Among the finishers were some Chico High alumni—Mike Buzbee with a time of 1:54.43, Pat Buzbee (1:58.37) and Bill Gregg (2:00:32)—as well as Chico Junior High Cougar Britt Brewer. Of interest in addition to Brewer's time of 2:03:49, was that he finished only four places behind much older, and future world-class triathlete Scott Molina who won the Ironman World Championships in 1988.

1-Brian Maxwell/BASC 1:45:09	33-Rick Brown/SRRC 1:56:09	65-Bill Andrews 2:00:34
2-Jim Nuccio/WVTC 1:45:20	34-Jim Casper 1:56:12	66-Perry Linn 2:00:36
3-Jan Sershen/ETC 1:46:28	35-Tom Standing 1:56:21	67-Sonny Reynaga/WVTC 2:00:42
4-Fritz Watson/WVTC 1:46:47	36-Mike Wheeler 1:56:23	68-Ed Nicholson 2:00:43
5-Pete Flores/AGRC 1:47:52	37-Kevin Kirby/AGRC 1:56:34	69-Robert Hedges 2:00:47
6-Dennis Rinde 1:48:31	38-Ross Smith/WVJS 1:56:39*	70-William Jenney 2:01:01
7-Michael Van Horn 1:50:05	39-Chris Little 1:56:57	71-Robert Wellck/WVJS 2:01:04*
8-Bruce McInturf 1:50:15	40-Adam Ferreira 1:57:01	72-Tom Hayes 2:01:11
9-Tim Farrell 1:51:10	41-Walt Lange/BC 1:57:34	73-Michael Garrett 2:01:15
10-Tom Laris/WVTC 1:51:14	42-Peter Demarais 1:57:42	74-Dan Hounchell 2:01:15
11-Art Baudendistel 1:51:51	43-Michael Conroy/ETC 1:57:46	75-Richard Martinez 2:01:24
12-Gary Goettelmann/WV 1:52:03	44-Bob Myers/PMK 1:57:51	76-Paul Holmes/BC 2:01:56*
13-Jim Barker/WVTC 1:52:08	45-Bert Johnson 1:57:57	77-Abe Underwood/BC 2:02:05
14-John Swift 1:52:10	46-Jim Hopkins 1:58:14	78-Robert Coleman 2:02:13
15-Tim Donovan 1:52:25	47-Jim O'Neil/SFOC 1:58:23*	79-Kees Tuinzing/TAM 2:02:14
16-Tom O'Neil/BC 1:52:47	48-Doug Butt/WVTC 1:58:23	80-Jack Hackmann/VMTC 2:02:26
17-Nick Nickols/HHS 1:52:51	49-Patrick Buzbee 1:58:37	81-Michael Deatherage 2:02:32
18-Chris Hamer/WVTC 1:53:03	50-Bob Bourbeau/WVJS 1:58:37*	82-Bob Costa 2:02:33
19-Jan Makowski 1:53:25	51-Tony Baccelli 1:58:54	83-Steve Finn 2:02:38
20-David Dunbar 1:53:37	52-Doug Rennie/BC 1:59:05	84-Frank Hutchinson 2:02:39
21-Greg Jewett 1:53:55	53-Dennis Gustafson 1:59:07	85-Tom Arnez 2:02:57
22-Ron Barker 1:54:07	54-Ken Harvey 1:59:26	86-Dan Williams 2:03:02
23-David Kiley (whlchr)(2:04:07)	55-Abraham Sun 1:59:31	87-Tom Hannickel 2:03:09
24-Mike Smith/WVTC 1:54:15	56-Paul B. Hamilton 1:59:33	88-Dennis Dillie 2:03:12
25-Michael Buzbee 1:54:43	57-Ralph Anievas 1:59:39	89-Douglas Latimer 2:03:25
26-Bradley Brown 1:55:13	58-Jay Cook/WVTC 1:59:43	90-Harold Crangle 2:03:27
27-David Bronzan/HSTC 1:55:15	59-Frank Lemus 1:59:47	91-Scott Molina 2:03:33
28-Paul Thompson 1:55:24	60-Larry Pugh 1:59:48	92-Mike Warr 2:03:36
29-Michael Gulli 1:55:33	61-Rodney Mowbray 2:00:09	93-Frank Turner/Clfx 2:03:39
30-Terry Hughes 1:55:52	62-Chris Samson 2:00:22	94-Dennis Kroll 2:03:44
31-Mike Wright 1:55:58	63-Keith Kruse 2:00:31	95-Britt Brewer/CRC 2:03:49
32-Darryl Beardall/TAM 1:56:04*	64-Bill Gregg 2:00:32	96-Jim Bowles/WVTC 2:03:49

Photo 21-7

Jacket earned by Mike Buzbee in one of these annual 20-mile road races.
Courtesy of Mike Buzbee

22

Suzanne Richter 5th at State Meet

Photo 22-1

Suzanne Richter finishing a race.
Courtesy of Suzanne Richter

> *For several years we have essentially built the [track] team around the distance events. In long distance running we can take an average athlete and develop him into someone who can score well in meets.*
>
> *We make up a lot of points in the distance events. We can usually score 20-25 in the 880, mile, and 2-mile.*
>
> *We can't compete in the sprints with Sacramento High or Grant, but we do well in the distances.*
>
> —Chuck Sheley in an *Enterprise-Record* article titled, "Formula Works Chico Utilizes Stamina, Not Speed."

Photo 22-2

Chico Enterprise-Record sports page drawing.

PACERS AND RACERS REVISITED

> *Heading the distance corps will be Williams, who ran a 1:58 880 and 4:28 mile last year as a sophomore. In addition to endurance, Greg has exhibited good speed, having run a 51.8 440 on a relay lap.*
>
> *Steve Growdon, a junior, has turned in 4:38 and 10:17 mile and 2-mile times this season. We're expecting a lot out of him. He doesn't have Williams' speed but he can set a fast pace so a lot of people won't be able to outkick him at the finish.*
>
> —Chuck Sheley quoted in the *Enterprise-Record* "Formula Works Chico Utilizes Stamina, Not Speed" article, published early in the 1978 Track season, regarding Chico's two best boys distance runners.

Chico High's distance running corps thinned out between the end of the 1977 Cross Country Season, and the ensuing 1978 Track Season. There was nothing unusual about this occurrence. If asked, a majority of runners will likely indicate that they much prefer the former over the latter sport, preferring to run over "hill and dale" instead of circling a track. Absent from this track season were seniors Chris Johnson and Julie Selchau and junior Darcy Burleson.

The Charlie's Angels were effectively disbanded. Stacy Shols and Luanne Park, who possessed great leg speed, would be winning sprints and the quarter-mile, and running legs on relay teams to best help the Panthers. Suzanne Richter and Jill Symons would dominate the middle-distance and distance events in the North Section.

It's a rare athlete that has both the endurance to run a very good mile time, and the leg speed to outkick their competitors at race's end. Among male runners, Chico had only two in the 1970s, Kent Pease and Greg Williams; Paradise two, Rob Erb and Larry Greer; and Las Plumas one, Toni Ruggle. Of the three greatest Panthers ever—Doug Avrit, Suzanne Richter, and Jill Symons—Richter had the most leg speed. These three talented and fierce competitors would each earn NCAA All-American honors in college: Avrit in cross country and for the 10,000 meters in track; Symons in cross country; and Richter in track for the 5,000 meters.

LEAGUE CHAMPIONSHIPS, MAY 17TH

Panthers Take Title, Anyway
Vikes Triumph in EAL

—Headline of an article in the *Enterprise-Record* sports pages.

Pleasant Valley High School won the Eastern Athletic League (EAL) Varsity Boys Track Meet at Butte College, but could not wrestle the league championship away from rival Chico. The Panthers went unbeaten in the dual meet season with a 10-0 record and ten points toward the team title. Pleasant Valley was 8-2, so, in order for the Vikings to even gain a title tie, Chico would have to finish third or less at the league championships—something that was not going to happen.

The Vikes scored 77 points in the meet to Chico's 71, while the rest of the league's teams were far behind. Although they came up second in the meet, the Panthers won their fifth straight championship as a result of points associated with a better dual meet record. Five EAL athletes in each event qualified to move on to the section championships.

NORTH SECTION MEET, MAY 27TH

> *In a performance befitting one of the finest female tracksters in the nation, junior Tonya Alston (Chico) set three personal records and three meet standards in winning the 110-yard low hurdles (14.6) and the high jump (5-9), while placing second in the shot (42-5) and third in the discus (130-8).*
>
> *Suzanne Richter established three meet records—880 (2:20.0), mile (5:07.4) and 2-mile (11:26.9). Stacy Shols (Chico) also set a meet record in winning the 100 at 11.2.*
>
> —*Northern California Running Review* July/August 1978.

The 1978 North Section Finals at Yreka High on May 26th, marked the first time that the Varsity Boys and Girls Championships were held concurrently on the same day and at the same location. Chico's girls easily won the team competition with a score of 63 points, followed by Shasta 31, Lassen 13, Nova 11, Pleasant Valley 11, and Corning 10, rounding out the other top teams.

Chico was led by Tonya Alston who, as highlighted in the book's preface, would become the greatest ever female athlete from Chico. She was the California State high jump champion in 1979, UCLA Track athlete and NCAA Division I high jump champion, and walk-on to the UCLA women's basketball team. Racking up points in other events was Suzanne Richter, who won the 880, mile, and 2-mile; Stacy Shols, victor in the 100; Luanne Park (59.1) the 440; and Jill Symons (5:16.7) who was second in the mile.

Chuck Sheley said about Richter's performance:

> Those who saw Suzanne's distance triple plus three section records can safely be assured that they saw a performance that will not be duplicated in many years if ever in North Section Championship competition.

Dale Edson, Richter's coach, added her own accolades:

> Her records were spectacular. She has worked harder than any athlete I've ever coached. Her recognition and success are long overdue.

Richter easily won the mile and 2-mile. Her intervening 880 victory was typical of her determination to win. She was third with a

220 to go, but sprinted past defending champion Shawn Hoose of Shasta and Anderson's Tracey Prince to prevail in the race.

440-Yard Dash

#	Name	Time
1	Luanne Park, Chico	59.1
2	Todd, Corning	59.4
3	McMannus, Shasta	60.4
4	Dori Parker, Nova	61.0
5	Graffery, CHE	61.6

880-Yard Run

#	Name	Time
1	Suzanne Richter	2:20.0
2	Tracey Prince, Anderson	2:20.6
3	Shawn Hoose, Shasta	2:22.0
4	Voss, Lassen	2:27.9
5	Shanks, Quincy	2:29.1

Mile Run

#	Name	Time
1	Suzanne Richter, Chico	5:07.4
2	Jill Symons, Chico	5:16.7
3	Cindy Claiborne, PV	5:23.6
4	Peikert, Shasta	5:35.0
5	Billison, Shasta	5:42.7

2-Mile Run

#	Name	Time
1	Suzanne Richter, Chico	11:26.9
2	Cindy Claiborne, PV	11:43.0
3	Kathy Sweeney, Nova	11:51.8
4	Knedler, Red Bluff	11:54.9
5	Shanks, Quincy	12:10.3

VARSITY BOYS COMPETITION

Our team performance was mediocre at best. We would have run better if the meet were held at the Senior Prom where most of our kids had their minds.

—Coach Sheley commenting on his squad's disappointing afternoon in an *Enterprise-Record* article titled, "CHS Gals Win Viking Boys Second; Chico Third in NSCIF Finals."

In the Boys competition, Chico scored 18 points; fourth among the top six teams behind Enterprise 32, Pleasant Valley 26, and Quincy 18; and ahead of Gridley 17, and Las Plumas 16.

The top five finishers in the middle-distance and distance races, and their times, are identified in the tables.

880-Yard Run

#	Name	Time
1	Seth Roberts, Paradise	1:56.4
2	Jim Antone, Chico	2:00.2
3	Wattenburg, Modoc	2:01.1
4	Dave Martin, Enterprise	2:01.8
5	Ward, Cummings	2:03.2

	Mile Run			2-Mile Run	
#	Name	Time	#	Name	Time
1	Mike Brand, Paradise	4:28.3	1	Frank Turner, Colfax	9:43.9
2	Steve Hadley, Anderson	4:32.4	2	Ellison, Enterprise	10:00.6
3	Chris Hood, PV	4:33.4	3	Robert Mazzei, Weed	10:03.5
4	Greg Williams, Chico	4:35.6	4	Bob Dipple, Paradise	10:04.7
5	Fernandez, Weed	4:39.5	5	Steve Growdon, Chico	10:06.5

CALIFORNIA STATE MEET

The State Meet was held June 2nd-3rd in Bakersfield, a city near the southern end of the San Joaquin Valley, roughly equal distance between Fresno and Los Angeles. In the mile, Suzanne Richter ran a lifetime best of 4:52.42, set a Chico High School girls record, and finished fifth in the fastest girls mile ever run in California. National 2-mile record holder Cheri Williams of Livermore won in 4:44.95—a state record—and also the 2-mile in an amazing 10:17.71. Tonya Alston, the only other CHS girl to reach the finals in any event, cleared 5-6 in the high jump and tied for sixth place. (She won this event the following year.)

Photo 22-3

Suzanne Richter.
Enterprise-Record photograph and excerpt from article

SUZANNE RICHTER EARNS SCHOLARSHIP TO CAL

I keep thinking. This is me running, I'm getting first, and I don't believe it.

I've never been No. 1 before. It seems I've always been in athletics, always competed, and all of a sudden, I got good.

I used to dread Tuesdays.

You can't think about names. You can't think at all, you just go.

—Comments by Suzanne Richter in an *Enterprise-Record* article, titled "Suzanne Richter Surprised" about finally achieving great success; previously dreading hill workouts on Tuesdays; and about the prospects of competing against some of the top runners while at Cal Berkeley.

Suzanne Richter was offered and accepted an athletic scholarship to UC Berkeley. The previous autumn, after she won the Girls Varsity race at the San Ramon Invitational, Coach Sheley told her there'd been a scout there from Berkeley and that he was going to call her. She didn't want to go to a big city, but the campus was really beautiful and the coach seemed interested in her. Moreover, her sister Karen went to UC Davis, which wasn't too far away, and her boyfriend, David Santos was at Cal. Suzanne was the first female Mid-Valley athlete to earn this type of scholarship—and one to a NCAA Division I school.

PARADISE 8.83-MILE RIDGE RUN

Road racing during and after the track season included the First Annual Paradise Ridge Run on May 7th, held in warm 85-degree weather. Lee Ferrero of Weed finished first over the 8.83-mile course, of which the first 3.5 miles were uphill, in a time of 49:01. Evidencing how diverse the field could be in a road race, Chico Junior High freshman Britt Brewer was fourth in 51:54, followed by Chico State professor Walt Schafer in 52:12. Finishing in fifteenth was former Chico State 4:01 miler, and current Paradise High teacher and coach, Kim Ellison. Merill Cray was the women's winner in 59:25.

In a companion three-mile race, Chico High's Steve Growdon was a sixteen-second winner over Steve Harney, 16:33 to 16:46.

1-Lee Ferrero/SWEAT	49:01	9-Bobby Dippel	53:57	17-Andy Jacobson			
2-James Bowles/WVTC	49:57	10-Lyle Freeman	54:23	18-Myron Klotz			
3-Rick Sanders	50:35	11-Bob Malain/BC	54:47*	19-Steve Haxby			
4-Britt Brewer/CRC	51:54	12-Dean Harper	54:58	20-Doug Riggle			
5-Walt Schafer/CRC	52:12	13-Michael Deatherage	55:37	21-Randy Lamb			
6-Mike Souza	52:44	14-Kim Ellison	56:01	22-Tom Roney			
7-Arvid Kretz/WVTC	53:35	15-Steve Daniels	56:07	23-Tim Chavez			
8-Noel Lincicome	53:36	16-James Claesgens	56:22	24-Charles Hansell			

TOP-OF-THE-STATE 7-MILE RACE

> *Hill, a product of Oregon State University and a one-time participant in the US-USSR track meet, dueled briefly with Weed's Lee Ferrero, who also served as the meet director. But he soon broke away for good at two miles to obliterate the all-time record for the 7-mile circuit, notching a great 38:03.*
>
> *On the distaff side, Merill Cray of Chico posted a fine 46:29 to place 17th overall, setting a new women's mark in the process.*
>
> —Excerpts from the *Northern California Running Review* September/October 1978 issue describing the results of the Top-of-the-State 7-Miler.

Ideal weather conditions and a record field of entries marked the third Annual Top-of-the-State footraces on August 19th at Weed. Leonard Hill of Phoenix, Oregon, and Paul Resignato of Chico won the seven- and four-mile races, respectively. The high caliber of the field was evident as 16 of the 24 age-division records were broken. Among the top finishers in the longer race were Chico Running Club members Walt Schafer, Merill Cray, and former Wildcat and All-American Mark Shuman.

1-Leonard Hill/SOS	38:03	8-Steve Daniels/SWEAT	44:12	15-Michael Gourley/CWTC	45:54
2-Lee Ferrero/SWEAT	39:41	9-Jack Frost/SWEAT	44:46	16-Gary Lampson/VMRC	46:20
3-John Frank/SWEAT	42:25	10-Fernie Fernandez/Un	44:49	17-Merill Cray/CRC	46:29F
4-Walt Schafer/CRC	42:33	11-Wayne Moss/SWEAT	44:58	18-Mark Shuman/CRC	46:30
5-Keith Forman/SteilStr	42:34	12-Scott Brazil/SWEAT	45:02	19-Leo Young/Un	48:02
6-Allen Masterson/SWEAT	43:24	13-Harry Daniell/SWEAT	45:12*	***MASTERS***	
7-Jim Quick/Un	44:10	14-Robert Mazzei/Un	45:37	23-Lee Bunnel/SWEAT	49:11*

23

1978 Wildcat Track & Field

Photo 23-1

I feel running carries you over in life. It has given me more confidence in myself. I know because of my success in track I can do the same in the classroom and on the job.

There are more guys on the streets who have more talent than me but they don't put in the time I do.

—Toni Ruggle in a *Chico Enterprise-Record* article by Barry Punzal, titled "CSU's Ruggle Battles to Be Best."

Wildcat Track & Field

Toni Ruggle competing as a Wildcat on the track. *Chico Enterprise-Record* photograph

In 1978, Toni Ruggle and high school classmate Scott Fairley, a pole vaulter, were co-captains of the Wildcat track team. Midway through the season, while relaxing in a home he shared with Scott and three other friends, Toni Ruggle described to a *Chico Enterprise-Record* reporter his remaining goals as a Wildcat. Arriving at Chico State in autumn 1973 (from Las Plumas High School in nearby Oroville), Ruggle was used to winning. As a prep athlete, he had twice represented the North Section in the California State Track & Field Championships and had a best of 4:18.8 in the mile.

PRECEEDING COMPETITIVE SEASONS

As recounted in Chapter 8, in the fall of his freshman year at Chico State, Toni was a member of the Wildcat team that finished sixth at the 1973 NCAA Division II Cross Country Championships at Wheaton, Illinois. Continuing to train hard and race well, at the conclusion of both the 1974 and 1975 track seasons, he qualified for and competed in the 1,500-meters at the Nationals. Toni wanted to earn All-American honors in these races, as presumably did the other competitors, and he considered that he had not performed well either year.

Then came a very discouraging junior year. Ruggle did not speak at length about it in the interview, only that 1977 had played a role in his current success, both in track and his life, commenting, "I've changed my attitude and reevaluated my training habits." He attributed his lack of success to inadequate training between the cross country and track seasons. As a result, distance runs during the track season were challenging. Moreover, the lack of sufficient base-conditioning hurt him physically and mentally. Toni summed up the preceding season thus, "I didn't run under 4:10 for the 1,500 meters all season and didn't qualify for the Nationals." (He finished fifth in the Far Western Conference Championship race.)

FINAL TRACK SEASON

The 1978 Season brought a resurgent Toni Ruggle as a result of increased work, who noted, "I have more confidence this season because I know I've done the training. The hard runs and the early morning training have paid off." By mid-point in the current season, Toni has won more races than in all the previous ones combined. His best seasonal marks were a 3:56 in the 1,500 and 4:13 in the mile (which is equivalent to a 3:54 1,500).

On February 18th at the *San Francisco Examiner* Games in Daly City, Toni had run a very impressive 4:18 to finish second in the mile, an event he characterized as "the biggest meet of my life." Although the time may not seem particularly impressive, one has to understand the conditions under which the race took place to appreciate it. The *Examiner* Games are held at the Cow Palace, an indoor arena in Daly City, situated on the city's northern border with neighboring San Francisco, and athletes must compete on a small track with tight turns.

In the "Devil Mile" (Devil Take the Hindmost), competitors must negotiate tight turns while circling the track eleven times. Ten of the runners cannot finish the race, because at the conclusion of each lap, the person in last place must step off the track. Because of this rule, running an even pace necessary to achieve best times is impossible, and spectators witness the excitement of a survival of the fittest contest, instead of a typical "tactical kickers race." Stanford's Tom Lobsinger won in 4:13.8, and Toni Ruggle was second (4:18.9), nipping Eric Hurst (4:19.0) of the Pacific Track Club in third.

Photo 23-2

Although of poor quality, this photograph of the "Devil Mile," which Toni Ruggle was then leading, evidences the excitement the event generates for fans, and for the runners competing in front of a loud and boisterous crowd.
Courtesy of Toni Ruggle

On March 18, 1978, against national-caliber competition in the Stanford Relays, Ruggle just missed qualifying for the Nationals in the 5,000 meters. In a field of twenty-five, he finished eighth in 14:40. The winner, Wysocki of the University of Nevada crossed the finish line in 14:07. In third place was Stanford's Roy Kissin (14:27.2) who while in high school at San Ramon had routinely ventured north to participate in and win the 2-mile race at the Chico Invitational Track & Field Meet.

WEST COAST RELAYS

After years of times of 4:11 to 4:14 for the mile, Toni finally went under the 4:10 barrier with a lifetime best of 4:08.1 at the West Coast Relays, May 5th-6th, in Fresno. It was an invitational mile with a loaded field on a dirt track won by Clifford from Cal Berkeley in 4:03.3. Ruggle's time qualified him for the national championships in Macomb, Illinois.

FAR WESTERN CONFERENCE MEET
The Far Western Conference Championships, hosted by the UC Davis Aggies, were held on May 11th-13th in Davis, California. Heide of Humboldt won the 3,000-meter steeplechase in 9:05.1, followed by Wildcat Tom Olson (9:19.5) in second place. Humboldt's Hammer, and Davis' Pratt finished 1-2 in the 1,500-meter race with times of 3:53.8 and 3:55.1, respectively.

NCAA DIVISION II NATIONAL CHAMPIONSHIPS
The national championships were held May 25th-27th at Macomb, Illinois. The participants included three Wildcats: Toni Ruggle and two "weightmen" (competitors in the shot put and/or discus throw). Interestingly, the distance events were dominated by athletes from Cal Poly San Luis Obispo, for whom Doug Avrit would later compete. Jim Schankel from San Louis Obispo won both the 5,000- and 10,000-meter races with times of 14:12.6 and 30:01.5; and teammate Mitch Kingery (30:45.9) was third in the 10,000 meters.

In the 1,500-meter run, Cal Poly's Dan Aldridge raced to victory with a time of 3:45.4. Toni narrowly missed making the final, his 3:51 in his heat falling one place short. He had done his best in his final season as a Wildcat, and was nominated for Chico State Track & Field Outstanding Male Athlete.

24

1978 Cross Country Season

This is the year we should win the section on the boys level. I'll be disappointed if we don't win.

We've had a rare opportunity the last two years. The success we've had is a once in a lifetime thing. We'll have to rebuild this year but will be competitive in the EAL [Eastern Athletic League].

—Chuck Sheley assessing his teams' chances in an *Enterprise-Record* article titled, "Can Chico's Panthers Keep Running Forever?" The Chico boys team had only finished third at the previous year's Section Meet, following graduation of the Avrit-led squad, and the girls, ranked second in the nation the previous year, had lost their top six runners.

Photo 24-1

Chico High Panthers relaxing on race day.
Chico High School 1978-79 yearbook

The 1978 Cross Country Season broke with Greg Williams, Chico's top boys runner, slowed by a summer bout with mononucleosis. Until he regained top form, Steve Growdon would lead the team with Williams running second, easily.

CHICO INVITATIONAL

This is the largest invitational in the North Section. Every school that has a team will be here.

—Chuck Sheley quoted in an *Enterprise-Record* article titled, "Chico Invitational Draws Top Talent."

Photo 24-2

Steve Growdon finishing a race.
Enterprise-Record photograph

Varsity Boys Race, September 30th
Vacaville High (1st, 71 points)
Chico High (2nd, 80 points)

Top Panthers
Steve Growdon – 3rd place, 13:05
Greg Williams – 5th place, 13:15
Britt Brewer – 20th place
Scott Lape – 26th place
Robbie Sylvester – 50th place

Girls Division Race
Pleasant Valley High (1st, 43 points)
Del Oro High (2nd, 75 points)

Top Vikings
Cindy Claiborne, 1st, 11:17
Darcy Burleson, 2nd, 11:35

DUAL MEET AGAINST PV, OCTOBER 19TH

They (the Panthers) won't go 1-2-3 on us this year.

—Concluding remark by Charlie Griffin, Pleasant Valley High's coach, and former Wildcat distance runner (quoted in an *Enterprise-Record* article), about a forthcoming dual meet between Chico and Pleasant Valley high schools after first expressing that he expected individual honors to be contested by Viking Rich Stensrud and Panther Greg Williams.

Amid excitement in the Chico running community about an impending showdown between the city's two rival high schools, coach Charlie Griffin of Pleasant Valley knew that his boys team lacked sufficient depth to prevail against Chico, but expected that his top runner would win the race or finish second. Griffin expected his undefeated girls squad, led by seniors Cindy Claiborne and Darcy Burleson, to beat Chico's team (3-3 this season) which had lost its top six runners.

Signifying the importance placed on this meet, a plaque was to be presented to the team champions in both the Varsity boys and girls divisions—something unheard of, except in the case of teams winning invitationals or championship meets.

#	Name	Time	#	Name	Time
1	Greg Williams, Chico	15:16	6	Rob Sylvester, Chico	16:21
2	Rich Stensrud, PV	15:23	7	Howard Waugh, Chico	16:35
3	Britt Brewer, Chico	15:51	8	Terry Wise, Chico	16:35
4	Brad Koehley, PV	16:07	9	Scott Lape, Chico	16:39
5	Calvin Dillon, Chico	16:14	10	Scott Sturb, Chico	16:40

As expected, the boys competition was not close. Chico Panthers took eight of the top ten spots to win 22-39 over the Vikings. In the race for individual honors, Williams pulled away from Stensrud on the Vikings home course to win by seven seconds. Griffin said about this effort in an *E-R* article titled "Favorites Pace Teams to X-Country Wins," "Rich hasn't been that close to Williams so far this year. They both broke the course record, which was 15:50."

In the girls 2.35-mile race, PV took five of the top six spots to easily win team honors. Burleson and Claiborne crossed the finish line together in 15:22, followed by Lori Wright in third place (16:11), Jan Lodge in fourth (16:24), and Nella McGuire in sixth place (16:35).

Chico's top five runners were Robin Cushman (6th, 16:28), Vicki Whitburn (7th, 16:55), Ruth Kroeker (8th, 17:01), Penny Cummings (9th, 17:05), and Tammy Denny (10th, 17:07).

LEAGUE CHAMPIONSHIPS

The second place by Growdon was super, and I've never seen Greg run as well as he did. He looked as smooth as he has ever been.

—Chuck Sheley quoted in an *E-R* article titled, "Vikinggals Take EAL Cross Country Meet."

The League Championships were hosted by Paradise High on October 26th in Paradise. In the Varsity boys 3-mile race, Chico High garnered its sixth consecutive EAL crown. Greg Williams took 31 seconds off the course record and, with strong performances from Steve Growdon and Britt Brewer, the Panthers rolled to an easy 38-58 victory over runner-up Las Plumas High.

In the girls 2.25-mile race, the Pleasant Valley Vikings captured their first EAL championships with a 36-point edge over second place Lassen. The top seven runners in each of these races made All-League.

Boys and Girls All-League Teams

#	Name	Time	#	Name	Time
1	Greg Williams, Chico	16:03	1	Cindy Claiborne, PV	14:08
2	Steve Growdon, Chico	16:22	2	Darcy Burleson, PV	14:47
3	Rich Stensrud, PV	16:28	3	Denise Weaver, Paradise	15:05
4	Britt Brewer, Chico	16:49	4	Smith, Lassen	15:14
5	Bob Ingram, Paradise	16:49	5	Lori Wright, PV	15:20
6	Boehm, Oroville	16:50	6	Brigitte Bass, Paradise	15:27
7	McKendrick, LP	16:57	7	Jan Lodge, PV	15:30

In a sea change from the past several years, five Vikings made their respective All-League teams, and only three Panthers.

CHICO WINS NORTH SECTION CHAMPIONSHIP

Photo 24-3

1. Greg Williams	Chico	16:49
2. John Frank	CV	16:50
3. Steve Growdon	Chico	17:20
4. Wingate	Shasta	17:24
5. Ellison	N.T.	17:28
6. Jordan	Shasta	17:32
7. Rich Stensrud	PV	17:34
8. Boehm	Oroville	17:36
9. Manauil	Truckee	17:47
10. Andrew	Anderson	17:54
11. Britt Brewer	Chico	17:55
12. Calvin Dillon	Chico	17:58
13. McKendrick	LP	18:03
14. Bob Ingram	Paradise	18:11
15. Weidenhoeft	Enterprise	18:14
16. Brad Koehly	PV	18:19
17. McTimmonos	Enterprise	18:20
18. Keller	Shasta	18:21
19. Eddie Byers	Paradise	18:22
20. Gazzilli	Enterprise	18:23

Greg Williams leading John Frank. *Enterprise-Record* photograph

On November 4, 1978, at Shasta College in Redding, the Chico Varsity boys team took their fifth North Section Championship in the past six years. In Chico's 52-73 win over runner-up Shasta High, Greg Williams and John Frank of Central Valley ran away from the field as they dueled the length of the 3.2-mile course. At the end, Williams sprinted to a five-yard victory. Steve Growdon finished in third place behind Frank. Sophomores Britt Brewer and Calvin Dillon were Chico's next two scorers in 11th and 12th place, and Howard Waugh's 28th-place finish (18:26.6) sealed the win for the Panthers.

Cindy Claiborne of Pleasant Valley won the Varsity girls 2.5-mile race in 15:17.2, besting teammate Darcy Burleson (15:39.2) who finished second. Pleasant Valley's next three runners—Lori Wright (11th, 16:24.3), Jan Lodge (15th, 16:35.2) and Nella McGuire (18th, 17:03.1)—all finished in the top twenty. The Vikings' laudable efforts were not enough to prevail over a strong Shasta team, whom they finished eight points behind in second place (26-34).

Chico's girls did not have a runner in the top twenty, but bunched five from 22nd to 30th to finish third in team competition. Robin Cushman's 22nd place (17:26.4) led the Panthergals. Close behind her were Ruth Kroeker (26th, 17:52.7), Penny Cummings (27th, 18:01.3), Vicki Whitburn (29th, 18:14.4), and Kathleen Richter (30th, 18:22.1).

POSTSEASON HONORS

> *A summer bout with mononucleosis meant a slow start for the 17-year-old Williams, but once recovered the Panther senior was unbeatable. Included in his achievements are titles from the Eastern Athletic League, Rio Linda Invitational large school and North Section runs. Additionally, he was SupCal's [Superior California's] best by finishing eighth in the north state meet, dominated by Mission San Jose.*
>
> —*Sacramento Bee* article titled, "Matadors Top X-County Stars" announcing that Jeani Fuller of Mira Loma High School and Chico's Greg Williams had been chosen girl and boy runner of the year on the 1978 *Sacramento Bee* All-Superior California Cross Country Team.

As indicated by the quoted material, Greg Williams was selected as the boy runner of the year on the 1978 *Sacramento Bee* All-Superior California Cross Country Team. This honor came after the Northern California Championships were held on November 25th at Crystal

Springs in Belmont, located on the San Francisco Peninsula about halfway between San Francisco and San Jose.

The boys race was won by Tom Downs from Skyline High School of Oakland in 14:44; seven spots behind him came Greg Williams who finished eighth in 15:11. In the girls race, San Mateo's Kim Schnurpfeil raced to victory with a time of 12:23.6. Cindy Claiborne (12:34) finished only eleven seconds back in fifth place. Jeani Fuller (12:28), a 14-year-old Mira Loma High School freshman who finished in third, was the *Sac-Bee* All-Superior California girl runner of the year.

COURSE SNOW-COVERED; 20° WITH WIND-CHILL

It gets lonely sometimes running every day. I think about school work or sing songs. I hum the tune "Rocky" and the next thing I know I'm stumbling over a rock on a hill.

You know, I had already decided who was going to beat me and at which races. But then I decided I didn't have to let them beat me.

—Cindy Claiborne, in an *E-R* article titled, "Local Runners Bound for KC," discussing her workouts, and about winning consistently after deciding that this was her year to do so.

Photo 24-4

Cindy Claiborne and Greg Williams running together, before leaving for the Nationals.
Chico Enterprise-Record photograph

National AAU Jr. Olympic X-C
Shawnee Mission Park, Kansas
December 9, 1978

Boys 16-17 Age Group
Greg Williams, 23rd, 14:42

Girls 16-17 Age Group
Cindy Claiborne, 8th, 17:29

Boys 9-and-Up Age Group
Mike Wall, 1st, 8:20.9

Cindy Claiborne and Greg Williams ended their 1978 Cross Country seasons at the very cold National AAU Junior Olympic Championships in Kansas, in which she placed 8th and he 23rd in their respective races.

25

Chico High Graduates' Seasons

Photo 25-1

Left: 1980 Lady Wildcat Cross Country Team member Jill Symons, then a junior in college. At right: Symons as a young Aqua Jet swimmer in 1972.
The Record 1980 – Chico State Yearbook Collection, and *Chico E-R* photograph.

In autumn 1978, college freshmen Suzanne Richter and Jill Symons were running cross country. Richter was now at Cal Berkeley leading a powerhouse team, and Symons at Chico State was leading a relatively new women's team. Often competing in the same meets, the former Panthers had occasion to see one another during warmups before races and would visit afterward. Three of these meets were the UC Berkeley, Fresno State and Stanford University Invitationals. A summary of their individual results in these races follows. Greater details about Richter's season and her time at Cal may be found in the book's concluding chapter, titled "What Came Later."

Berkeley Invitational	Fresno State Invitational	Stanford Invitational

September 23rd	September 30th	October 14th
Cal 1st (19)	Cal 1st (23)	Cal 1st (28)
Chico 4th (123)		Chico 4th (131)

Name	Time	Name	Time	Name	Time
Richter (2nd)	18:00	Richter (2nd)	17:15	Richter (2nd)	17:37
Symons (6th)	19:10	Symons (12th)	17:57	Symons (10th)	18:36

GOLDEN STATE CONFERENCE CHAMPIONSHIPS

Running for Chico State, Jill Symons captured first place at the Golden State Conference (GSC) Cross Country Championships, clocking 18:04 over the 5,000-meter course. She had been unbeaten against CSC competitors throughout the season. Among the eight teams competing, Chico State finished third with 65 points behind Sacramento State (41) and Cal State Hayward (56).

In addition to Symons, the Lady Wildcats had three other finishers in the top fifteen. Julie Mastain was fifth, Catherine Oddone tenth, and Colleen Conners fifteenth. Other Wildcat finishers were Janet Wilson (34th), Alicia Munoz (36th), Kim Woodland (39th), Linda Wieking (40th), Cathie Fries (48th), Ann King (50th), and Carrie Herd (52nd).

Symons, Oddone, and Conners qualified for the Region Eight finals in Long Beach the following weekend. From that meet the top three teams, plus the top ten individuals would qualify for the national championships in Boulder, Colorado.

Disappointment awaited in Long Beach. Symons, Oddone, Conners, and their coach arrived at the cross country course only five minutes before the gun—leaving no time to warmup either physically or mentally. The coach, who believed the race was at 11 a.m. instead of 10 a.m., later said about the incident, "I messed up, I really messed up." Symons failed to qualify for the Nationals, but would bounce back the following XC season, when she had the highest ever finish to date of any Lady Wildcat in a National Cross Country Championship.

Photo 25-2

Lady Wildcats competing in a cross country race in 1980. Sophomore Darcy Burleson is the second runner from the left in the photograph.
The Record 1980 – Chico State Yearbook Collection

WYSOCKI SHATTERS ALMOND BOWL RECORD; SYMONS GETS WOMEN'S RECORD

Both great athletes, Suzanne Richter was a little faster afoot in shorter distances than Jill Symons, who did quite well in longer road races. As headlined in an article in the *Northern California Running Review* Winter 1979 issue, Jill set a new women's record in the 6-mile race at the Almond Bowl on November 11, 1978.

Among the competitors were many former Wildcat runners, such as Dave Wood, Tom Olson, Mark Shuman, Jim Price, and Pat Finn. There were also current and former Panthers Mike and Pat Buzbee, Bill Gregg, and current young star and high school sophomore Britt Brewer. Jill Symons finished in 37th place with a time of 34:59, nearly two minutes ahead of Merill Cray.

1-Tom Wysocki/Un	28:48	7-Mark Shuman/Chico	30:50
2-David Wood/Chico	30:30	8-John Frank/Summit	30:59
3-Tom Olson/Chico	30:37	9-Jim Price/Anderson	30:59
4-Perry Linn/BC	30:41	10-Pat Finn/Chico	31:32
5-Hans Menet/UNR	30:43	11-Glenn McCarthy/ER	31:46
6-Pat McGuire/UNR	30:50	12-Mike Buzbee/Chico	31:56

13-Miguel Tibaduiza/UNR	31:59	19-David Luckengill/Chico	32:38
14-Frank Krebs/BC	32:04	20-Pat Buzbee/Blairsden	32:46
15-David Mills/Orinda	32:10	21-Mike Jordan/Redding	32:55
16-Craig Van Sickel/UNR	32:15	22-Richard Cental/Liv.	32:56
17-Britt Brewer/CRC	32:33	23-Bob Conradt/UNR	32:58
18-Bill Gregg/Davis	32:35	(Continued on page 48...)	

(Almond Bowl Run, cont'd.)		34-Dave Cargill/Suisun	34:43
24-Mark Cyr/Chico	33:11	35-Sam Simmons/Chico	34:47
25-Tom Phillips/Oroville	33:17	36-Buckley Hulseman/RBlf	34:58
26-Tom Hayes/Redding	33:21	37-Jill Symons/Chico	34:59F
27-Jose Solorio/Reno	33:39	38-Glenn Reed/SWEAT	35:00
28-Lee Young/CenValley	34:03	39-Ken Garber/Redding	35:07
29-Jack Frost/SWEAT	34:14	40-Mark Bunnell	35:13
30-Scott Brazil/PaloCedro	34:23	41-Greg Schutz/Chico	35:18
31-Larry Pugh/Suisun	34:30	42-Jim Fisher/SWEAT	35:21
32-Mike Andrews/Chico	34:35	43-A.J. Ferguson/Chico	35:49
33-Henry Tushar/Chico	34:41	44-Kent Casto/Chico	36:01

Photo 25-3

Pat Finn, while still a Wildcat, and teammates in a cross country race.
Left to right: Mike Leonard, Mike Fornaciari, Pat Finn, and Scott McVay.
Courtesy of Pat Finn

CLARK SPLASHES TO VICTORY AT PEPSI-20; SYMONS NIPS ULLYOT TO CAPTURE WOMEN'S TITLE

> *Jill Symons, who had won a quick six-mile race the week before in Chico, steadily closed the gap on leaders Joan Ullyot and Penny DeMoss and kicked in hard over the last few hundred yards to record an excellent 2:09:14, some 11 seconds in front of Ullyot. DeMoss was 2:10:44 in third place.*
>
> —Description below the headline above, in an article in the *Northern California Running Review* Winter 1979 issue.

As indicated in the preceding quoted material, a week after her race in Chico, Jill Symons won the women's division of the Pepsi 20-miler on November 19th, besting, among others, the well-known and very accomplished Dr. Joan Ullyot. Ullyot had begun running long distance at age 30, four years after graduating from Harvard Medical School. From her first major competition, the 1971 Bay to Breakers race in San Francisco, to her final Boston Marathon in 1996, she led the way for women runners, including as an advocate who helped spur the introduction of a 3,000-meter race and a marathon for women at the 1984 Olympic Games.

Bill Clark (West Valley Track Club) was the overall race winner in 1:48:24. Also finishing well were Mike Buzbee in thirteenth place (1:54:03) and Pat Buzbee in thirty-seventh (1:57:28).

STATE JC CROSS COUNTRY CHAMPIONSHIPS

One day before the Pepsi 20-miler, the California State Junior College Cross Country Championships had been held November 18th at San Diego, in which West Valley finished seventh with 188 points. Dyer of West Valley led the team with a 16th place finish and time of 20:27 over the 4-mile course. Ex-Panther Kurt Graves in 32nd (20:56), was the team's number two runner. Finishing 39th (21:55) was former Pleasant Valley High School Viking Jim Scott, Butte College's number one runner.

Photo 25-4

1978 All-Golden Gate Conference team. Kurt Graves is in the back row, fourth from the left, wearing a striped racing singlet and cap like his teammates.
Courtesy of Kurt Graves

Doug Avrit, who had run for West Valley his freshman year of college (1977-78), was taking this year off to help out with his family's dairy farm in Chico, before transferring to Cal Poly San Luis Obispo. Doug and Kurt's post-West Valley College running are taken up in their respective segments of "What Came Later."

1979 Track Season

Greg Williams was one of the finest milers in Chico history and Steve Growdon ran some great two miles.

—Jack West, former Oroville High, Butte College, and Chico State track star, reflecting back on his time as an assistant coach at Chico High when Williams and Growdon were seniors.

Photo 26-1

Jack West winning a race on the track, while competing for Butte College. Courtesy of Jack West

Chico High Boys Track ended the 1970s as it started the decade, with middle-distance and distance runners a bedrock of team success. Of the 1,571 total points scored by twenty-one team members over the course of the season, 407 (26 percent) came from milers Greg Williams, Steve Growdon and Calvin Dillon, who also competed in other events. These individuals were the 2nd, 6th, and 7th highest "point getters" for the Panthers. Howard Waugh, who contributed the most points, and Scott Lape, ninth overall, were solely middle-distance runners.

Possessing greater leg speed, Williams and Dillon routinely ran the mile/880 double (and 4x440 relay legs as required), while Growdon shouldered the mile/2-mile double. Williams, like Kent Pease before him, was content to run with or behind race leaders—then outkick them at the end. Growdon generally led from the start, "shedding kickers" well before the finish in order to win contested races.

Bottom line, these five athletes scored 44 percent of all team points.

Chico High Boys 1979 Best Marks

Name and Points Scored	440	880	Mile	2-Mile
Calvin Dillon (7th, 111 points)	53.3	2:00.6	4:46.7	
Steve Growdon (6th, 119 points)		2:02.0 relay	4:27.8	9:34.31
Scott Lape (9th, 98 points)	51.9	2:01.2		
Howard Waugh (1st, 180 points)	50.7	2:00.5 relay		
Greg Williams (2nd, 177 points)	52.9 relay	1:59.7	4:21.6	9:52.3

Former Wildcat distance runner Jack West served as an assistant coach that season which benefited the Panthers greatly. (A list of other Wildcats that coached Panthers in the 70s, and ex-Panthers that were later coaches may be found in Appendix D.) *Toe the Mark* previously introduced readers to four stellar Wildcats who hailed from the town of Oroville. These were Gene Meyers, Tom Brown, Toni Ruggle, and Calvin Lantrip. A fifth was Jack West who ran a 9:49 2-mile at Oroville High, before graduating in 1970 and moving on to Butte College. There he met Kim Ellison, who was "dipping his toes" back into running, after returning home from Army service in Vietnam.

West recently described Butte College's Cross Country team:

> The team was good from the start, but not championship material. However, [coach Karl] Springer had a secret weapon, an older runner who could not begin running with us until the second meet. Springer was from southern California, and our future star was his idol, since he was a senior when Springer was a sophomore. Springer was so excited about our new runner, that we were sick of this new guy by the time he arrived. After the first meet, Kim Ellison showed up and we were ready to give him hell on the first run. He was heavy and out of shape, but he hung with us on the first long run, and we all became Ellison fans within the first week.

> With Kim improving, we were getting to be a good team. We were rated 4th in the league, but considered a dark horse by league organizers. The powerful Shasta team, led by Mike Leonard and Jim Price, were favorites. However, everyone on the Butte team had their best races and we crushed the competition, winning the first Butte College [Golden Valley Conference] league championship in any sport. I finished in second place and Ellison was third. We took second in the [California] Small Junior College Championships the following week.

Following additional success at Butte College, West graduated and moved on to Chico State, where his collegiate running was truncated by injuries and illness:

> The 1973 track season looked good after running 4:12.1 in one of the first meets, not far behind Bobby King and just ahead of Dave Wood. I ran a few races, but ended up injured. I took 4th in the conference mile. The next year, I ran 4:12.8, but was ill most of the year and watched the league meet from the stands.

WOODLAND INVITATIONAL

Jack West's influence was immediately felt, but particularly later in the track season. It was cold and windy at the Woodland Invitational on May 5th. Despite these conditions, Steve Growdon ran a lifetime best in the 2-mile, finishing fourth in a very strong field with a time of 9:34.31. This effort made him the third-best-ever Panther in that event, behind record holder Doug Avrit (9:11.6) and Jack Forrester (9:24). Showing their strength, the Panthers won both the distance medley (10:41.3) and the two-mile relay (8:12.81).

In the distance medley, Dillon led off with a 2:03.7 for the 880; then handed off to Waugh, who ran a 51.6 440. Growdon ran the third leg, a 1,320 in 3:15.5; and then Williams anchored the Panthers with a come from behind 4:31 mile. Williams (2:03.0), Lape (2:02.9), Dillon (2:04.4), and Waugh (2:02.5) teamed up to win the two-mile relay.

Highlighting the Chico girls efforts, Tonya Alston won the high jump with a leap of 5-5, and placed third in the 110-yard hurdles.

MEET BETWEEN CHICO, PARADISE, AND OROVILLE

On May 10th, five days after Woodland Invitational, and a week before the League Championships, Chico easily outscored Oroville 80-57, with Paradise third at 33 points. The meet counted as a dual meet win over Oroville. Particularly significant were Greg Williams and Steve Growdon's performances in the mile. Greg won in 4:21.6, besting Paradise's Robert Ellsworth (4:22.4), with Steve third in 4:27.8. These times were personal bests for the two Panthers, and Williams' the third best CHS mile time ever, behind Doug Avrit (4:16.5) and Kent Pease (4:19.1). Williams and Growdon then doubled-back in the 2-mile, running 1-2 (10:12.8 and 10:13.8), respectively.

LEAGUE CHAMPIONSHIPS, MAY 17TH AND 18TH

Chico High School garnered the Varsity Boys League Championship after, a day earlier, the girls tied with Pleasant Valley High School for this honor. Neither win came easily. Oroville High with 73½ points, actually won the boys championship meet over Chico (66). However, because the EAL championship was decided on a point system by which both dual meets and the league championship meet counted, Chico won as a result of two wins over the Tigers in the dual season.

In the girls competition, Pleasant Valley won the championship meet with 69 points, with Chico trailing by three points. Chico was 2-1 against PV in dual meets, their record was now 2-2, and they tied for league honors. A summary of the top five finishers in the girls and boys 440, 880, mile, and 2-mile follow.

The Vikings dominated the girls distance races; winning both the mile and 880, and having three of the top five finishes in these events as well as in the 2-mile. Despite suffering from a painful, sprained left ankle, Cindy Claiborne won the 880, and took third place in both the mile and 2-mile races.

Girls 440-Yard Dash

#	Name	Time
1	Tammy Denney, Chico	1:00.6
2	Silva, Bidwell Jr.	
3	Anderson, PV	
4	Holderbein, Chico	
5	Kathleen Richter, Chico	

Girls 880-Yard Run

#	Name	Time
1	Cindy Claiborne, PV	2:28.5
2	Anderson, PV	
3	Harvey, Lassen	
4	Darcy Burleson, PV	
5	Nelson, Paradise	

Girls Mile Run

#	Name	Time
1	Darcy Burleson, PV	5:32.5
2	Lori Wright, PV	
3	Cindy Claiborne, PV	
4	Thompson, Chico Jr.	
5	Brigitte Bass, Paradise	

Girls 2-Mile Run

#	Name	Time
1	Brigitte Bass, Paradise	12:20.9
2	Darcy Burleson, PV	
3	Cindy Claiborne, PV	
4	Lori Wright, PV	
5	Brown, Paradise	

Boys 440-Yard Dash

#	Name	Time
1	Kevin Brown, Oroville	50.2
2	Brannon, PV	50.6
3	Howard Waugh, Chico	50.7
4	Baker, Oroville	51.2
5	Scott Lape, Chico	51.9

Boys 880-Yard Run

#	Name	Time
1	Kevin Brown, Oroville	1:59.3
2	Rob Ellsworth, Paradise	1:59.5
3	Mason, LP	2:00
4	Calvin Dillon, Chico	2:00.6
5	Scott Lape, Chico	2:01.2

Boys Mile Run

#	Name	Time
1	Greg Williams, Chico	4:30.7
2	Rob Ellsworth, Paradise	4:31.1
3	Steve Haxby, Paradise	4:36.9
4	Boehm, Oroville	4:38.6
5	Richardson, Lassen	4:42.6

Boys 2-Mile Run

#	Name	Time
1	Steve Growdon, Chico	9:41.9
2	Ralph Tedford, LP	9:42.3
3	Greg Williams, Chico	9:52.3
4	Bob Dipple, Paradise	9:55.9
5	Eddie Byers, Paradise	10:12

NORTH SECTION CHAMPIONSHIPS

> *It was a good, even team performance. We wanted no mistakes, and we didn't make any. The thing was consistency in performance. Eleven Panthers went to the meet, and 10 came away with points. You can't get away from a team which chips away with points all down the line. I think we won it handily.*
>
> —Coach Chuck Sheley quoted in an *E-R* article, "Consistency Carries Chico to Section Title," regarding the Varsity boys capturing their fifth North Section title in the past eight years.

The 1979 North Section Championship Meet was held on May 25th at Mitchell Field in Oroville. As indicated in the preceding quoted material, the Panthers won easily, amassing 42 points to finish ahead of runnerup Las Plumas and Modoc, both of which scored 29 points.

Greg Williams won the mile in 4:24.3 after taking charge of the race about midway through it, and he also qualified for the state meet as a member of the 4x440 relay team after being called into service owing to illness of one of the regular members. Four other Panthers middle-distance and distance runners finished in the top five in their races:

- Steve Growdon: 2nd in the 2-mile (9:47.5)
- Howard Waugh: 3rd in the 440 (51.5)
- Calvin Dillon: 4th in the 880 (2:01.8)
- Scott Lape: 5th in the 880 (2:02.1)

"Panthergals Win Third Title" headlined an *Enterprise-Record* article describing Chico winning the Girls Section Meet with 50 points to finish ahead of Pleasant Valley (39). Team victory followed three wins by Tonya Alston, and two from lightning bolt Robin Cromwell. Cindy Claiborne led Pleasant Valley to a second-place finish with two individual victories. Leslie Deniz of Gridley was another double winner, with victories in the shot put and discus throw. These athletes' winning times and/or marks are identified in the table.

Name	Event	Time or Mark	Name	Event	Time or Mark
Alston	110 hurdles	14.9	Cromwell	100 yards	11.7
	long jump	17' 4"		220 yards	26.8
	high jump	5' 6"			
Claiborne	mile	5:23.6	Deniz	Shot put	45'4"
	2-mile	11:53.0		discus	157' 8"

Pleasant Valley's Darcy Burleson (12:02.9) and Lori Wright (12:11.8) finished second and third in the 2-mile behind Claiborne. Other local athletes finished in the top five in the 440 and 880:

- K. Anderson, Bidwell Jr. (3rd in the 880)
- S. Anderson, Pleasant Valley (4th in the 440, 62.0)
- Tammy Denny, Chico High (5th in the 440, 62.6)

STATE MEET IN SACRAMENTO, CALIFORNIA

> *Hughes Track Gets Cool CIF [California Interscholastic Federation)] Reception.*
>
> —Headline of a *Sacramento Bee* article about CIF Council members' unhappiness after viewing the condition of the Hughes Stadium track for the California State Track & Field Championships.

Due to a slow clay track, many performances were not outstanding (timewise) at the California State Meet, held June 1st-2nd at Hughes Stadium in Sacramento. Highlights for North Section athletes were victories by Chico's Tonya Alston in the high jump, and Gridley's Leslie Deniz in the discus. Alston leaped 5' 9" to defeat the defending champion. She also qualified for the finals of the hurdles, but pulled a hamstring during the race. In the finals for the discus, Deniz threw 167' 1" breaking the national record set two years earlier.

BIDWELL CLASSIC MARTHON, MARCH 3RD

Before departing spring 1979 activities, it's appropriate to highlight the performances of a Panther and ex-Panther in the Bidwell Classic Marathon and Half-Marathon in Chico. As reported in an article in the *Northern California Running Review* Spring 1979 issue:

> [Sophomore] Britt Brewer, who is only 15, placed eighth in 2:37:55...he moved to Spokane shortly after the race so he will be NorCal's loss and Washington's gain.
>
> At the half-marathon distance... Jill Symons ran a swift 1:21.42 to lead all women.

```
***FULL MARATHON***           5-Tony Baccelli/Sac'to 2:34:57    10-Mike Buzbee/YubaCty 2:39:00
1-Bill Sevald/ETC    2:23:59   6-James Rocha/SRRC     2:37:40    11-Ross Rowley/SUND    2:41:36
2-Ron Nabers/WVTC    2:25:04   7-Phil Sanfillippo/WVJ 2:37:41    12-Scott Mellberg/Ch   2:43:39
3-Chris Hamer/WVTC   2:29:43   8-Britt Brewer/Chico   2:37:55    13-Cecil Lashlee/Colo  2:44:23
4-Tim Swezey/PMK     2:30:39   9-Doug Latimer/Un      2:38:32*   14-Gary Nathanson      2:45:30
```

27

1979 Cross Country Season

No empire lasts forever, no dynasty continues unbroken.

—Krishna Udayasankar

For the first time in seven years, a team other than Chico High is wearing an Eastern Athletic League varsity cross country crown.

—Opening sentence of an *E-R* article, titled "Paradise, Lassen Harriers Triumph," describing the results of the League Championships on October 25, 1979, a prelude to the North Section Championships.

Chico High's nearly decade-long dominance of North Section distance running came to an abrupt end on November 3, 1979, on Chico's home course at Hooker Oak Park. Paradise and Shasta High took the Varsity boys and girls crowns, and Anderson and Nova the Jayvee and Freshman boys titles. Chico Junior High's girls won the Jayvee title, providing hope for the future after the hemorrhaging of so many great Panther runners as a result of high school graduations.

1979 North Section Team Champions

Boys Teams			Girls Teams	
Varsity	**JV**	**Freshman**	**Varsity**	**JV**
Paradise	Anderson	Nova	Shasta	Chico Jr.

The boys and girls that filled the ranks of the Panther teams had fought hard all season, with a highlight being Chico's Rena Thompson finishing sixth at the league finals and making the All-EAL team. Herb Bladorn, Chico's top varsity boy, narrowly missed this honor; finishing in eighth place, he was one spot shy of making the team.

NORTH SECTION CHAMPIONSHIPS

At the North Section Meet held in Chico, the Chico High boys finished seventh in the team competition led by Herb Bladorn in 21st place. The Chico girls did better, with Rena Thompson (9th) and Tammy Denny (15th) leading the Panthergals to a third-place team finish.

Bob Noe's Chico Junior High girls team easily prevailed over Bob Wall's Lassen High 9th grade Grizzles (45-69) to earn the Freshman title. It could have been 1971 (instead of 1979) when Chico Junior had taken its first North Section crown from powerhouse Lassen High School.

Photo 27-1

Mural, which no longer exists, of the mascot of Chico Junior High School adorning an area on the outside of the gymnasium. Artwork by Edwin "Ed" Logan, an art teacher at Pleasant Valley High School who did murals on several Chico-area schools.

Photo 27-2

T-shirts designed by Chico Junior High School art teacher and cross country and track & field coach Bob Noe. Reproduction of this fine art in black and white does not do it justice. Courtesy of Bob Noe

28

Jill Symons and Greg Williams' 1979 Cross Country Seasons

Northern California road races in summer 1979 beckoned runners, included two relatively new ones. One of these was in San Francisco, and the other 275 miles to the north at Mt. Shasta near the Oregon border. Among the competitors in these races were Wildcat Jill Symons, preparing for her second cross country season at Chico State, and professor Walt Schafer. Separately, recent high school graduate Greg Williams was preparing to follow Doug Avrit and Kurt Graves to West Valley College in the San Francisco Bay Area, and run for WVC.

SAN FRANCISCO 10-MILE CLASSIC

> *Blume leads three under 50 minutes in S.F. 10-Mile classic; Jill Symons breaks one hour.*
>
> *Jill Symons of Chico became the first PA-AAU runner (we think) to dip under one hour for 10 miles, clocking a swift 59:55, over four minutes ahead of runnerup Diane Killen.*
>
> —Headline and excerpt from the associated article in the *Northern California Running Review* September/October 1979 issue.

On August 12, 1979, a large field of 1,421 runners finished the Second Annual San Francisco 10-Mile Classic, over a fairly challenging, rolling course, under sunny 60-degree skies. Cal Berkeley's Gary Blume won the race in 49:22 and in the process pulled his coach Brian Maxwell and Pete Sweeney under the 50-minute barrier. Equally impressive was Jill Symons. She easily won the women's division and in doing so broke 60 minutes, an accomplishment on par or exceeding that of these men.

TOP-OF-THE-STATE RACE AT MT. SHASTA

Six days after Jill Symons raced in San Francisco, Walt Schafer competed on August 18th in the Fourth Annual Top-of-the-State 7-mile race, contested at the foot of Mt. Shasta. Finishing fifth overall with a time of 43:03, Walt (a newly turned masters' runner from the Chico Running Club) easily won that division, clobbering the existing 45:12 record.

QUALIFYING MEET FOR AIAW NATIONALS

Near the end of her cross country season, Jill and her teammates who had qualified to compete in the AIAW (Association for Intercollegiate Athletics for Women) Region 8 Meet, travelled to Rocklin, California. Symons ran to victory in the Division III race with a time of 17:44, leading Chico to a fourth-place team finish. Teammate Catherine Oddone finished in 15th place (19:01), joining Symons in qualifying for the AIAW National Championships.

NATIONAL CHAMPIONSHIPS AT TALLAHASSEE

The AIAW Nationals were held at Tallahassee, Florida, on November 17, 1979. Jill Symons finished in 14th place (18:31) in the Division III race, easily making All-American. (As of this writing, her finish that day remains the highest ever by a Lady Wildcat at the Nationals.) Catherine Oddone was 58th with a time of 19:28.

The following *Nor-Cal Running Review* results identify finishers from northern California in the top fifty-eight places.

```
/DIV. III/ Hywd St. 56...6-Sac'to St. 161. 1-Benoit/Bwdn
17:14, 2-Ensrud/SO 17:50, 3-Aubuchon/CSH 18:01 ..9-Hester/CSH
18:24, 11-Foy/Sac 18:27, 14-Symons/Chico 18:31, 20-Brandt/UCD
18:43, 24-Castro/CSH 18:48, 31-Stoutt/CSH 18:59, 35-Robinson/
CSH 19:05, 39-Scannell/Sac 19:10, 47-Pappas/Sac 19:17, 51-
Felix/CSH 19:19, 55-Seibel/Sac 19:24, 58-Oddone/Chico 19:28,
```

GREG WILLIAMS LEADS WEST VALLEY TEAM

A week before Symons' superlative run, Greg Williams finished second at the Northern California Junior College Championships held at Crystal Springs, Belmont, on November 10th.

```
NORCAL JC CHAMPS (Nov. 10, Belmont): /MEN, Div. I/ SRJC 77,
SJCC 92, Marin 96, COS 103, ARJC 104. 1-Hernandez/SJ 20:32, 2-
Williams/WV 20:35, 3-Will/AR 20:39, 4-Royal/SR 20:43, 5-Thorn-
ton/FCC 20:44, 6-Jones/SR 20:52, 7-Arago/COM 20:53, 8-Beruman/
SJ 21:00, 9-Baumsteiger/COM 21:00, 10-Otis/CR 21:02, 11-Lozano/
COS 21:10, 12-Jenkins/WV 21:12, 13-Baldocchi/CSM 21:13, 14-Pow-
```

Photo 28-1

West Valley Cross Country team, circa 1979. Greg Williams is on the right side of the photo, in the third tier of four runners. After a year and a half at West Valley, former Chico High Panther Kurt Graves had by then transferred to Oral Roberts University. Courtesy of Kurt Graves

Williams and teammate Greg Jenkins, who finished 12th, made the All Northern-California Team. Williams, the most valuable runner, had led his team to a perfect dual meet season against Chabot, San Francisco, San Jose, Canada, Diablo Valley, Foothill, San Mateo, and De Anza junior colleges. Earlier, he, Greg Jenkins, Jim Thylin, Mark Gyorey, Curt Karbowski, and Tom Dorst had been named to the All-Golden Gate Conference team. A team roster follows:

1979 CROSS-COUNTRY ROSTER 1979

Chris Amaral	Branham High School	Frosh
Chris Back	Blackford High School	Frosh
Don Barber		Soph
Tom Dorst	Branham High School	Frosh
Mark Gyorey	Saratoga High School	Frosh
Greg Jenkins	Leigh High School	Soph
Curt Karbowski	Pioneer High School	Soph
Charles Lighty	West Florence, SC	Soph
Dennis Maloney	Leigh High School	Frosh
Gerald McPeak	Westmont High School	Frosh
Bob Mende	Del Mar High School	Frosh
John Mendoza	Bellarmine	Frosh
Dan Nieckarz	Buchser High School	Frosh
Ron Palermo	Del Mar High School	Soph
Russell Richardson	Del Mar High School	Soph
Rick Riordan	Saratoga High School	Soph
Jim Thylin	San Lorenzo Valley High School	Soph
Bob Trocha	Valley Christian	Frosh
Greg Williams	Chico High School	Frosh

STEVE GROWDON

Photo 28-2

Steve Growdon, and his bike packed with gear,
at Hoosier Pass in the Rocky Mountains of central Colorado.
Courtesy of Steve Growdon

After graduating from Chico High School (CHS) in 1979, Steve Growdon and teammate Scott Lape attended Stanford University. Steve did not run competitively for the Cardinal, but remained engaged in athletic pursuits. Following graduation from Stanford in 1983, he spent two plus years serving in the Peace Corps in the Philippines.

After returning to the United States, Growdon earned an MBA from Dartmouth College, then moved to Seattle. He spent a summer bicycling across the country (4,600 miles) with a group of friends. Married and in Seattle, he worked in management for Starbucks in its early days, before earning a teaching credential.

Since then, Steve has taught Social Studies at a Seattle-area public high school, and also served as an assistant coach for the school's cross country team for the past six years. One of school's alumni, Joe McConaughy, has gone on to set the fastest known time for the Pacific Crest Trail, the Appalachian Trail and other long runs.

Since graduating from CHS, Steve had continued running, competing in ten half-marathons, many Ragnar Relay series races, Hood-to-Coast relays, and other road races. He recently noted about his continued training, "Over the years I have run more than 60,000 miles. None of this would have occurred without Chuck Sheley, Bob Noe and the others who created the CHS running dynasty of the 1970s. Thanks, guys!"

29

End of the 1970s, End of a Dynasty

Autumn 1979 brought an end to Chico High dominance in distance running in the North Section with, most notably, Paradise High taking the Varsity Boys Cross Country crown from Chico High. There were several factors responsible for this occurrence; one was former Wildcat 4:01 miler Kim Ellison teaching English and coaching at Paradise High. There, he had begun developing powerhouse runners.

Three exceptional Paradise athletes from the late 1970s set marks from 1977 through 1980 which remain among the best ever run in the North Section. The times shown below were converted from the 880, mile, and 2-mile distances of that era, to equivalent ones for the 800-meter, 1,600-meter, and 3,200-meter races contested today.

Year	Athlete	Time	Year	Athlete	Time
	800-Meter Run			**1,600-Meter Run**	
1977	Larry Greer	1:55.3c	1977	Larry Greer	4:09.2c
1978	Seth Roberts	1:55.7c		**3,200-Meter Run**	
1980	Paul Carrozza	1:53.3	1977	Larry Greer	9:17

Larry Greer's time in the mile (4:09.2 when converted to 1,600m) was the fastest ever run in the North Section, until 1983 when Yreka's Jim Frey broke it with a 4:08.82 for 1,600 meters. Today, Frey and Greer are still ranked first and second on the North Section all-time best performances list for this event.

These and related factors contributed to the ascendance of other schools' teams. Simply stated, providing that training areas adequate for the development of distance runners are available and easily accessible, the following is generally true:

Good athletes	+	good areas in which to train	+	good coaching	=	Good teams
Good athletes	+	good areas in which to train	+	very good coaching	=	Very good teams
Exceptional athletes	+	good areas in which to train	+	exceptional coaching	=	Exceptional teams

Good places to train, such as Bidwell Park in Chico and dirt trails in hilly areas of Paradise, Oroville, and Susanville, were conducive to developing fitness and avoiding injury. Good coaches can produce good teams with good athletes. Very good coaches better able to recruit, develop and motivate athletes, can field very good teams comprised of good athletes. Exceptional teams result from exceptional coaches guiding exception athletes, as was the case with the "Charlie's Angels." There are of course, other contributing factors leading to great teams such as team chemistry and cohesiveness.

As shown in the table, Paradise High first dipped its toe into the "XC Section Championship pool" in 1977, with a Junior Varsity boys win. Two years later in 1979, this group, augmented by other talented runners being developed behind them, took Chico High's Varsity boys crown. In 1977, Pleasant Valley High School had also prevailed over cross-town rival Chico High's Varsity boys team, following graduation of the Avrit-led group of distance runners.

The following year, 1978, the Chico Varsity team regained the title, before it was later snatched away by Paradise. Years of dominance in the 1970s—18 of 24 possible North Section Varsity, Junior Varsity, and Freshman Championships from 1971 through 1978—were over.

North Section Boys Cross Country Championship Teams, 1970-1979

Varsity	JV	Freshman	Varsity	JV	Freshman
1970			**1975**		
Lassen	Lassen	Lassen	Chico	Chico	Chico Jr.
1971			**1976**		
Lassen	Lassen	Chico Jr.	Chico	Chico	Chico Jr.
1972			**1977**		
Lassen	Chico	Chico Jr.	PV	Paradise	Chico Jr.
1973			**1978**		
Chico	Chico	Chico Jr.	Chico	Lassen	Chico Jr.
1974			**1979**		
Chico	Chico	Chico Jr.	Paradise	Anderson	Nova

PV: Pleasant Valley High School

There were no Girls North Section Cross Country Championships until 1974, and then only varsity competition. Beginning in 1977, junior varsity competition was added to the section meet. Chico High School and Chico Junior High won four of the nine team titles contested from 1974 through 1979.

North Section Girls Cross Country Championship Teams, 1974-1979

1974		1976		1978	
Varsity	**JV**	**Varsity**	**JV**	**Varsity**	**JV**
Enterprise		Chico		Shasta	Lassen

1975		1977		1979	
Varsity	**JV**	**Varsity**	**JV**	**Varsity**	**JV**
Lassen		Chico	Chico	Shasta	Chico Jr.

The 1977 Varsity girls team was ranked second in the nation, and three of its members—Suzanne Richter (14), Julie Selchau (18), and Jill Symons (20)—were named to the twenty-two-member All-Northern California Girls Cross Country Team (First Team). Darcy Burleson received Honorable Mention. The All-Northern California Team included six sections of California: North, North Coast, Central Coast, Sac-Joaquin, San Francisco, and Oakland. This geographic area extended north to the Oregon border, and south to Merced in central California.

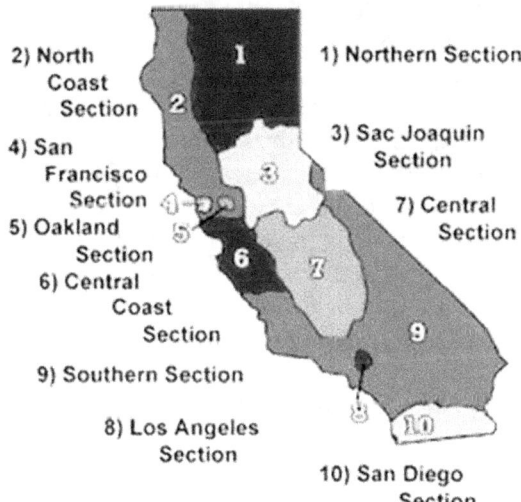

CALIFORNIA'S CIF SECTIONS

1) Northern Section
2) North Coast Section
3) Sac Joaquin Section
4) San Francisco Section
5) Oakland Section
6) Central Coast Section
7) Central Section
8) Los Angeles Section
9) Southern Section
10) San Diego Section

A year earlier, Doug Avrit (2) had been selected as a member of the 1976 All Northern California Boys Cross Country Team (First Team);

Kurt Graves (9) the Second Team; and Santos Cervantes Honorable Mention. Darcy Burleson (5) was a member of the Girls First Team, and was also named "Girls Runner of the Year."

The following year, 1978, Greg Williams was the *Sacramento Bee* Boys Runner of the Year.

SUMMATION

As the 1970s drew to a close, the collective Chico running community had many things not available to local athletes in the previous decade, including good running shoes, all-weather tracks, and membership in the Chico Running Club. It also had many accomplishments of the 70s in which to take pride. These included a 4:01.4 mile by Kim Ellison—a Chico State record which would stand for thirty-seven years until Scotty Bauhs broke it in 2008 with a time of 3:59.81. Kim also earned All-American honors in track in 1971.

Chico State Men's Cross Country team finished sixth at the 1973 NCAA Division II National Championships. During the decade, two Wildcats—Mark Shuman (1973) and Jill Symons (1979)—earned All-American honors in NCAA Cross Country Championships. Gene Meyers (1971), Tom Brown (1973, 1974), and Karl Schaechterle (1976) were All-Americans in Track & Field. Meyers earned this honor for the mile race, and Brown and Schaechterle in the steeplechase race.

Marathoners Pat and Mike Buzbee broke the existing 1972 Olympic Trials Marathon qualifying standard of 2:30:0 with times of 2:28:2 and 2:29:55, respectively. Chico State professor Walt Schafer ran a 2:37:51 at age thirty-seven, and Britt Brewer a 2:37:55 at age fifteen.

Chico High School Boys and Girls Cross Country and Track & Field teams collectively won numerous North Section Championships and, as previously highlighted, the 1977 Girls Cross Country team was ranked second in the nation by *Harrier* magazine.

Suzanne Richter finished fifth in the mile at the 1978 California State Track & Field Championships with a best of 4:52—a record that still stands at Chico High. Richter was the first mid-valley female athlete to receive an athletic scholarship to a Division I university and began competing at Cal Berkeley in autumn 1978. She was a NCAA Division I Track & Field All-American in the 5,000-meter race in 1979.

Doug Avrit finished 10th in the 2-mile at the State Meet in 1977. As of this writing, his best times of 4:16.5 and 9:11.9 in the mile and 2-mile remain school records. Running for Cal Poly San Luis Obispo in college, he was twice an NCAA II All-American: in Cross Country in 1981, and in 1982 for the 10,000-meter race at the Track & Field National Championships.

30

What Came Later

DOUG AVRIT

Photo 30-1

Doug Avrit on the track while competing for West Valley College.
Courtesy of Doug Avrit

Following their graduation from Chico High School in 1977, Doug Avrit and Gene Antone headed to the San Francisco Bay Area to attend and compete for West Valley Junior College. Ex-Panther pole vaulter Jerry Mulligan led the way to the school. Avrit and Antone were later followed by Panthers Kurt Graves and Greg Williams. This migration resulted from Chuck Sheley's relationship with West Valley Coach Bill Campbell, who he knew would take his former athletes to a high level.

At the completion of the 1978 Track Season, Doug placed fourth in the 5,000m at the Junior College State Meet. His season best time of 14:34 had come during the conference championship, at which he lost the race on a lean at the finish by Paul Mello from San Mateo.

Following a year at West Valley, Doug returned to Chico to help out with the family dairy for a year. In autumn 1979 he transferred to Cal Poly San Luis Obispo to join the Mustangs. He was already running at a high level, but through hard work, he steadily improved while there and throughout the remainder of his competitive running career, which culminated in a thirteenth place finish in the marathon at the 1984 U.S. Olympic Trials.

At the conclusion of the 1980 Track Season, Avrit ran the 5,000 meters at the NCAA Division II Championships hosted by Cal Poly Pomona at Pomona, California. Cal Poly San Luis Obispo took the team title among 78 schools from across the country. Their great distance runner Jim Schankel won the 5,000 meters in 14:07.50. At one point during this race, all four Mustang entrants—including Doug—were in the top four positions. Schankel pulled away, from the other competitors "still glued to him," during the final 200 meters to set a new meet record.

That autumn, Doug finished 8th at the Western Regional Cross Country Championships, held at Morro Bay State Park on November 1st. The Mustangs won the team competition with a score of 36 points. Their fifth scoring runner crossed the finish line in twelfth place, attesting to the strength of the team. Two weeks later, Cal Poly San Luis Obispo was third at the NCAA II National Championships at Kenosha, Wisconsin. Avrit finished 69th in the race with a time of 32:09.

TWICE AN ALL-AMERICAN AT CAL POLY

> *Avrit was a two-time NCAA All-American at Cal Poly, placing 15th in the 1981 NCAA Division II Cross Country Championships, and seventh in the 10,000 meters at the 1982 NCAA Div. II Track and Field Championships.*
>
> —From a San Luis Obispo *Telegram-Tribune* article describing the New York Marathon (discussed in the next section), which also provided readers information about Doug Avrit, one of the competitors.

Doug Avrit made All-American for the first time on November 14, 1981, competing in the NCAA II Cross Country Championships. This meet, hosted by the University of Massachusetts Lowell, was at the Hickory Hill Golf Course in Methuen, Massachusetts. The winner, Mark Conover from Humboldt State, completed the course in 31:45.7. Doug ran 32:51.5 to finish in fifteenth place, trailing teammate Andy Diconti in eighth (32:43.6).

1983 NEW YORK CITY MARATHON

> *New Zealand's Rod Dixon, fighting off leg cramps and a sore hamstring, wore down first time marathoner Geoff Smith of Britain and won the New York City Marathon in dramatic fashion Sunday—the first foreigner to capture the prestigious event in the race's 14-year history.*
>
> *Former Cal Poly cross country and track standout Doug Avrit placed 20th in the 26.2-mile race, clocked in 2 hours, 13 minutes, and 57 seconds.*
>
> —San Luis Obispo County (Calif.) *Telegram-Tribune*,
> Monday, October 24, 1983.

In autumn 1983, Doug Avrit raced to a time of 2:13:57 in the New York City Marathon, run through all five boroughs of the city: the Bronx, Brooklyn, Manhattan, Queens and Staten Island. Finishing twentieth overall, after averaging 5:06 mile pace for nearly two and one-quarter hours; he was in rarified company.

New Zealander Rod Dixon, the winner in 2:08.59, had been the Bronze Medalist in the 1,500 meters at the 1972 Olympics in Munich. Dixon, who was very colorful, once remarked something like, "All I want to do is train like an animal and drink lots of beer." He had finished fourth in the 5,000 meters at the 1976 Montreal Olympics, and would be tenth in the 1984 Los Angeles Olympics Marathon. Geoffrey ("Geoff") Smith, the second-place finisher at the New York Marathon had represented Great Britain at the 1980 Olympics in the 10,000 meters and would do so again in the marathon in 1984.

Doug Avrit later described the race to Gregor Robin who penned an article titled, "Avrit has a long run on Broadway." The following excerpts from this piece, observations by Doug, provide a hint of the excitement of the race:

> When we were warming up we looked around, and we kept hearing about more and more guys who were going to be there.
>
> In the last three years everyone watched [Alberto] Salazar instead of going for it themselves, because Salazar was head and shoulders above the field. This time, the race was wide open....
>
> We were trying to run halfway under control, but we were passing people who were fading from the early pace.

From miles 5 to 12 I was just running, not trying to be competitive. People were going by me and I just let them. At 12 miles a pack came by me of about four runners. I looked at these guys and told myself 'I can run with these guys.'

When we turned on the wet road into Central Park, the crowd lining the course cheered like it was the Olympics.

What New York did for me was a lot.... Now I can go out at a five-minute mile pace and hold it for 20 miles, then see what happens.

1984 U.S. OLYMPIC TRIALS MARATHON

The qualifying standard to toe the starting line at the 1984 U.S. Olympic Trials Marathon was 2:19:04. If you couldn't average 5:18 per mile, you weren't invited to compete for an Olympic team berth. The conditions in Buffalo, New York, the site of the race on May 26th, were not conductive for distance running, and particularly not very fast and demanding prolonged racing. It was both hot and humid and when a runner's core temperature approaches a critical threshold, their nervous system intentionally induces fatigue, slowing the body down to protect itself from excessive heat buildup.

The first three finishers—Pete Pfitzinger, Alberto Salazar, and John Tuttle—made the Olympic team. Doug Avrit finished thirteenth.

1984 Olympic Trials Marathon Partial Results

Finisher	Time	Finisher	Time
1. Pete Pfitzinger	2:11:43	8. Bill Rodgers	2:13:30
2. Alberto Salazar	2:11:44	9. Sal Vega	2:14:18
3. John Tuttle	2:11:50	10. Tom Raunig	2:16:02
4. Dave Gordon	2:11:59	11. Duncan MacDonald	2:16:56
5. Dean Matthews	2:12:25	12. David Hinz	2:17:18
6. Tony Sandoval	2:12:41	13. Doug Avrit	2:17:45
7. Greg Meyer	2:13:29	14. Bill Weidenbach	2:17:45

AMY HARPER AVRIT

Amy was a fearless and tough competitor who won races when at times it didn't seem possible. From a coaching perspective, she would be one of those athletes that comes along only once in a great while.

—Husband and Calaveras High School track coach Doug Avrit discussing his wife's great athletic successes during an interview associated with her selection to the NCAA II Hall of Fame.

As good as Doug was while competing for San Luis Obispo, fellow Mustang, and future wife, Amy Harper was even better. Amy Harper Avrit was inducted into the NCAA Division II Hall of Fame in 2013. A four-time national champion, she claimed NCAA Division II individual national championships in cross country in both 1982 and 1983, leading Cal Poly to team titles both years, and captured NCAA Division II titles in both the 1,500- and 5,000-meter runs in 1983, also leading the Mustangs to the team title.

MIKE BUZBEE

Photo 30-2

At left: Cover of one of the many yearbooks Coach Mike Buzbee has created for Yuba City High Cross Country team members. At right: Coach Buzbee.

Recently, Mike Buzbee traveled to hometown Chico from Yuba City to compete in the Bidwell Classic. Now seventy years old, he won his age group for the half-marathon as well as finishing ahead of scores of younger runners. He had never stopped running and racing. After high school, Mike and Pat were both self-coached and, despite this limitation, achieved great success. A few months earlier when in Chico for the Almond Bowl, I noticed a 26.2 decal on his car, and commented, "Shouldn't there by a "100 x" in front of that? Haven't you run about a hundred marathons in your life?" He replied, "I'm pretty close."

In 1975, the Buzbees had begun teaching; Mike in Yuba City and Pat in Turlock. Mike taught mathematics and science in the Yuba City Unified School District for 45 years while coaching/competing. During this period, he and wife Karen raised two sons; he was involved with the Boy Scouts of America as an assistant scoutmaster; and he earned a Master's Degree in Mathematics Education.

For forty-five years, Mike had served as an exemplary role model and influenced generations of students through his teaching and coaching, and continues to do so today. In his early years, he coached wrestling and soccer at Barry School; distance runners at Yuba High School under future Chico State head track & field coach Kirk Freitas; and was later assistant coach under John Orognen.

Beginning in 1998 and continuing today, Mike is the Cross Country head coach at Yuba High. During his tenure, Yuba has boasted League Championships, and advanced individual athletes to the powerful Sac-Joaquin Section Championships and to the State Meet. Until 2021, Mike was also concurrently the head track & field coach with the same results, League Championships, and the development of Section and State Meet competitors.

PAT BUZBEE

> *For me, physically, I started breaking down in my early 30's. This told me that I could probably not train sufficiently to run any more good marathons (I did 20 total). This would now guide my running if I wanted to continue.*
>
> *There was a time I think in the early 90's (now age 40+), I ran a race every weekend to see if I could do it. I ran against some very good runners who I grew up with in the sport of road racing, and others who I was not familiar with. I discovered it generally to be very competitive. I tried to tap into this somewhat but discovered I was running against some who were very talented, and others who didn't seem to have a life outside of running. Some were even high school and college nemeses. After getting married and being blessed with a daughter in 1989, and work also being quite competitive/consuming, life seemed "too competitive."*
>
> —Pat Buzbee reflecting on limiting competitive running owing to injuries, work-related demands, and family responsibilities.

In 1979, Pat Buzbee left teaching and enrolled in graduate school at Chico State. After earning a Master's Degree in Computer Science, he accepted a software engineer position at IBM in San Jose, moved there, and entered the "corporate world."

Photo 30-3

Pat Buzbee participating in a 1991 San Jose State Spartan fund raiser, by running as many sponsor-funded laps as possible on its track. In 1999, he competed in the USCAA National Corporate Track & Field Championships.
Courtesy of Pat Buzbee

In the decades following, Pat has retained his lifelong love with running. Following are a few of his recent running-related musings.

Different Running Loops
"In Chico, Mike and I had many different running loops around town. Our main 'bread-and-butter' runs were in Bidwell Park. However, we also took running to the streets! We had the 'river loop,' the 'Christmas loop,' the 'Rio Lindo loop,' several 'orchard' loops, 'Bidwell Avenue loop,' '(Neil) CUSACK Avenue loop,' 'Bell Road loop,' and many originating from our home, then known as 'Warner Street AC,' aka WSAC. After we moved from our parents' house in Chico, new runs would form or former ones would be slightly modified to incorporate a new start/end. To this day, I have running loops from my home in San Jose."

Keeping Your Running Fun
"Most important. I enjoy running track, cross-country, and road races. They are each different and bring out the best in you. Nothing is more savoring than a cold fall morning lining up on the starting line for a cross-country challenge. Like in San Francisco Golden Gate Park, and

some vintage music is playing in the back ground, and the course is always wet."

Expressing Gratitude
"Mike and I owe so much appreciation for what Chuck Sheley did for us in our early years."

Thanking Additional Members in the Chico Community
"Among the individuals who were very instrumental and supportive of my running (and twin brother Mike) in the 1970s were, in no particular order: Mel Jones, Willie Simmons, Jack Yerman, George Wright, Don Fridshal, Larry Dion, Les Fredrickson, Mike McGie, Frank Burk, Walt Schafer, Gene Gilligan, DuWayne Ray, Skip McDonald, Bill Peck, Betty Best, and many others."

The Competition Never Ends
"Some of the most wonderful people I have ever met are older athletes I have met at track meets for 'seniors.' That is, age 50+. These are accomplished people in many disciplines. Some are new athletes and have discovered the love of sport. Others are continuing athletes or are renewing their past glory by lacing up the shoes once again."

KURT GRAVES

Photo 30-4

Kurt Graves in second, following leader Mark Curb in a 10,000-meter race on the track at the University of Arkansas. Graves ran a lifetime best of 29 minutes and 59 seconds in this race.
Courtesy of Kurt Graves

In early 1978, Kurt Graves, following Doug Avrit and other former teammates to West Valley College, attended the spring semester, then the 1978-1979 school year. While competing for West Valley Vikings, Graves had a personal best of 30:52 for the 10,000-meter race. In 1979, he ran in this event at the California State Junior College Track & Field Championships. Kurt doesn't recall his time or finishing place, only that, "It was slow, because it was hot. And my blisters were enormous."

Photo 30-5

Kurt Graves (left) and two friends relaxing on the water after he and Doug Avrit ran legs on a team competing in the 1978 Lake Tahoe Relays. This race followed the completion of their freshman track season at West Valley College in Saratoga, California.

After two years at West Valley, Kurt completed his education at Oral Roberts University in Tulsa, Oklahoma. While a student there, he ran for the ORU Titans (today the Golden Eagles), competing in distance races on the track. His bests in the 3,000-meter steeplechase, indoor 3-mile, and 10,000 meters, were 9:26, 14:09, and 29:59, respectively. The steeplechase and 3-mile personal records came at different Midwestern City Conference Championships in which he won these races.

Graves also road raced, competing in distances from 10,000 meters (6.2 miles) through the marathon (26.2 miles):

Distance	Time	Year	Race / Location
10K	29:59	1981	Napa Fair, Napa Valley, California
15K	46:49	1980	Tulsa Run, Tulsa, Oklahoma
20K	1:04:24	1982	20K Road Championships
25K	1:19:17	1982	Mohawk Park, Tulsa, Oklahoma
½ marathon	1:09:50	1982	Jenks Half-Marathon, Jenks, Oklahoma
marathon	2:24:49	1982	Drake Relays, Des Moines, Iowa

Most significantly, Kurt received recognition as a student/athlete while attending Oral Roberts University:
- 1982 Male Student Athlete, Oral Roberts University (D1)
- 1982 Midwestern City Conference Male Student Athlete Award
- 1982 Southland Corporation Olympia Award

The Olympia Award was commissioned by The Southland Corporation in Dallas, Texas (and sanctioned by the U.S. Olympic Committee) to be presented to athletes in the 31 summer and winter Olympic sports who excel in athletics, leadership and scholarship. Olympic athletes, including familiar names like Mary Lou Retton and Greg Lougainis received the award).

CRAIG LARSEN

Photo 30-6

Craig Larsen at the top of Mt. Haleakala in Maui, December 2015.
Courtesy of Craig Larsen

Craig Larsen did not run competitively in college, but trained on his own and engaged in some road racing. In the 1980s after suffering a right knee injury, he found that running even as little as three miles at a time resulted in pain, but that he could bike 100 miles with no pain. That cemented a transition to cycling (a common one for ex-runners with bad knees).

Fast forward a couple of decades. In 2013, Craig lived in the San Francisco Bay area and rode for Monta Vista Velo based in Cupertino, California. This year marked the most races for him in the period 2010 through 2021, during which he rode twenty-two races. One of the 2013 races involved him returning to his hometown to compete in the Chico Stage Race sponsored by the local Chico Corsa cycling club.

During this visit, Craig briefly discussed his training with me. It included in addition to cycling on the road, some periodic training in a wind tunnel and morning runs on a treadmill. Craig was then 57 years old. In the Master 55+ category of the Chico Stage Race, held April 13-14, 2013, he won two of the three components: the Road Race and Time Trial. Everyone in the Criterium received the same time. His times for each race are identified below, as well as their summation under General Classification, for which he finished first as a result of his places.

Road Race	Time Trial	Criterium	General Classification
02:01:46193	00:23:39193	00:35:04193	03:00:20193

CONCURRENT ROAD RACING

The desire of runners to run, dies hard. Craig began running lightly in 2015, and wanted to explore the possibility of more aggressive training, and some racing as well. He signed up to participate in the Golden Gate Relays on his company's corporate team (NetApp). The NetApp team placed third in the 190-mile race from Calistoga to Santa Cruz, during which Craig experienced no knee pain during his leg of the relay.

A plunge into road racing followed; 10Ks he ran are not included in the following summary of competitive events.

Date	Race	Division	Place	Time
3/6/2016	Bidwell Classic Half-Marathon	M60-64	2nd	1:36:22
6/15/2016	Grand Canyon, South Rim to Colorado River and back			4:35
11/6/2016	Almond Bowl Half-Marathon	M60-64	3nd	1:58
3/4/2017	Bidwell Classic Half-Marathon	M60-64	2nd	1:38:40
4/23/2017	Bend Half-Marathon	M60-64	1st	1:41:44
11/1/2017	Chico HOT Half-Marathon	M60-69	1st	2:04:49
11/5/2017	Almond Bowl Half-Marathon	M60-64	3rd	1:39:36
11/4/2018	Almond Bowl Half-Marathon	M60-64	1st	1:36:58

Four and one-half months after the self-supported Grand Canyon run, he injured his left calf during the Almond Bowl Half-Marathon. After healing, he participated in a half-marathon in Bend Oregon, involving climbing 700 feet over the course. No problem for someone with very well-developed quads (strong quadriceps aid both cycling and running up hills); Craig set an age-group course record.

Next stop Chico, for the Hooker Oak Trail (HOT) Half-Marathon, which he characterized as his toughest race yet. Unlike other Chico half-marathons involving loops of a paved road in lower Bidwell Park, this one takes runners to rugged trails in upper park.

Craig is back on step, and in step so to speak, regarding running. He hasn't raced since Covid hit, but intends to toe the starting line again before 2022 wraps up at year's end.

KENT PEASE

> *I ran only a couple races at Chico State. We'd transferred to metric rather than miles so they were 1,500 meter runs. Best was 3:56.2 which equates to around a 4:12 mile. Disappointed that I couldn't continue competitive running and have a chance at sub-4.*
>
> —Kent Pease, succinctly describing his short-lived competitive college running career.

Following high school graduation in 1976, Kent enrolled at Chico State, and briefly ran for the Wildcats. However, the aspirations of the former two-time North Section mile champion were truncated by a knee injury which prevented him from training sufficiently to remain a competitive athlete.

After three semesters at Chico State, Kent transferred to UC Berkeley completing his degree in civil engineering, then on to Cornell on scholarship earning a master's degree.

Following his formal education, Kent moved to Colorado for a job and for the recreational activities in the area. He worked for several civil engineering consulting companies specializing in geotechnical engineering, especially tunnels. He noted that "Colorado and most of western North America is a great outdoor playground." His primary activity is rock climbing, but he also frequently participates in other sports such as mountain biking, cross-country skiing, mountaineering, boating river trips, fishing, and descending technical slot canyons.

Photo 30-7

Rock climbing and, in the center photo, canyoneering.
Courtesy of Kent Pease

As a climber, Kent ascended several of the big walls in Yosemite and elsewhere, established about 250 new routes, and authored an instruction book titled *The Crack Climber's Technical Manual*. He said, "It's nice to be well-rounded and participate in a range of activities—it's all fun—and although not competitive, it's still challenging."

Photo 30-8

  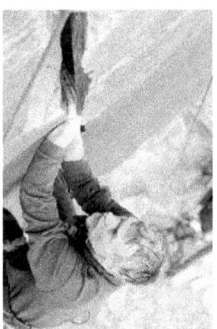

Additional climbing-related photographs and one of Kent engaged in a much less dangerous activity.
Courtesy of Kent Pease

A common thread in all these activities is that running in high school started him on an active lifestyle. Recalling his formative years, Kent remarked, "The team coached by Mr. Sheley was fun and a good community, and it just felt natural." Kent named a climbing route he established in honor of his former coach, and wasn't happy to learn that someone had taken steps to make it less challenging, as expressed by a missive he posted at a mountaineering website:

> "Mr. Sheley" is a proud line standing as a testament to long hard workouts inspired by my high school track and X-country coach. As noted above, the climb is 150 feet long and ends on top of the pillar. Shortening the climb with an intermediate anchor is like dropping out of a race. Also, the addition of bolts where removable protection is available violates our basic standards for the sport and is an unwarranted intrusion on nature. I request that the persons who placed the bolts reverse the process and return the route to its original condition.

SUZANNE RICHTER

> *Heading the list of recruits who have turned the program around is freshman Suzanne Richter from Chico.... She is now Cal's number-one runner. In Cal's five meets, Richter has won one, finished second three times, and third once. In the UCLA meet, in which Cal runners finished 1-2-4-5-6, Richter broke the course record with a time of 17:31.9, more than 48 seconds under the old mark for the 5,000-meter distance.*
>
> —Excerpts from an article by Larry Stone titled, "An Undefeated Cal Team."

Photo 30-9

Suzanne Richter and teammate Jan Oehm shaking hands after Richter had run the time of 16:24 in the 5,000 meters. Courtesy of Suzanne Richter

In 1978, Suzanne Richter's first cross country season as a UC Berkeley "Cal Bear," Jill Campbell was the only returning member of the previous year's squad. That team had never finished higher then third in a meet, and that was in three-way meets. This year, on the eve of the Western Regional AIAW (Association for Intercollegiate Athletics for Women) Championships at Long Beach, Cal was ranked third in the nation behind Iowa State and Penn State.

Cal easily won the meet on November 4th with a score of 32, ahead of Cal State Northridge 58, Cal Poly San Luis Obispo 62, UCLA 102, and Univ. of Hawaii 188. Northridge's Brown won the race in a time of 17:02; Richter, a half-minute behind at 17:38, finished in tenth place. Prior to the Nationals on November 18th at Denver, Colorado, Suzanne caught a virus and was really sick. She finished 101st and, without her in the fore, UC Berkeley was seventh in the team competition.

1979 TRACK SEASON ALL-AMERICAN

THIS IS Cal TRACK & FIELD.
ALL-TIME TOP PERFORMERS

6. Suzanne Richter 16:24.10 1979
7. Rowena Tam 16:24.35 2011
8. Sabrina Han 16:25.41 1990
9. Jan Oehm 16:26.80 1979
10. Lynne Hjelte 16:28.20 1980

Undeterred, Suzanne bounced back from this malady, and earned All-American honors in her first track season at Cal. The AIAW National Championships were held May 23rd-26th at Michigan State University, where she finished sixth in the 5,000-meter race with a time of 16:59.8. As of this writing, Suzanne's best of 16:24.10 places her sixth among the Top 10 Cal Bears for that event.

CAL CROSS COUNTRY, 1979-1981

In the years 1975–1981 the AIAW conducted national championships in cross country, overlapping in the fall of 1981 with the inaugural NCAA National Championships Meet. Cal's best team finish at the Nationals during Suzanne's time at UC Berkeley, and incidentally her best finish as well, came at the 1981 AIAW National Cross Country Championships at Pocatello, Idaho. Suzanne ran 18:56 to finish 47th in the race. For team scoring purposes, she was 31st and Cal's number three runner. As shown below, Cal finished fifth in the team competition.

TEAM RANK	TOTAL POINTS	NAME	SCORING FINISHERS					PUSHERS	
			1	2	3	4	5	6	7
1	80	Iowa State University	1	6	11	29	33	56	86
2	110	Purdue University	5	15	22	30	38	57	65
3.	114	University of Wisconsin	3	8	14	36	53	54	66
4	148	University of Montana	4	18	20	44	62	79	97
5	165	U. of California - Berkeley	9	16	31	39	70	88	96

MEETING UP AGAIN IN THE SAME RACE

Earlier that season at the Cal Berkeley Invitational on September 19th, former Chico Panther Suzanne Richter had once again toed the line with ex-Pleasant Valley Viking Cindy Claiborne. Cindy Grant, Suzanne Richter, and Cindy Schmandt ran 1-2-3 to lead the Golden Bears to victory. Suzanne clocked 18:27.1 over the course in Tilden Park, and Cindy Claiborne 19:39.9 to finish seventeenth. Claiborne was the second runner for the Humboldt State "Jacks," coming in behind teammate Claudia Bergsohn (19:21.2) in eleventh place.

Photo 30-10

Cindy Claiborne and Suzanne Richter while they were still in high school.
Courtesy of Suzanne Richter

INJURIES TAKE THEIR TOLL / REFLECTIONS

I had a lot of injuries that hampered my running career. I think I ran one race in my sophomore year of cross country before I injured my sciatic nerve and missed the entire season. My sophomore track season I had on and off issues with my Achille's tendon. I ramped up my mileage and it took a toll on me. More is not always better.

My fondest memories from high school and college are from my cross-country and track experiences. The life lessons that I learned on the cross-country course and through sports competition surpassed anything I learned in a classroom. Hard work, diligence, confidence, dedication, and perhaps most important, dealing with disappointment, failure and defeat, enriched my whole life's journey. I still run and I still love it. It is my sanctuary. It is where I go to relieve stress and it always makes me happy.

—Suzanne Richter remarking on increased mileage negatively impacting her aspirations and running viability. Despite setbacks in college, she has retained her great love and deeply-felt appreciation for running.

TONI RUGGLE

In 1982 I joined the Aggie Running Club based out of Davis. Our first shoe sponsor (don't laugh they provided free shoes) was Converse. Then one of our teammates, Angelo Martinez, helped develop the Rebook Aerobic shoe, which put Rebook on the map. Rebook was our sponsor for several years, followed by Asics. What was cool about that was we became friends in a sense with Steve Scott who was sponsored solely by Asics. Steve Scott was a great miler who held the American outdoor mile record for more than 26 years and also was the former American indoor record holder in the same event. Angelo who helped get Hoka shoes off the ground became our current sponsor (Hoka Aggie Running Club).

—Toni Ruggle describing being part of a group of runners, whose members never stopped training and racing after college, and the group's running shoe company sponsorship.

Following the completion of his collegiate eligibility in 1978, Toni took the summer off to rest and reflect on his running career. He emerged from this relatively short respite with renewed spirit to resume training and competing. Most of his college teammates had graduated and left Chico to pursue employment opportunities elsewhere, so he started training on his own and quickly found other training partners.

Some included Pat Buzbee, Dave Wood, Bill Elliot, Chris Hood, Tom Olson, Mike Wright and others. Members of this group were successful in winning local races in and around Chico. As the years passed, members came and went. Some of the more recent members included Roger Dix, Tom Peet, Jim Walker, Todd Hamel, Mike Smith, Greg Meadows, Mike Thorpe, Tom Tucker, Dana Kriz, Ernie Freer,

Kevin Barry, Tony Granados and others. Toni remarked about this shared comradeship, "Having that group of training and racing fellowship was amazing."

Photo 30-11

In 1982, Tom Cushman arrived in Chico. He was raised in Oregon and ran for Oregon State with bests of 14:54.0 and 31:16.49 for the 5,000m and 10,000m. He came to Chico to work as a meteorologist, and joined the northern California road racing circuit with great success. Over the years, he won several races, established numerous age group records, and was an age group winner in the 10,000 meters at the 2003 USA National Masters Championships in Eugene, Oregon.

Courtesy of Toni Ruggle

In Toni's first race against Tom, a Run for Life 3-miler around downtown Chico, Cushman won and Ruggle was second (14:16 and 14:23, respectively). Tom joined the Aggie Running Club in 1992. He and Toni have been teammates since then and ran several Pacific Association cross country and national championships together.

The group of local runners, of which Tom and Toni were a part, became known as the A-Team, which stuck until they got older and slower. As much younger, Gary Towne-coached, Wildcats took over winning the open division of local road races, they changed their name to the Original A-Team. With age, training seven days a week was reduced to four to five days in order to stay healthy.

Over the years, the A-Team/later Original A-Team has competed in all the local races, and won the Whiskey Town Relays several times. Once, seven members ran the Bidwell Half Marathon in a centipede outfit. Able to proceed only at the pace of its slowest pair of legs, the arthropod finished 7th through 13th place with a time of 1:18. At the Tahoe Relays, teamed-up members of the group have finished in the top three in their age group several times.

A tradition, continued over the years, has been the group's annual Christmas Eve Run in downtown Chico. Dressed in holiday attire, members run through town handing out candy to the crowds. Locals have dubbed them the Running Elves—spreading a little cheer to all.

JIM WALKER

Quitters don't tri. Triathletes don't quit.

—Anonymous from Race Omaha website.

That triathlon isn't going to train for itself.

—A triathlon slogan from thelongroadtoironman sports blog.

From his time as a Chico High Panther, Jim Walker is proudest of what his year group did for CHS Cross Country. His fondest running memory is when Chico won the varsity section title for the first time, during his junior year. Today, Jim still wears a Chico High School T-shirt when running in Bidwell Park.

Following high school, Jim ran cross country and track for Butte College, saying about the experience:

> I was never an outstanding runner but did make All-Conference in track due solely to having three of the fastest 400-meter runners on our 4 x 400 relay team.

Jim got interested in triathlons around 1980 and found that he was a better cyclist than runner and became an adequate swimmer. He won a handful of triathlon and duathlon competitions in the local area (Paradise, Sacramento, and Cool, California), and had cycling success winning the local Chico to Forest Ranch hill climb in 1983 in a time of 39:32. (This was on the longer course that started on El Monte Avenue.) The Sierra Nevada brewery in Chico used to sponsor this race, with each competitor having an opportunity to take home a case of beer, providing they finished the course in a time less than their chronological age. Since Jim was then about twenty-five years old, he was well under the standard, in addition to being the race winner.

In the early days of triathlon competitions born in San Diego, California, The World Triathlon Corporation organized an Ironman triathlon in Hawaii. The length of its legs (and those of other ironman races since) was a 2.4-mile swim, 112-mile bike ride, and a concluding 26.2-mile run. Jim noted about this race:

> I competed in the Hawaiian Ironman triathlon in 1982 and 1983. Although I did not do great, I was in about the top 20 percent of

finishers. Training for and competing in these races helped me in many other aspects of my career.

Photo 30-12

Jim Walker competing in an unofficial or promotional relay, judging by the Bud Light beer bottle he's carrying as a baton.
Courtesy of Jim Walker

After completing his studies at Butte College, Jim moved on to Chico State, and later UC Davis. Initially a paramedic, his additional education resulted in him becoming a physician's assistant. Jim was also involved in local politics, rising to vice mayor before leaving public service to focus on patient care.

He still considers himself a runner, and often trains in Chico with Toni Ruggle and other local "vintage" runners.

Postscript

There was always a strong team spirit and feeling of being in a family, although I was conscious of it only later in life with time for reflection. Part of Coach's draw was well placed observations of people or encounters which were presented in humorous terms. And yes, the green van! Even then I suspected that he bought it more for the track and XC teams than for his family use.

—Former Chico High great Kent Pease, reflecting back on his experiences running for Chuck Sheley in the 1970s. Kent went on to earn a bachelor's degree in civil engineering at UC Berkeley, and a master's at Cornell University before embarking on a career as an engineer.

My competitive running ended in late autumn 1976 after, while running on a muddy trail along the American River early one morning, I slipped and slid into the river. I remember that the air temperature was in the 30s, and I just wanted out of the cold water. Apparently, I had torn the ACL in my left knee, but didn't know this until decades later when a surgeon, after dealing with a torn meniscus, told me that I also had a torn ACL, as well as arthritis in the knee.

I was then attending American River College (ARC) in Sacramento, and running cross country for legendary coach Al Baeta. We knew that he had run for Cal Berkeley while in college, but not that he had run a leg on the two-mile relay team at the LA Coliseum Relays in 1954 that broke the world record with a 7:28.5, only to lose the competition to Fordham's new mark of 7:27.3. Knowing this now provides an answer to how, in 1976, he could hang with us for a good portion of our distance workouts. We would cruise along on a six-mile run at about 5:30 mile pace, look back, and see our coach, who would remain there for three miles or so.

I had run bests of 4:25 (mile), 9:38 (2-mile), and 15:15 (5,000 meters) at Butte College. I improved tremendously under Coach Baeta, but that season, I was forced to face the truth that I did not have sufficient talent to ever be a great runner. Twice we ran an 8-mile time trial along a measured stretch of a paved bike path. On the second occasion, Jim Mebust, our best runner, ran a time of 40:40. Mine was 41:04—a 5:08 mile pace for eight miles. A world-class marathoner could run that pace for another 18 miles, in addition to the first eight.

After each cross-country meet, Coach Baeta would post our rankings on the team, based on our average finishes in races to date. At season's end before being injured, I was third man on the team. The best times of my teammates for the events listed below (achieved during the 1976-1978 track seasons) still rank in ARC's top ten marks ever.

1,500-Meter Race			3,000-Meter Steeplechase		
Name	Time	Year	Name	Time	Year
Loran Ringo	3:51.1	1976	Tim Farrell	8:58.2	1978
Mike Brown	3:51.1	1978	Bill Weed	9:04.4	1977

2-Mile Race			10,000-Meter Race		
Name	Time	Year	Name	Time	Year
Tim Farrell	9:03.0	1978	Tim Farrell	30:58.00	1978
Jim Mebust	9:06.2	1977	Earl Lagomarsino	31:34.00	1977
Arthur Baudenistal	9:08.4	1977			
Gary Sutherland	9:08.9	1977			

I was hurt between the California North State Championships and the State Championships. At the former, Steve Henson, who was running for the College of the Siskiyous, wasn't anywhere close enough to use his kick against me. The head coach at Fresno State, Gene "Red" Estes, had talked to our top runners about the possibility of scholarships if we ran for him. I loved training and racing with my teammates, and everything was great; then it wasn't. I went to a doctor about my injury, and he told me that I would never compete at my best again.

Having no particular goals in college, other than running, I went down to the Navy recruiter's office and enlisted. Best thing I ever did. Following my tour, I attended Chico State, finished a degree in two years, and earned a commission via Officers Candidate School. A few months later, on a Friday night at the Officers Club on the Amphibious Base in Coronado, California, I met my future wife, Nancy. She was a Navy Nurse Corps Officer and I a "ship driver" (Surface Warfare Officer). A year later we married—best decision of my life!

The lessons I learned from coaches Chuck Sheley and Al Baeta, and the work ethic gained from being a part of their programs, would put me in good stead throughout my naval career. Coach Baeta, who was a master of "psyching us up" before big meets, would speak about the importance of having ivory tower memories (meaning good results that particular race day) to draw upon later in life. Running in Chico in the 1970s is one of those memories.

Appendix A: Top Times of CHS Boys Track Athletes in the 70s

The following individuals are all former Chico High School athletes. Top performers in the 1970s from other Butte County high schools, may be found on the following page.

880-Yard Race

Name	Time	Name	Time
Steve Payne (1970)	1:55.7	Santos Cervantes (1977)	2:02.5
Dave Garner (1970)	1:58.1	Robert McKay (1974)	2:03.3
Kent Pease (1976)	1:58.4	Brian Millis (1973)	2:03.4
Greg Williams (1977)	1:58.8	Brad Marzolf (1976)	2:04.2
Craig Herendeen (1971)	1:59.7	Chris Lambert (1976)	2:05.8
Jim Antone (1978)	2:00.2	Kurt Graves (1977)	2:06.2
Calvin Dillon (1979)	2:00.6	Pat O'Connell (1974)	2:07.0
Howie Waugh (1977)	2:00.5 ®	Dave Bruhn (1974)	2:07.8
Chris Shols (1976)	2:01.0	Britt Brewer (1978) CJHS	2:08.5
Scott Lape (1977)	2:01.2	Bill Gregg (1973)	2:09.0
Doug Avrit (1977)	2:01.8	Mark Burch (1974)	2:09.2
Steve Growdon (1979)	2:02.0 ®	Ray D'Amato (1975)	2:09.2

® relay-leg

Mile Race

Name	Time	Name	Time
Doug Avrit (1977)	4:16.5	Robert McKay (1974)	4:40.0
Kent Pease (1976)	4:19.1	Bruce Eggleston (1972)	4:41.7
Greg Williams (1977)	4:21.6	Kurt Graves (1977)	4:42.9
Steve Growdon (1977)	4:27.8	Pat O'Connell (1973)	4:44.5
Santos Cervantes (1977)	4:29.0	Calvin Dillon (1979)	4:46.7
Bill Gregg (1974)	4:32.1	Kevin Boone (1977)	4:46.8
Dave Bruhn (1974)	4:33.7	Britt Brewer (1978) CJHS	4:47.4
Dana Miller (1970)	4:36.2	Steve Zicker (1974)	4:57.8
Mark Burch (1973)	4:37.5		

2-Mile Race

Name	Time	Name	Time
Doug Avrit (1977)	9:11.9	Bruce Eggleston (1971)	10:08.6
Steve Growdon (1979)	9:34.8	Bill Gregg (1973)	10:11.3
Kurt Graves (1976)	9:37.0	Chris Johnson (1978)	10:20.2
Dave Bruhn (1975)	9:45.4	Robbie Sylvester (1977)	10:22.1
Santos Cervantes (1976)	9:46.8	Mark Burch (1973)	10:25.9
Greg Williams (1977)	9:52.3	Dana White (1976)	10:32.3
Kevin Boone (1976)	9:53.6	Steve Zicker (1975)	10:31.0
Britt Brewer (1978) CJHS	9:59.0	Greg Robertson (1972)	10:46.8
Bernie Fricke (1970)	9:59.9		

Photo Appendix A

Two-mile race at the 1978 Eastern Athletic League Championship Meet. The competitors are from left to right: Curt Boehm (Oroville High), Bobby Dippel (Paradise High), Eddie Byers (Paradise, obscured), Chris Johnson (Chico High), Rich Stensrud (Pleasant Valley High), Steve Growdon (Chico High), and leading the race, freshman Britt Brewer from Chico Junior High School.
Courtesy of Britt Brewer

Top Performances in the 1970s
(From other Butte County High Schools)

880-Yard Race

Name	Time	Name	Time
Larry Greer, Paradise, 1977	1:56.0	Rob Erb, Paradise, 1974	1:56.6
Seth Roberts, Paradise, 1978	1:56.4	Toni Ruggle, LP, 1973	1:57.5

Mile Race

Name	Time	Name	Time
Larry Greer, Paradise, 1977	4:10.8	Dave Meyers, Oroville, 1976	4:23.9
Toni Ruggle, LP, 1973	4:18.8		

2-Mile Race

Name	Time	Name	Time
Larry Greer, Paradise, 1977	9:17.0	Jack West, Oroville, 1970	9:49
Calvin Lantrip, Oroville, 1973	9:30		

LP: Las Plumas High School

Appendix B: Top Times of CHS Girls Track Athletes in the 70s

Individuals highlighted by shading were members of the 1977 Chico High School Girls Cross Country team (nicknamed "Charlie's Angels"), which *Harrier* magazine ranked second in the nation.

100-Yard Dash

Name	Time	Name	Time
Stacy Shols (1977)	11.19	Tonya Alston (1977)	11.3
Robin Cromwell (1977)	11.3	Carol Hartman (1975)	11.6

220-Yard Dash

Name	Time	Name	Time
Stacy Shols (1978)	26.0	Teresa Bradley (1976)	26.4
Robin Cromwell (1979)	26.2	Beth Ghio (1975)	29.6

440-Yard Dash

Name	Time	Name	Time
Luanne Park (1978)	58.9	Suzanne Richter (1977)	60.6

880-Yard Race

Name	Time	Name	Time
Suzanne Richter (1978)	2:20.0	Jill Symons (1978)	2:21.9
Darcy Burleson (1977)	2:20.8	Luanne Park (1978)	2:23.3

Mile Race

Name	Time	Name	Time
Suzanne Richter (1978)	4:52.45	Jill Symons (1978)	5:16.7
Darcy Burleson (1977)	5:01.7		

2-Mile Race

Name	Time	Name	Time
Suzanne Richter (1978)	11:13.5	Jill Symons (1977)	11:36.2
Darcy Burleson (1977)	11:33.6		

Appendix C: Best Times by Panthers on Chico's Home Course in the 1970s

Chico Boys 2.55-Mile Cross Country Course
(Course changed in 1979 to 3.0 miles)

Name	Time	Name	Time
Doug Avrit	12:29	Mark Burch	13:23
Greg Williams**	12:40	Kevin Boone	13:24
Kurt Graves	12:45	Bill Gregg	13:29
Santos Cervantes	12:48	Craig Larson	13:35
Chris Johnson	13:03	Britt Brewer	13:40
Steve Growdon	13:05	Josh Strong	13:47
Dave Bruhn	13:07	Pat O'Connell	13:53
Bruce Eggleston	13:14	Chris Shols	13:58
Kent Pease	13:20		

** *Sacramento Bee* Boy Runner of the Year (1978)
   NSCIF Cross Country Champion, who beat Central Valley's John Frank (2nd)

Chico Girls 1.87-Mile Cross Country Course
(Course changed in 1979 to 2.16 miles)

Name	Time	Name	Time
Darcy Burleson	10:30	Stacey Shols	12:02
Suzanne Richter	10:50	Joan Gregg	12:05
Jill Symons	11:03	Kathy Jo Bernadett	12:09
Luanne Park	11:41	Vicki Whitburn	12:16
Julie Selchau	11:55	Tammy Denny	12:29

The first seven girls listed in the table were members of the 1977 Chico High School Girls Cross Country team (nicknamed "Charlie's Angels") which *Harrier* magazine ranked second in the nation.

Appendix D: Chuck Sheley's Student Teachers, Assistant Coaches, and Athletes who later Coached

Student Teachers who went into Coaching

Ron Caminada	Bob Hooper	Eric Reichel
Lefty Chell	Paul Johnson	Jon Robinson
Mike Clark	Rich Kemp	Karl Schaechterle
Marty Dockendorf	Don Lytle	Bob Smith
Kathy Donecho	Will Matthews	Jerry Strangio
Mike Finney	Rick Moitoza	Alex Varga
Jim Gilbert	John Morton	Craig Vogensen
Emett Grijalva	Bob Noe	
Glenn Hayes	Terry Pagni	
Jan Hill	Mike Pena	

Chico High School Assistant Coaches

Lefty Chell	Joe Hall	Tom Peet
Tammy Denney	Mark Jones	Karl Schaechterle
Pat Finn	Darren Marshall	Julie Van Dyke
Bill Green	Ralph Patten	Jack West

Former Chico High School Athletes Who Coached

Doug Avrit	Mike Buzbee	Carolyn Kurnizki
Britt Brewer	Bill Gregg	Sondra Norris
Dave Bruhn	Steve Growdon	

About the Author

Commander David D. Bruhn, U.S. Navy (Retired) served twenty-two years on active duty and two in the Naval Reserve, as both an enlisted man and as an officer, between 1977 and 2001.

He is a graduate of California State University, Chico, and has Masters Degrees from the U.S. Naval Postgraduate School and U.S. Naval War College.

During his career, Bruhn served aboard six ships including command of the mine countermeasures ships USS *Gladiator* (MCM-11) and USS *Dextrous* (MCM-13) in the Persian Gulf. Ashore, he did two three-year tours in the Pentagon. During the first one, he was assigned to Secretary of the Navy and Chief of Naval Operation staffs as a budget analyst and resources planner. His final assignment was to the Secretary of Defense staff as executive assistant to a senior (SES 4) executive at the Ballistic Missile Defense Organization in Washington, D.C.

Following military service, he was a high school teacher and track coach for ten years, and is now a USA Track & Field official. He lives in northern California with his wife Nancy and has two grown sons, David and Michael.

A prolific writer, Bruhn has authored over twenty books on naval history. This is his first sports-related book.

www.ingramcontent.com/pod-product-compliance
Lightning Source LLC
Chambersburg PA
CBHW060558230426
43670CB00011B/1876